DESTROYING AMERICA

THE CIA'S QUEST TO CONTROL THE GOVERNMENT

Anthony R. Frank

DESTROYING AMERICA

*THE CIA'S QUEST
TO CONTROL
THE GOVERNMENT*

Anthony R. Frank

Anthony Frank

Copyright © 2022 Anthony R. Frank

All rights reserved.

ISBN: 9781080797530

Table of Contents

Chapter 1: The CIA - Operating Domestically and Targeting Americans 1

Chapter 2: CIA Officers in the Secret Service Planning Presidential Assassinations 32

Chapter 3: The Blatant Cover-Up of a Presidential Assassination..67

Chapter 4: KGB Asset and Future President George H. W. Bush..80

Chapter 5: How to Kill Members of Congress and How to Empower the CIA 118

Chapter 6: The Big Picture 143

Chapter 7: Learning from the KGB, Killing More Members of Congress, & Taking Control of the United States Government 158

Chapter 8: Orchestrating the Assassination of a President 184

Chapter 9: Preparing for President Johnson's Assassination and a Goldwater Presidency 195

Chapter 10: The KGB, the CIA, & Oswald's Feigned Defection to Russia 215

Chapter 11: Goldwater's Prospects for the Presidency, Help from George W. Bush's Father and George W. Bush's Grandfather ...231

Chapter 12: Getting the United States Government to Cover Up an Obvious Conspiracy in a Presidential Assassination 244

Chapter 13: The KGB's Chosen Patsies in the Assassination 283

Chapter 14: The CIA Continues Trying to Control the Presidency 307

Chapter 15: An Even Bigger Picture 329

Chapter 1: The CIA – Operating Domestically and Targeting Americans

In 1975, President Ford's "Commission on CIA Activities Within the United States" (the Rockefeller Commission) stated that the CIA's Directorate of Science and Technology had been putting "LSD and other potential behavior-influencing substances" into the food of "unsuspecting" Americans from 1953 to 1963.[1]

CIA officers started drugging unsuspecting Americans "on the West Coast" in 1953, and by 1961, they were drugging unsuspecting Americans "on the East Coast."

The Rockefeller Commission, which consistently tried to gloss over the CIA's domestic operations, claimed that the ten-year program of putting LSD and other drugs into the food of unsuspecting Americans "in normal social situations" was some kind of CIA "testing" operation, but the CIA eventually acknowledged that the alleged testing "made little scientific sense."[2]

In one drugging incident in 1953, a CIA officer met with Dr. Frank Olson, a civilian biochemist working for the Department of the Army, and surreptitiously slipped LSD into his drink. Dr. Olson was none-too-pleased with it and made an issue of it with his immediate superior, Colonel Vincent Ruwet.

Five days after the drugging incident, Olson was still making an issue of it and not getting any answers, which resulted in Colonel Ruwet calling the CIA officer who drugged Dr. Olson.

---

[1] Rockefeller Report, p. 227
[2] U.S. Senate Report - Project MKULTRA - Senate Select Committee on Intelligence, p. 2

The CIA officer then took Olson to New York, allegedly for "psychiatric treatment," but they instead met with an "allergist and immunologist."

Three days after arriving in New York, the CIA officer and his victim checked into a tenth-floor hotel room. The CIA officer wrote in his intelligence report that Dr. Frank Olson, who would not keep his mouth shut about the CIA putting LSD into his drink, "crashed through" a "closed window blind" and a "closed window" and "fell to his death" at 2:30 a.m.[3]

Someone wrote a CIA "Field Office Report" claiming that Dr. Olson committed "suicide," and the Rockefeller Report maintains that Olson "jumped" from the tenth-floor window. But the CIA officer who drugged Olson and reported on his death a week later never said anything about Olson committing "suicide," nor did he say anything about Olson "jumping" from the tenth-floor window.

The Rockefeller Report maintains that the CIA "destroyed" its records of the LSD operation, stating that "all the records" were "ordered destroyed in 1973," and the Rockefeller Commission allegedly accessed only a "limited" number of records, but having access to any of the records clearly means "all the records" had not been destroyed.[4]

A CIA Inspector General's report, which had not been "destroyed," addressed the LSD operation in 1957, four years after it was launched and six years before it would end.

The Inspector General wrote, "Precautions must be taken to conceal these activities from the American public . . . . Knowledge that the Agency is engaging in unethical and illicit activities would have serious repercussions."[5]

And while the CIA's Directorate of Science and Technology was in the midst of its LSD program, Richard Helms, "Chief of Operations" in the CIA's Directorate for Plans, sent a memorandum to all CIA

---

[3] U.S. Senate Report - Project MKULTRA - Senate Select Committee on Intelligence, pp. 77-78
[4] Rockefeller Report, p. 226
[5] U.S. Senate Report - Project MKULTRA - Senate Select Committee on Intelligence, p. 74

Division Chiefs and their staffs on August 17, 1959 titled, "Clandestine Services Operations in the United States."[6]

Helms's memorandum states, "All clandestine operations carried out by the Clandestine Services in the United States will be coordinated in advance with the CI [Counterintelligence] staff," but such coordination would happen only if it is "necessary to prevent jurisdictional conflicts with other departments and agencies within the United States or to obtain assistance and cooperation from them for domestic operations."

In other words, when the CIA secretly targets U.S. citizens with "clandestine operations," CIA officers have the option of getting "assistance and cooperation" from "other" U.S. departments and agencies if they need it, and the CIA will take "advance" steps to prevent other government agencies from complaining that the CIA has no "jurisdiction" in the United States.

One agency with which the CIA has had "jurisdictional conflicts" when secretly conducting its operations inside the United States is the FBI.

A high-ranking FBI official met with CIA Director John McCone in May 1964 and brought up the CIA's "DDP operations," which are conducted by the CIA's Deputy Director for Plans. The FBI official told McCone that "DDP operations in the United States" are "taking up much of my time these days," adding, "Your people are more operational than ever in the U.S. right now."[7]

Richard Helms, who wrote the 1959 memorandum on the CIA's "Clandestine Services Operations in the United States," had been the CIA's Deputy Director for Plans (DDP) for two years before the FBI official noted the huge "DDP operations in the United States."[8]

In May 1973, nine years after the FBI official met with McCone and just a few months after Helms wrapped up a seven-year

---

[6] National Archives Record Number 104-10310-10193
[7] National Archives Record Number 104-10306-10023, pp. 17-18
[8] National Archives Record Number 104-10301-10000, p. 33

tenure as CIA Director, the new CIA Director, James Schlesinger, "issued instructions to each directorate to come forward with descriptions of activities, especially those involved in the domestic scene, that had flap potential."[9]

1973 was the year that the CIA allegedly destroyed "all the records" of its ten-year LSD operation, but the Rockefeller Commission clearly had access to the LSD records. Even the report of the CIA officer who drugged Dr. Frank Olson and then reported on his death a week later had not been "destroyed."

Some of the CIA's "flap potential" activities were brought to light two years after Schlesinger's memorandum. Both the Senate and the Ford Administration produced reports in 1975 following public revelations about the CIA's illicit activities inside the United States.

The *New York Times* reported in December 1974 that a "check of the CIA's domestic files" revealed "illegal activities by members of the CIA inside the United States, beginning in the 1950s, including break-ins, wiretapping and the surreptitious inspection of mail."[10]

Seven days later, Senator William Proxmire stated, "I can say on the basis of the information I have, and I think it is very good information," that the stories and allegations about "people who had been under investigation by the CIA, about the surveillance, about the breaking and entering, and about wiretaps, that those are accurate and correct."[11]

To deal with the exposure, President Ford established the previously cited Commission on CIA Activities Within the United States, chaired by Vice President Nelson Rockefeller, and three weeks later, the U.S. Senate established the Senate Church Committee, headed by Senator Frank Church.

CIA Director William Colby testified to the Church Committee that Watergate conspirator E. Howard Hunt had at one time been a CIA officer with the CIA's "Domestic Operations Division," adding that

---

[9] CIA "Family Jewels, June 25, 2007 Release, p. 403
[10] New York Times, 12-22-74, p. 1
[11] New York Times, 12-30-74, p. 1

the "Domestic Operations Division" conducts "our operations here in this country."¹² (The "Watergate scandal" originated in June 1972 when operatives in the Nixon re-election campaign broke into the Watergate Hotel in Washington, D.C.)

Hunt, himself, submitted an affidavit to the Rockefeller Commission stating that back in November 1963, he was "an employee of the Central Intelligence Agency assigned to the Domestic Operations Division, located in a commercial building in Washington, D.C." adding that the "Domestic Operations Division" was part of the CIA's "Deputy Directorate for Plans."¹³

Regarding the CIA's domestic operations, the Rockefeller Commission stated that CIA officers operate in the United States with "official covers" and "nonofficial covers."¹⁴

CIA officers with "official covers" are detailed to be employees of "other United States government agencies," which means they are given "official" positions that provide them with "cover" while they carry out the CIA's agenda.

Those with "nonofficial covers" have "no official" position to "cover" their secretive operations targeting Americans, hence, the term "nonofficial cover."

CIA officers are required to fill out intelligence reports every day. Those with "official covers" fill out intelligence reports on the federal employees and government officials with whom they interact. They will also enlist federal employees as "assets" when targeting government officials and private citizens.

CIA officers with "nonofficial covers" fill out intelligence reports on the private citizens with whom they interact, and they will use private citizens as "assets" when targeting U.S citizens.

The 1975 Rockefeller Report disclosed that there are U.S. businesses that are "created and controlled" by the CIA and used for CIA "activities" and "operations" in the United States. "Many"

---

[12] National Archives Record Number 157-10011-10025, p. 9
[13] National Archives Record Number 180-10110-10064, pp. 21 & 25
[14] Rockefeller Report, p. 215

CIA officers have "nonofficial covers" as employees of companies that are "owned" by the CIA and "operated" by CIA officers.[15]

There are also "United States citizens" who "assist" the CIA by serving as "officers and directors" of some of the CIA-owned companies. All CIA-owned companies are "legally constituted corporations, partnerships, or sole proprietorships." (Any location where the CIA sets up shop in the United States becomes a CIA "field station.")

CIA officers also operate in the United States with "nonofficial covers" as employees of "privately owned American business firms," and "cover arrangements" for many of the CIA officers operating domestically require the "management of a variety of domestic commercial entities."[16] No one would think that normal, everyday, working Americans are actually CIA officers gathering intelligence and conducting secretive operations targeting U.S. citizens.

CIA officers can use "official covers" without actually being employed by "other United States government agencies." The CIA simply issues fake documentation to make it appear as such.

A memorandum to the CIA's "Central Cover Group" in May 1962 states, "It is requested that a U.S. Army credential be issued to the identity under the alias William Walker. This document will be used within the continental U.S."[17]

CIA officers with "nonofficial covers" similarly use fake documentation. A CIA officer named Charles Ford was "issued alias documentation under the name of Charles D. Fiscalini" in March 1962, after which Ford was to "travel to New York to meet with an unidentified attorney."[18]

As an "operations officer" in the CIA's "Western Hemisphere Division," Ford was "reissued this alias documentation in February 1963 to be utilized 'in the continental U.S. for operational purposes.'"

---

[15] Rockefeller Report, p. 208
[16] Ibid., p. 215
[17] National Archives Record Number 104-10106-10559
[18] National Archives Record Number 104-10310-10196

Charles Ford himself wrote a memorandum in 1975 stating that he "frequently carried identification in that name and used it on several occasions."[19]

"Nonofficial covers," like the one Charles Ford used, allow CIA officers to blend in as normal, everyday Americans while targeting U.S. citizens, whereas "official covers" allow CIA officers to blend in with the huge federal work force, which includes the FBI, the Department of Justice, the Department of Defense, the IRS, and every other U.S. Department and federal agency.

In addition to exposing the CIA's ten-year program of putting LSD into the food of "unsuspecting" Americans and exposing the intricacies of how CIA officers operate inside the United States, the Rockefeller Report, which, again, consistently tried to gloss over the CIA's domestic operations, confirmed that the CIA engages in the illegal inspection of mail, stating that the CIA began doing it "during the early 1950s."[20]

A CIA document alleges that the mail intercept operation was "terminated" on February 15, 1973,[21] but three months later, on May 16, a CIA memorandum stated that the mail intercept operation was officially "in a dormant state," contradicting the earlier claim that it had been "terminated."

The memorandum of May 16, 1973, states that "a decision" was "pending" on whether or not the operation "will be continued" after the "dormant state" had passed.[22]

Back in 1960, the CIA Inspector General foresaw the possibility that the CIA's mail intercept program might someday be exposed, and he "recommended preparation of an 'emergency plan' and 'cover story.'"[23]

---

[19] National Archives Record Number 104-10310-10119
[20] National Archives Record Number 104-10431-10124, p. 12
[21] National Archives Record Number 104-10418-10069, p. 4
[22] CIA "Family Jewels," June 25, 2007 Release, page 28
[23] Rockefeller Report, p. 107

The Rockefeller Report states that the CIA Inspector General's job is to "investigate reports of wrongdoing,"[24] which means the CIA Inspector General's job is to recommend "preparation of an 'emergency plan' and 'cover story'" to gloss over any CIA "wrongdoing."

On February 1, 1962, the Deputy Chief of Counterintelligence wrote, "Existing Federal Statutes preclude the concoction of any legal excuse for the violation. It must be recognized that no cover story is available to any government agency . . . . A flap would put us out of business immediately and give rise to grave charges of criminal misuse of the mail by government agencies."[25]

Regardless of not having a "legal excuse" or a "cover story" for illegally intercepting U.S. mail, the CIA took steps to prepare an "emergency plan" should the secret operation ever be exposed.

CIA Director Richard Helms spoke with Attorney General John Mitchell about the mail intercept operation on June 1, 1971, and four years later, Helms told the Rockefeller Commission that the Attorney General of the United States "fully concurred in the value" of the CIA intercepting and reading U.S. mail, and the Attorney General "had no 'hang ups' concerning it."[26]

But contrary to Helms's claim, a notation in the Rockefeller Report states that Attorney General John Mitchell maintained "they had only discussed mail covers," which is examining the outside of an envelope to determine the recipient and the sender.

And all they did is "discuss" mail covers. The Attorney General does not have the authority to dictate that the CIA can legally spy on Americans by intercepting their mail to determine the recipient and sender. Under the National Security Act of 1947, the legislation creating the CIA, the CIA is expressly prohibited from engaging in

---

[24] Rockefeller Report, p. 88
[25] Rockefeller Report, p. 107
[26] Rockefeller Report, p. 110

any "internal security functions," and it is expressly prohibited from having "internal security powers" and "internal security duties."[27]

Pursuant to further preparing the CIA's "emergency plan," Helms also "met with Postmaster General Blount" on June 2, 1971, one day after meeting with the U.S. Attorney General, and CIA Director Richard Helms allegedly told the Postmaster General of the United States all about the CIA intercepting and reading U.S. mail since "the early 1950s."

The 1975 Rockefeller Report states, "Blount, according to Helms, was 'entirely positive regarding the operation and its continuation.'"[28]

But again, a notation in the Rockefeller Report states, "Blount said he could not recall the specifics of his conversation with Helms."

Presidential aide Jack Marsh wrote a memorandum to President Ford in 1975 stating that the CIA used a "description" of the mail intercept operation to "hoodwink senior postal officials."[29]

Lieutenant General Samuel Wilson, Chairman of a CIA "Task Group," wrote a memorandum to CIA Director William Colby in November 1975 titled "Future Handling of Mail Opening Problem" in which General Wilson vouched for the "mail intercept project," stating that "useful operational leads" were obtained from it.

The General also bemoaned a "widespread awareness of CIA's activities in this field," and he made it a point to tell Director Colby, "It is far from certain at this stage whether this will result in

---

[27] National Security Act, section 104d and section 308a
https://www.dni.gov/index.php/ic-legal-reference-book/national-security-act-of-1947
(Also archived from the CIA's own website at the link below)
https://web.archive.org/web/20180606172154/https://www.cia.gov/library/readingroom/docs/1947-07-26.pdf
[28] Rockefeller Report, p. 110
[29] National Archives Record Number 178-10004-10121, p. 8

any public pressures on Congress that 'something be done about it.'"³⁰

Vouching for the operation and wondering if Congress might "do something about it" would indicate that the CIA was either intercepting mail again, five months after the Rockefeller Report exposed it, or the CIA had every intention of intercepting mail in the future, which would necessitate "Future Handling" of the "Mail Opening Problem."

The CIA's February 1973 claim that the mail intercept operation had been "terminated" was obviously part of the "cover story." The illegal operation had to be temporarily put into a "dormant state" to avoid "flap potential."

The CIA, according to its own documents, "controlled and operated the mechanics of procurement with members of the Post Office,"³¹ and by the time the operation went into a "dormant state" in 1973, one CIA document stated that the CIA had illegally "opened" 192,000 pieces of mail and they had "photographed" 2.7 million pieces of mail.³²

Besides an official policy of opening and reading mail, there is nothing to prevent individual CIA officers from acting on their own to intercept and read U.S. mail. A CIA document states that in 1955, "A CIA officer, on his own initiative, opened and photographed 900 letters."³³

In 1967, eight years before just some of the CIA's nefarious domestic operations were temporarily thrust into the limelight, the CIA's Counterintelligence Division established a "Special Operations Group" for specific CIA operations inside the United States, one of which was called Operation CHAOS.

This particular operation "recruited persons from domestic dissident groups or recruited others and instructed them to associate

---

[30] National Archives Record Number 104-10310-10030
[31] National Archives Record Number 104-10408-10245
[32] National Archives Record Number 104-10418-10069, p. 6
[33] Ibid., p. 12

with such groups in this country,"[34] and it was apparently ultra-secret. The Rockefeller Report states, "Knowledge of its activities was restricted to those individuals who had a definite 'need to know.'"[35]

Operation CHAOS targeted "the United States Peace Movement" during the Vietnam War and "immediately set about collecting all the available government information on dissident groups." All CIA "field stations" in the United States supplied Operation CHAOS with "any information" they had on the Peace Movement.[36] (As noted earlier, CIA field stations are locations where the CIA sets up shop. The CIA can set up "field stations" anywhere in the United States.)

Operation CHAOS also had a project that "concentrated on antiwar demonstrations" called "Demonstration Techniques."

The Rockefeller Report exposed very little about the CIA's Operation CHAOS but did cite "the addition of more and more resources" to Operation CHAOS. It also stated, "The excessive secrecy surrounding Operation CHAOS, its isolation within the CIA, and its removal from the normal chain of command, prevented any effective supervision and review of its activities by officers not directly involved in the project."[37]

By August 1973, Operation CHAOS alone had a computer system with "over 300,000 names and organizations which, with few exceptions, were United States citizens and organizations apparently unconnected with espionage."[38]

Operation CHAOS's massive intelligence gathering was allegedly going to pinpoint "foreign involvement" in the anti-war movement, which was obviously just a cover story for a CIA operation targeting more than 300,000 "United States citizens and organizations apparently unconnected with espionage."

---

[34] Rockefeller Report, p. 131
[35] Rockefeller Report, p. 145
[36] Rockefeller Report, p. 133
[37] Rockefeller Report, p. 131
[38] Rockefeller Report, p. 148

Not surprisingly, in May 1973, the CIA Inspector General determined that there was a "high degree of resentment" among "many Agency employees" who were "expected to participate" in Operation CHAOS.[39] (As will be seen throughout this book, the CIA has never stopped conducting its illegal operations inside the United States, and they have only gotten worse.)

When the Rockefeller Commission addressed the "Domestic Activities of the Directorate of Operations,"[40] they blatantly tried to avoid acknowledging the existence of the CIA's "Domestic Operations Division," choosing instead to refer to what they termed "the division" in the Directorate of Operations that allegedly carried out only minimal domestic activities.

"The division" carried out an operation targeting "Activities of United States Black Militants," and it was completely separate from the ultra-secret Operation CHAOS until someone with Operation CHAOS read "the division's reports" on "militant activities." Operation CHAOS then began working with "the division" to gather intelligence on "a broader range of dissident or militant groups."[41]

The information on "Black Militants" was invaluable to corrupt elements of the CIA who focused on inciting "racial" unrest in the United States. As will be seen later in this book, the Commission on *CIA Activities Within the United States* disclosed that the CIA was behind massive rioting across the United States from 1963 to 1968.

In 1969, the CIA's "Special Operations Group," which initiated Operation CHAOS, asked the Domestic Operations Division to report on the activities of "radical student and youth groups, radical underground press, and draft evasion/deserter support movements and groups." The "division's field officers," or more specifically, CIA "field officers" in the Domestic Operations Division, were told to report on "the purely domestic activities of these groups and their members."

---

[39] CIA "Family Jewels," June 25, 2007 Release, p. 327
[40] Rockefeller Report, p. 208
[41] Rockefeller Report, p. 211

In 1970, twenty-three years after the National Security Act prohibited the CIA from engaging in any "internal security functions," and prohibited it from having "internal security powers" and "internal security duties,"[42] Operation CHAOS and "the division" met several times to "discuss what one memorandum describes as 'over-aggressive positive actions' by the division's personnel in the collection of CHAOS information."[43] This is clear evidence that the CIA's Domestic Operations Division assisted Operation CHAOS when this one operation alone targeted "over 300,000" United States citizens and organizations that were "unconnected with espionage."

The Rockefeller Report acknowledges the existence of the "Domestic Operations Division" but claims it is responsible only for "developing contacts with foreign nationals."[44]

The Directorate of Operations was previously known as the Directorate for Plans,[45] which had been "organized around regional geographic divisions" of the world.[46] The geographic division where "the division" operates is the United States, and the Rockefeller Commission's desperate attempt to avoid acknowledging that "the division" is actually the CIA's "Domestic Operations Division" is utterly transparent.

The Rockefeller Report blatantly glosses over the CIA's illicit activities and its massive domestic operations by implying that they are either legitimate and necessary or they are simply past abuses that will never happen again.

The 1975 Rockefeller Report also disclosed, "Police cover in the form of badges and other identification has, on several occasions, been obtained from local police departments,"[47] and when the CIA

---

[42] National Security Act, section 104d and section 308a
https://www.dni.gov/index.php/ic-legal-reference-book/national-security-act-of-1947
[43] Rockefeller Report, p. 212
[44] Rockefeller Report, p. 221
[45] Rockefeller Report, p. 84
[46] Church Committee: Interim Report, p. 11
[47] Rockefeller Report, pp. 297-298

conducted "the surreptitious entry of a business establishment" in Fairfax, VA (meaning CIA officers broke into a place of business), the Fairfax City Police Department provided them with a "badge" to use as "flash identification" in the event they were caught.

Any CIA officer using a "police cover" is violating the National Security Act of 1947, the legislation that created the CIA. It specifically prohibits the CIA from having any "police" or "law enforcement powers."[48]

"Virtually all of the Agency activities" addressed in the Rockefeller Report "were known to top management," but there are no outsiders in the CIA hierarchy to disrupt its nefarious activities because "a distinct feature of the CIA is the absence of 'outsiders' in top-level management."[49]

In any other United States "executive agency," the "chief officer" and "top-level assistants" are "appointed from the outside," but "no such infusion occurs in the CIA."

Besides having "official covers" as employees of "other United States government agencies," CIA officers are also detailed to a wide variety of positions at the White House, where they gather intelligence on the President, White House officials, and the federal employees with whom they interact.

In the 1973 documentation of "domestic activities" with "flap potential," the CIA's Director of Personnel wrote, "For many years the Central Intelligence Agency has detailed employees to the immediate office of the White House."[50]

He also wrote that CIA officers are assigned to "components associated intimately with the immediate office of the President."

---

[48] National Security Act, section 104d
https://www.dni.gov/index.php/ic-legal-reference-book/national-security-act-of-1947
(Also archived from the CIA's own website at the link below)
https://web.archive.org/web/20180606172154/https://www.cia.gov/library/readingroom/docs/1947-07-26.pdf
[49] Rockefeller Report, pp. 83 & 85
[50] CIA "Family Jewels," June 25, 2007 Release, p. 105

The CIA also "furnished secretaries, clerical employees, and certain professional employees" to the White House, and at the time the memorandum was written in 1973, a CIA officer was "detailed" to the "White House Communications Section."

The Director of Personnel wrote that CIA officers had been "detailed" to the White House as "couriers" and "telephone operators." A CIA officer was also assigned to be a "laborer" on the White House grounds, and another CIA officer was assigned to be a "graphics man who designed invitations for State dinners" at the White House.

The CIA is not some government "Temp" agency that sends employees on various assignments because there is a temporary need for them as couriers, telephone operators, secretaries, and clerical employees. The CIA is in the business of gathering intelligence and conducting secretive operations, and as noted earlier, all CIA officers are required to fill out intelligence reports every day on the people with whom they interact and on the information they gather.

When CIA officers are detailed to the White House, they gather intelligence on White House officials and White House personnel and conduct secretive operations targeting them, and they report back to the CIA.

"Most" of the CIA officers detailed to the White House were "hired as bona fide White House employees," which means they were given "official covers" as White House personnel. They were still working for the CIA and reporting to the CIA, just like all CIA officers with "official covers" who are employees of "other United States government agencies."

It is, in fact, preposterous to think that a slew of highly trained, college educated CIA officers would leave their prestigious, high-paying positions as CIA officers so that they could take on mundane jobs as telephone operators, couriers, laborers, and clerical employees, positions to which they had been "detailed" by the CIA on a supposedly temporary basis.

The CIA's Director of Personnel further stated in his 1973 memorandum that CIA officers "have been, and are at the present time, assigned to the National Security Council, and we have seven clericals on detail to the NSC [National Security Council]."[51]

The National Security Council issues directives on how the CIA will operate. The CIA most certainly wants to influence the thinking and decisions emanating from the NSC. CIA officers assigned to the National Security Council fill out intelligence reports on other NSC staff members and on what the National Security Council is doing, as do the CIA officers detailed to various "clerical" positions on the National Security Council.

The Director of Personnel also wrote that CIA officers had been "detailed" to "Congressional staffs," and a CIA document states that by the mid-1970s, the CIA had intelligence files on "some 30-40 U.S. Congressmen."[52] As will be seen later in this book, the CIA has much more effective ways of gathering intelligence on Members of Congress.

CIA officers are trained to endear themselves to people and win their trust. People will tell CIA officers things that they would never tell anyone else, and CIA officers then put that information into their intelligence reports, something that all CIA officers are required do on a daily basis.

Besides being detailed to the National Security Council, and the "immediate" office of the White House, and "components associated intimately with the immediate office of the President," and a wide variety of seemingly mundane positions at the White House, CIA officers function as Secret Service agents protecting the President "while he is in the United States."

A CIA document on November 2, 1964, states that the CIA had been providing "manpower support" to the Secret Service "since 1955." It also states that one of the "continuing problems" they were

---

[51] CIA "Family Jewels," June 25, 2007 Release, p. 106
[52] National Archives Record Number 104-10301-10011

having was the "legal status" of CIA officers that are "assigned" to function as Secret Service agents.[53]

Five months later, the CIA instituted an official policy to deal with the "legal status" problem.

In April 1965, Lieutenant General Marshall Carter, the Deputy Director of the CIA, wrote a memorandum titled "Agreement Between the United States Secret Service and the Central Intelligence Agency Concerning Presidential Protection *in the United States.*"[54]

General Carter's memorandum states that when CIA officers are assigned to Secret Service duty, "Such officers detailed by the CIA will be designated officers of the Secret Service," and they will be protecting the President "while he is in the United States."

The Secret Service obviously has police and law enforcement powers, but as noted earlier, the National Security Act of 1947 prohibits CIA officers from having "police" and "law enforcement powers."[55] They are prohibited from having "internal security functions" and "internal security powers" and "internal security duties."[56]

The Deputy Director of the CIA cannot make laws. He cannot overrule the legislation that created the CIA.

Just a few short years after the CIA was created, the National Security Council spent three years setting up "national policies" for the CIA, one of which was eventually brought to light.

The one national policy that was exposed was a money laundering operation that allows the CIA to channel "millions of dollars" through "foundations" to "a wide spectrum of youth, student, academic, research, journalist, business, legal and labor organizations" in the United States.[57]

---

[53] National Archives Record Number 104-10423-10332
[54] National Archives Record Number 104-10419-10046
[55] National Security Act, section 104d
[56] National Security Act, section 308a
https://www.dni.gov/index.php/ic-legal-reference-book/national-security-act-of-1947
[57] New York Times, 2-19-67, p. 1

When the operation was first exposed in 1967, groups that had been receiving money from the CIA since the 1950s included the American Newspaper Guild, the National Student Association, the National Education Association, the Institute of Public Administration of New York, and the Retail Clerks International Association of Washington.

The secretive money laundering operation was first publicized in the *New York Times* on February 19, 1967, and regardless of the massive domestic operations that had been taking place since at least 1953, it was the first exposure of any large-scale CIA activity in the United States.

President Johnson immediately appointed a three-man committee to deal with it. The chairman of the committee was Under Secretary of State Nicholas Katzenbach, who was himself a CIA officer with an "official cover" in the State Department, and it included CIA Director Richard Helms. Just a few days later, the committee issued a report stating that the CIA's multi-million dollar funding operation was in keeping with the CIA's "national policies established by the National Security Council in 1952 through 1954."[58]

The National Security Council clearly decided that establishing "national policies" for the CIA in the early 1950s would somehow nullify the Act of Congress that created the CIA in 1947.

Congress chose not to investigate the CIA's money laundering operation. On February 25, 1967, six days after the CIA foundations were exposed, "Congressional leaders said that there would be no special investigation of the Central Intelligence Agency by the legislative branch . . . . Republican leaders, who have been critical of the Johnson Administration on almost every other issue, said at a news conference that they saw no reason to look into the intelligence agency's involvement with private organizations and institutions."[59]

The Senate Republican leader, Senator Everett McKinley Dirksen, said the disclosures "amounted to 'little more than a Roman

---

[58] New York Times, 2-24-67, p. 1
[59] New York Times, 2-25-67, pp. 1 & 10

holiday,'" and the House Republican leader, Congressman Gerald Ford, stated, "There is enough Congressional surveillance of the CIA."

Democratic Senator Mike Mansfield, the Senate majority leader, took the position that "an investigation of the subsidies should be left to the intra-administration committee appointed by President Johnson and directed by Under Secretary of State Nicholas Katzenbach."

One day before Congress shrugged off how American tax dollars were being spent, Katzenbach's three-man committee reported that the CIA's multi-million dollar funding operation is one of the "national policies established for the CIA from 1952 through 1954."

The rest of the CIA's "national policies" are apparently still classified.

In 1977, the Senate Intelligence Committee disclosed that the CIA used its money laundering foundations to secretly finance the LSD operation. The CIA had "standing arrangements" with "universities, pharmaceutical houses, hospitals, state and federal institutions, and private research organizations" in which the CIA gave out "annual grants" that were channeled through the CIA foundations, "thereby concealing" the CIA financing.[60]

The CIA can arguably use American tax dollars to finance anything it wants with its money laundering foundations, and as will be seen in much of this book, corrupt elements of the CIA are very focused on who is elected to Congress and the Presidency. The CIA can easily finance the political campaigns of their chosen candidates by channeling money to groups that support their candidate, "thereby concealing" the CIA's support for the candidate.

In an effort to gloss over the CIA's money laundering operation (the first exposure of a CIA domestic operation), some anonymous

---

[60] U.S. Senate Report - Project MKULTRA - Senate Select Committee on Intelligence, pp. 70-71

"informed sources" told the New York Times that the CIA is enjoined "only from 'internal security functions,'" which the Times said contradicts "a widely held belief that the agency is prohibited by law from engaging in clandestine activities within the United States." The Times also stated that the anonymous informed sources claimed "there never had been a serious question about its authority to deal secretly in this country with home-based groups."[61]

The CIA has certainly done much more than deal secretly with home-based groups, and contrary to what the *New York Times* said, the CIA is most certainly banned from "engaging in clandestine activities within the United States." It was established only for "clandestine activities" in other countries.

It is beyond reason to claim that when the CIA clandestinely performs its "functions" inside the United States, the CIA is not part of the national security apparatus and the domestic operations are, therefore, not actually "internal security functions."

As for Senator Mansfield's acceptance of the CIA's "national policies" in 1967, thirteen years earlier he was the "leader of a bipartisan move for a joint committee on the CIA."

In 1954, seven years after the CIA was created under the National Security Act of 1947, Mansfield and his Senate colleagues had no idea whether the CIA was "engaging in domestic activities."[62]

Senator Mansfield introduced legislation to set up an Intelligence Oversight Committee in 1954, but Senator Leverett Saltonstall, Republican Chairman of the Senate Armed Services Committee, persuaded the Senate Rules Committee to "shelve" the resolution so that it could not come up for a vote, even though the resolution had "the support of twenty-seven Senators."[63]

Two years later, Congress made a second attempt at CIA oversight when the Senate voted on a resolution that would create a "joint Congressional watchdog committee."

---

[61] New York Times, 2-24-67, p. 16
[62] New York Times, 6-7-54, p. 16
[63] New York Times, 6-3-54, p. 13

But in 1956, the third year of CIA's the ten-year LSD operation, the attempt at CIA oversight went down in flames by a vote of 59 to 27 because "President Eisenhower's declared opposition, plus intensive behind-the-scenes opposition by the CIA itself, proved sufficient to turn the tide overwhelmingly against the resolution."[64]

A few days earlier, the resolution had "thirty-five cosponsors and pledges of support from other Senators" and "seemed assured of passage by a comfortable margin . . . . Ten of the original cosponsors switched to vote against it on final passage."

President Eisenhower's "declared opposition" clearly did nothing to prevent the bill from becoming immensely popular in the Senate. It was obviously the CIA's "intensive behind-the-scenes opposition" that brought Congressional oversight to a screeching halt in 1956.

When Senator Mansfield and the entire United States Congress acquiesced in 1967, the *New York Times* reported: "The general attitude in Congress was that the issue contained no political profit,"[65] which means that by the time the CIA's money laundering operation was exposed, political profits were more important to the esteemed Members of Congress than addressing the CIA's domestic operations.

Seven years after the CIA ran rampant on Capitol Hill and successfully blocked Congressional oversight, CIA Director John McCone documented that he told President Johnson that the "only problem" the CIA had in their relationship with Congress is "a continual harangue for a Joint Committee on Intelligence."[66]

A short nineteen days after McCone said Congressional oversight would be a "problem" for the CIA, Richard Helms, the CIA's Deputy Director for Plans, wrote a memorandum to the Deputy Director of the CIA in which he promoted the resumption

---

[64] New York Times, 4-12-56, p. 1
[65] New York Times, 2-25-67, p. 1
[66] National Archives Record Number 104-10306-10018, p. 20

of "testing" LSD on "unwitting" subjects, adding that if a "testing arrangement" is resumed, it "must afford maximum safeguards for the protection of the Agency's role in this activity."[67]

Helms also wrote, "While I share your uneasiness and distaste for any program which tends to intrude upon an individual's private and legal prerogatives, I believe that it is necessary that the Agency maintain a central role in this activity."[68]

Helms was appointed to be Director of the CIA less than three years after blatantly stating that it was "necessary" for the CIA to have a "central role" in drugging unsuspecting Americans with LSD.

It was, in fact, Richard Helms who "proposed" the LSD operation in a memorandum to CIA Director Allen Dulles back in April 1953, and Dulles "approved" the operation ten days later.[69] Dulles led the CIA during the first eight years of the LSD program.

In 1963, the last year of the CIA's LSD program, former CIA Director Allen Dulles wrote a book titled *The Craft of Intelligence* in which he boldly proclaimed, "Espionage is not tainted with any legality."[70]

Senator Barry Goldwater, a CIA officer and a Member of Congress in violation of the Constitution, chimed in on the issue of Congressional oversight in December 1974, within days of the *New York Times* reporting on the CIA's massive domestic operations.

The *New York Times* reported: "Congress will be making 'a big mistake' if it undertakes too strong an investigation of the Central Intelligence Agency for alleged domestic spying, Senator Barry Goldwater, Republican of Arizona, said today.

"Mr. Goldwater, holding his annual news conference from his home, said that he had no knowledge of domestic spying but that the CIA should be allowed to keep 'domestic subversives' under surveillance."[71]

---

[67] U.S. Senate Report Project MKULTRA - Senate Select Committee on Intelligence, p. 82
[68] U.S. Senate Report Project MKULTRA - Senate Select Committee on Intelligence, p. 74
[69] U.S. Senate Report Project MKULTRA - Senate Select Committee on Intelligence, p. 70
[70] Dallas Morning News, 10-13-63, p. 24
[71] New York Times, 12-28-74, p. 8

Information on Senator Goldwater and other Members of Congress being in the CIA is addressed later in this book, as are the clear and concise details on how it violates the Constitution.

The *New York Times* detailed the need for intelligence oversight back in January 1956, the third year of the LSD operation, stating: "Uncontrolled secret intelligence agencies are in a position to dominate policy making, and hence government. Their very secrecy gives them power . . . . Few, even in the Executive Branch, know what they do . . . . An over powerful secret intelligence agency is dangerous, not alone to the formulation of sound policy, but to the viability of democratic institutions."[72]

In 1966, the *Times* took cognizance of a Congressional subcommittee that had some dealings with the CIA, stating: "Even these establishment watchdogs can be told just as much as the CIA Director thinks they should know."[73]

The *New York Times* perspective was validated in a *Washington Post* article on October 12, 1963 stating: "Senator Saltonstall, who has been one of the nominal watchdogs, has remarked during a floor debate, 'The difficulty in connection with asking questions and obtaining information is that we might obtain information which I personally would rather not have.'"[74] (Saltonstall was the Senator who pushed to have the Senate Rules Committee "shelve" the 1954 legislation on CIA oversight so that Congress could not vote on it.)

Three days before the *Washington Post's* October 12 article, President Kennedy addressed Congressional oversight of the CIA at a news conference forty-four days before his assassination. The soon-to-be-assassinated President said that he is "'well satisfied with the present arrangement' of having the CIA's budget looked over by a selected few from the Senate and House Appropriations

---

[72] New York Times, 1-15-56, p. 24
[73] New York Times, 4-29-66, p. 18
[74] Washington Post, 10-12-63, p. 10

and Armed Services Committees, and its general activities looked over by his own Intelligence Advisory Council."75

When the CIA was being roundly criticized for interfering in foreign policy during the Administration of President Kennedy's successor, President Lyndon Johnson, it was suggested that "the Foreign Relations Committee set up its own 'special subcommittee on the CIA.'"76

Senator J. W. Fulbright, the Chairman of the Senate Foreign Relations Committee, "interjected that this had been proposed before but when the CIA Director, Admiral William F. Raborn, appeared before the Foreign Relations Committee, he 'took the position he was not authorized under the law to respond to our questions.'"

In other words, President Johnson's CIA Director told the entire Senate Foreign Relations Committee, "The people who made the laws before you made the laws said it is against the law for me to answer your questions. I am not in contempt of Congress and you will continue to pay me and everyone employed by the CIA with the tax dollars of your constituents, and you will continue to use American tax dollars to finance virtually everything we do."

Senator Richard Russell, Democratic Chairman of the Senate Armed Services Committee, openly stated at the time that there was "no justification whatsoever for any other committee to muscle in on the jurisdiction of the Armed Services Committee so far as the CIA is concerned." Russell claimed attacks on the CIA were "erroneous" and "calculated to deceive Members of Congress."77

In October 1973, more than a year and a half before any official government reports on the CIA's massive operations inside the United States, a House Armed Services subcommittee acknowledged the CIA's domestic operations, stating that henceforth the CIA operate domestically only with the President's "personal" permission. The subcommittee "recommended a ban on any CIA domestic

---

[75] Washington Post, 10-10-63, p. 10
[76] New York Times, 5-17-66, p. 6
[77] Ibid.

activity except with the personal consent of the President,"[78] but they could not recommend a "ban" on "domestic activity" without being acutely aware of it in the first place.

In 1977, President Jimmy Carter gave the hallowed "personal consent" to CIA domestic activity when he issued an Executive Order condoning the CIA's targeting of U.S. citizens.

"Under the Carter order, CIA infiltration of domestic organizations was limited to a publicly stated set of purposes, including recruitment of agents" and "development of cover."[79]

The *Washington Post* cited the Carter order in December 1981 when President Reagan issued an Executive Order giving the CIA even greater latitude in operating domestically. But the Congressional Intelligence Oversight Committees, which Congress finally established in the mid-1970s, realized that they had to make it look like they were limiting the excuses the CIA would use to operate domestically.

"As a result of protests by the Intelligence Committees, the White House abandoned a proposal that would have permitted the CIA to infiltrate and to influence purely domestic organizations. But the order would still allow the CIA and other intelligence agencies, aside from the FBI, to infiltrate such organizations for any one of a secret list of purposes to be prescribed by the Attorney General."[80]

Congress insisted on a hallowed "secret list of purposes" that would allow the CIA to run rampant inside the United States and allow it to "infiltrate and to influence purely domestic organizations."

President Reagan's 1981 order "changes the flat rule requiring the head of the CIA and all other intelligence agencies to report to the Attorney General evidence of possible violations of federal law by their employees. Instead, such reports are to be made only

---

[78] Houston Chronicle, 10-30-73, section 4, p. 26
[79] Washington Post, 12-5-81, p. 11
[80] Washington Post, 12-5-81, p. 11

when they would not interfere 'with the protection of intelligence sources and methods,'"[81] thus giving CIA officers Cart Blanche to violate "federal" laws as long as they use "intelligence sources and methods" when doing so.

Reagan's order also allows the CIA to use "'electronic surveillance, unconsented physical searches, mail surveillance, physical surveillance, or monitoring devices' within the United States."[82]

Regarding CIA violations of "federal" laws before Reagan's 1981 order officially condoned the violations, the 1975 Rockefeller Report states, "For a period of over twenty years, an agreement existed between the Department of Justice and the CIA providing that the Agency was to investigate allegations of crimes by CIA employees."[83]

As noted earlier, when the CIA investigates its own crimes, such as surreptitiously administering LSD to unsuspecting Americans, it results in warnings from the CIA Inspector General that "precautions must be taken to conceal these activities from the American public . . . . Knowledge that the Agency is engaging in unethical and illicit activities would have serious repercussions."

And when the CIA Inspector General investigates crimes like opening and reading the U.S. mail, he will recommend preparation of an "emergency plan" and "cover story."

The CIA is perpetually concerned with the "flap" potential of its secret nefarious activities inside the United States, and it is perpetually concerned with the "precautions" that "must be taken to conceal these activities from the American public."

For the Department of Justice to allow the CIA to investigate its own crimes is patently ridiculous, as is the idea that a CIA Director would report CIA officers to the Attorney General for committing "federal" crimes. And Reagan's Executive Order said nothing about CIA officers who commit state and local crimes.

---

[81] Ibid.
[82] U.S. Privacy and Civil Liberties Oversight Board (Executive Order 12333) https://documents.pclob.gov/prod/Documents/OversightReport/4f1d0d87-233b-4555-9b87-79089ad9845e/12333%20Public%20Capstone.pdf
[83] Rockefeller Report, p. 14

The Rockefeller Report states, "In 1954, the CIA pointed out to the Department of Justice that in many cases involving CIA, prosecution would require public disclosure of sensitive Agency operations and procedures."[84]

There obviously had been, or potentially were, by 1954 "many cases" of criminal activity in the CIA that warranted federal "prosecution," otherwise there would be no reason to point out that "in many cases," such prosecution would require disclosing the Agency's "sensitive" operations.

The fact that the CIA is prohibited from carrying out domestic operations under the National Security Act of 1947 means that all CIA operations in the United States are "sensitive," thus precluding the "prosecution" of any criminal activity.

The Rockefeller Report states that the "Office of General Counsel" is expected to "find legal techniques" that would "facilitate" CIA activities,[85] but "legal techniques" are not required when conducting operations in a foreign country. Foreign countries do not allow the CIA to legally spy on them. The CIA General Counsel is tasked only with manipulating U.S. law to make it seem "legal" when the CIA conducts illicit activities inside the United States.

President Reagan's Executive Order in 1981 also "permits" the CIA to "enter into arrangements with state and local police," which certainly facilitates violating state and local laws. CIA officers with such "arrangements" and "police cover in the form of badges and other identification" can obviously exercise "police" and "law enforcement" powers, both of which are prohibited by the National Security Act of 1947. CIA officers wearing police uniforms, carrying police badges, and driving police cars can obviously intimidate or harass anyone that the CIA targets inside the United States.

---

[84] Rockefeller Report, p. 75
[85] Rockefeller Report, p. 87

It would, of course, be convenient for CIA officers committing crimes if the police officers responding to investigate were actually CIA officers with "police covers." When the *New York Times* exposed some of the CIA's massive domestic operations in 1974 and a wide swath of illegal CIA activities, a CIA official "contended at length" that the domestic operations were "not illegal" because of the CIA's "legal" right to "prevent the possible revelation of secrets."[86]

Committing crimes is itself a secret that, as far as the CIA is concerned, cannot be revealed. The CIA considers all of its activities inside the United States to be "secret."

The National Security Act indeed states that the CIA Director is "responsible for protecting intelligence sources and methods from unauthorized disclosure," and as noted earlier, CIA officers can simply utilize "intelligence sources and methods" when engaging in criminal or unconstitutional activity, which would preclude any official disclosure of the activity.

The Senate Church Committee stated in 1975 that in targeting "American citizens in this country," the CIA employs "physical surveillance" and "electronic surveillance," and it inspects their "income tax records."[87] CIA officers with "official covers" as IRS officials would have no trouble inspecting "income tax records," and the CIA can certainly use the IRS to carry out a political agenda.

Renegade CIA officers and corrupt CIA officials clearly ignore the laws and Constitutional protections afforded American citizens whenever they see fit, including protection against "unreasonable searches" as described in the 4th Amendment and the "equal protection of the laws" put forth in the 14th Amendment.

CIA officers, in fact, committed felonies for ten years when they put LSD and "behavior-influencing substances" into the food of "unsuspecting" Americans, not to mention the death of Dr. Frank Olson, who plunged to his death in the middle of the night while he was alone with the CIA officer who drugged him a week earlier.

---

[86] New York Times, 12-22-74, p. 26
[87] Church Committee: Book III, p. 732

CIA operatives out in the field will break any law that a superior or ranking CIA official wants them to break, and individual CIA officers will clearly not be held accountable when they choose on their own to break the law.

As former CIA Director Allen Dulles stated, the CIA's actions are not "tainted" by "any legality."[88]

Under a "National Security Council Intelligence Directive" on February 12, 1948, just a few short months after the CIA went into operation, the CIA was instructed to establish "field offices within the United States" and engage in the "exploitation" of "individuals" and "non-governmental organizations" within the United States, including "business concerns."[89]

The Intelligence Directive repeatedly states that the CIA field offices must focus only on "foreign intelligence information" and on sources that have "foreign intelligence potential," but with the proverbial foot-in-the-door, corrupt elements of the CIA soon began carrying out massive operations inside the United States targeting U.S. citizens.

In 1975, CIA Director William Colby testified to the newly formed House Select Committee on Intelligence that CIA officers work "full-time" at "major domestic media outlets."[90]

Colby also testified that CIA officers are detailed to "major circulation American journals," which would be newspapers like the *New York Times* and the *Washington Post*.

When Colby was pointedly asked, "Has the CIA ever asked media networks or journals to kill a story," he boasted, "I spent a great deal of my time earlier this year trying to get that done."[91]

With full-time employees of the CIA having "nonofficial covers" in the media, the CIA can control the narrative for any story it sees

---

[88] Dallas Morning News, 10-13-63, p. 24
[89] National Security Council Intelligence Directive No. 7
https://history.state.gov/historicaldocuments/frus1945-50Intel/d427
[90] Hearings Before The Select Committee On Intelligence, Part 5, p. 1589
https://www.maryferrell.org/showDoc.html?docId=146901#relPageId=27&tab=page
[91] Ibid., p. 1593

fit, which obviously facilitates the CIA's political agenda. As will be seen later in this book, there are high-profile CIA officers using "nonofficial covers" with CBS News, NBC News, and Fox News.

A 1961 CIA document on "Security and Control of Operations" states: "Control is the capacity to generate, alter, or halt human behavior by implying, citing, or using physical or psychological means to ensure compliance."[92]

Renegade CIA officers operating inside the United States will "generate, alter, or halt" the behavior of U.S. citizens and government officials that they target, and they will do so "by implying, citing, or using physical or psychological means to ensure compliance."

President Truman, who signed the 1947 legislation creating the CIA, wrote an article published in the *Washington Post* on December 22, 1963, titled "Limit CIA Role to Intelligence." In detailing his concerns about the CIA, Truman stated that "for some time" he had been "disturbed by the way the CIA has been diverted from its original assignment."[93]

Truman also warned that the CIA "has become an operational and at times a policy making arm of the government."

Congress passed the National Security Act of 1947 and President Truman signed it into law believing that the CIA would most definitely not conduct operations inside the United States.

The National Security Act states in no uncertain terms that the CIA "shall have no police, subpoena, law enforcement powers, or internal security functions," and under "Definitions" in Section 308, it states, "As used in the Act, the term 'function' includes functions, powers, and duties,"[94] which means the CIA is expressly prohibited from performing "internal security functions" and expressly

---

[92] National Archives Record Number 104-10408-10241
[93] Washington Post, 12-22-63, p. 11
[94] https://www.dni.gov/index.php/ic-legal-reference-book/national-security-act-of-1947
(Also archived from the CIA's own website at the link below)
https://web.archive.org/web/20180606172154/https://www.cia.gov/library/readingroom/docs/1947-07-26.pdf

prohibited from exercising "internal security powers," and it is expressly prohibited from having "internal security duties." It is more than obvious that the CIA completely disregards these legal restrictions.

This book is an account of my first-hand knowledge of massive corruption in the government and the CIA. The CIA operations detailed thus far, as bad as they are, pale in comparison to the rest of the corruption laid out herein. It is not a "theory," and there are no "conclusions" drawn from the wealth of data presented in this book. The documentation speaks for itself.

Twenty-eight years after the CIA was created, the Commission on CIA Activities Within the United States (the Rockefeller Commission) addressed legal challenges to the CIA's unconstitutional activity and its widespread domestic operations, stating, "Practically all of the CIA's operations are covered by secrecy . . . . Few potential challengers are even aware of activities that might otherwise be contested; nor can such activities be easily discovered."[95]

---

[95] Rockefeller Report, p. 78

Chapter 2: CIA Officers in the Secret Service Planning Presidential Assassinations

KGB infiltration of the CIA was exposed in 1984, and the KGB officers admitted that they were behind the assassination of President Kennedy on November 22, 1963. Killing Kennedy was the first of multiple CIA efforts to control the Presidency. The KGB infiltration and how it was exposed is addressed in detail later in this book.

As cited in Chapter 1, CIA documents from 1964 clearly state that CIA officers are "detailed by the CIA" to perform Secret Service functions.[96]

Four of the eight Secret Service agents in the Presidential follow-up car when Kennedy was assassinated were Soviet KGB officers inside the CIA, all four of whom had been "detailed" to the Secret Service. It was confirmed in 1984 that these four CIA officers were, in fact, KGB officers. (The Presidential follow-up car, or Secret Service follow-up car as it is sometimes known, rides directly behind the Presidential limousine when the President travels.)

The four KGB officers' official Secret Service reports, cited in precise detail in this chapter, clearly attest to their participation in President Kennedy's assassination.

Four Secret Service agents rode inside the Presidential follow-up car, while four agents rode on the outside running boards on either side of the car. Agents on the running boards are expected to be the first to shield the President from any possible danger.

---

[96] National Archives Record Numbers 104-10423-10332 & 104-10419-10046

One KGB officer rode on an outside running board, and the other three KGB officers rode inside the car.

The highest-ranking Secret Service agent in the follow-up car was a KGB officer named Emory Roberts, who rode in the front passenger seat next to the driver, Agent Samuel Kinney. Roberts had the prime position for watching the assassination unfold, as President Kennedy was directly in front of him in the rear seat of the Presidential limousine.

Two of Roberts' KGB cohorts, Glen Bennett and Tim McIntyre, were assigned with Roberts to "work the Presidential follow-up car throughout this entire movement."[97] Bennett rode in the back seat on the right side while McIntyre rode on the left rear running board.

The fourth KGB officer was Special Agent George Hickey, who rode in the back seat with Bennett to his right and McIntyre to his left on the outside running board. Hickey's own report states that he was an "extra man" in the follow-up car, which means he had no business being there. Hickey arrived in Dallas the previous day on an Air Force cargo plane transporting the Presidential limousine and the Secret Service follow-up car.[98]

Special Agent John Ready, who was not a KGB officer, rode on the right front running board next to Roberts, the KGB officer in the front passenger seat. Ready was closest in proximity to President Kennedy and was expected to be the first agent to shield the President. He worked the "Presidential Detail" with KGB officers Roberts, Bennett, and McIntyre.

Special Agent Clint Hill rode on the left front running board next to Kinney, the driver. Hill was assigned to work "the First Lady's Detail" with Special Agent Paul Landis, who was on the right rear running board next to Bennett, one of the two KGB officers in the back seat.

---

[97] Warren Commission Document 3 - Secret Service Report of 18 Dec 1963, p. 171
[98] Warren Commission Hearings and Exhibits, Volume XVIII, p. 761

In KGB officer Emory Roberts' official report, he wrote that after a bullet struck President Kennedy in the head, he picked up the car radio and told Special Agent Lawson in the lead car, "The President has been hit. Escort us to the nearest hospital fast but at a safe speed."[99]

Roberts "repeated the message, requesting to be cautious, meaning the speed. I had in mind Vice President Johnson's safety," and Roberts added "as well as the President's, if he was not already dead." Roberts then "turned around to wave the Vice President's car to come closer."

"I said, pointing to McIntyre, 'They got him, they got him,' continuing I said, 'You, meaning McIntyre, and Bennett take over Johnson as soon as we stop.'"

Roberts did not punctuate his Secret Service report with exclamation points, but he was most definitely making an exclamatory statement when he explicitly told McIntyre, "They got him! They got him!"

Roberts wrote that at 12:30 p.m., before witnessing the fatal head shot, he witnessed the "first of three shots fired, at which time I saw the President lean toward Mrs. Kennedy."

With Special Agent John Ready standing just inches away on the right front running board, KGB officer Emory Roberts clearly saw that "they got him" with the "first" shot, and he clearly saw the President react to the shot, but according to his own Secret Service report, Roberts, the highest-ranking agent in the car, sat there and watched silently for at least five seconds and possibly as many as eight seconds while President Kennedy was being shot to death directly in front of him. Roberts said and did absolutely nothing until President Kennedy was shot in the head.

(There is an ongoing debate concerning the amount of time it took to fire all of the shots at President Kennedy, but the fact is that it took at least five seconds and possibly as many as eight seconds.)

---

[99] Warren Commission Hearings and Exhibits, Volume XVIII, pp. 734-735

Senator Ralph Yarborough of Texas, who was riding with Vice President Johnson directly behind the Presidential follow-up car, could plainly see the reactions of Secret Service agents during the assassination. Yarborough's affidavit to the Warren Commission states that when he heard the first shot, he "thought immediately that it was a rifle shot."[100]

Yarborough's affidavit also states, "All of the Secret Service men seemed to me to respond very slowly, with no more than a puzzled look. In fact, until the automatic weapon was uncovered, I had been lulled into a sense of false hope for the President's safety by the lack of motion, excitement, or apparent visible knowledge by the Secret Service men that anything so dreadful was happening. Knowing something of the training that combat infantrymen and Marines receive, I am amazed at the lack of instantaneous response by the Secret Service when the rifle fire began."

Senator Yarborough was actually witnessing the result of the KGB sabotaging Presidential protection. The KGB officers, one of whom was running board agent Tim McIntyre, knew that there would be a problem if the other three running board agents, Landis, Ready, and Hill, took action to protect the President when the gunfire began. Kinney, as a driver, certainly could not do anything during the assassination, but if it were going to be a successful assassination, the KGB officers would have to do something about the other three running board agents.

McIntyre's partner, Glen Bennett, took decisive action to make sure the three agents would not be a problem. Warren Commission Exhibit 1020 contains a news article stating that Secret Service agents were "in the Fort Worth Press Club the early morning of Friday, November 22, some of them remaining until nearly 3 a.m. . . . . They were drinking. One of them was reported to have been inebriated."[101]

---

[100] Warren Commission Hearings and Exhibits, Volume VII, p. 440
[101] Warren Commission Hearings and Exhibits, Volume XVIII, p. 677

It also states that after leaving the Press Club at "nearly 3 a.m.," the Secret Service agents went to "an all-night beatnik rendezvous called 'The Cellar.'"

Secret Service Chief James Rowley testified to the Warren Commission about the incident, stating, "There were nine men involved at the Press Club, and there were ten men involved at The Cellar."[102]

Rowley testified that Bennett and the three running board agents that needed to be disabled, Landis, Ready, and Hill, had participated in the drinking and late night activity. Out of the sixteen Secret Service agents in the Presidential motorcade, Bennett, the KGB officer, and the three running board agents were the only ones to participate in the drinking and late-night activity. The other five Secret Service agents who consumed alcohol at the Press Club were not in the Presidential motorcade on November 22, 1963. As noted earlier, the running board agents would be the first to shield the President from any possible danger.

Rowley claimed that someone, whom he did not identify, told the agents, "There was a buffet to be served at the Fort Worth Club," but when the agents arrived, "there was no buffet." Later in his testimony, he stated, "and they just thought while they were there, they would have a drink."[103]

Rowley glossed over it with one of three different versions of the drinking incident, testifying that he "ascertained in personal interviews" that three agents "had one scotch" and "others had two or three beers." He also testified that agents "were in and out" of the Press Club from "roughly around 12:30 until the place closed at 2 o'clock."

But in a letter to the Warren Commission several weeks prior to his testimony, Rowley put forth two versions of the drinking incident that were different from his Warren Commission testimony. In one version, Rowley wrote that Calvin Sutton, president of the Press

---

[102] Warren Commission Hearings and Exhibits, Volume V, pp. 451-452
[103] Warren Commission Hearings and Exhibits, Volume V, p. 458

Club, had said that "the Press Club has a closing curfew of 12 midnight," but Calvin Sutton, for some unknown reason, "kept the Press Club open until sometime after 2 a.m.," which is clearly more than two hours past the "closing curfew."

Sutton supposedly "ordered the bar at the Press Club closed" at "about 2 a.m.," and "as the bar was closing, a party of about four people arrived who were later identified to him as Secret Service agents. Mr. Sutton requested the bartender serve them one drink, after which the bar was again closed and the party left."[104]

The other version in Rowley's letter had at least something in common with his Warren Commission testimony. He wrote that what he determined "in the course of this investigation" was that "nine Special Agents of the White House Detail were in the Press Club at various times and departed at various hours up to 2 a.m.," which is what he told the Warren Commission. But Calvin Sutton, president of the Press Club, admitted that four Secret Service agents were there until sometime after 2 a.m. and it was reported that Secret Service agents were in the bar "until nearly 3 a.m."

Rowley also claimed, "The amount of beer and liquor consumed by any of them did not exceed one and a half mixed drinks, or in one case, three glasses of beer," which is different than his Warren Commission testimony that three agents "had one scotch," and "others had two or three beers," and it is completely different from the claim that "about four" Secret Service agents showed up at 2 a.m. and "Mr. Sutton requested the bartender serve them one drink."

The claim that the bar was closing when about four agents got there and that it stayed open so they could have a drink is nowhere in his Warren Commission testimony. Also, his letter to the Warren Commission did not mention anything about Secret Service agents showing up for a buffet at 2 o'clock in the morning. His letter did not say anything at all about a buffet, but it did say they were having a "party" at the Press Club, and after the bar

---

[104] Warren Commission Hearings and Exhibits, Volume XVIII, p. 667-668

finally closed, they obviously took the "party" over to the "all-night beatnik rendezvous," otherwise known as The Cellar.

After testifying that the agents did not find a buffet and were "in and out" of the Press Club until it closed, Rowley stated, "After that, some of them went to The Cellar."

KGB officer Glen Bennett and the three running board agents, Landis, Ready, and Hill, all admitted to consuming alcohol at the Press Club and then going to The Cellar afterward.[105] As noted earlier, they were the only Secret Service agents assigned to the Presidential motorcade who participated in the drinking and late-night activity.

Rowley claimed they went to The Cellar after leaving the bar in the early morning hours of November 22 "out of curiosity, because this was some kind of a beatnik place." He acknowledged that "there was someone connected with the group who was intoxicated," but he claimed that it was just someone that the agents "ran into" at the Press Club. He claimed the intoxicated man who was "connected with the group" was not a Secret Service agent.[106]

KGB officer Tim McIntyre wrote in his report that Secret Service agents assigned to the Presidential follow-up car were working the "8 a.m. to 4 p.m. shift" on November 22, 1963.[107]

Chief Justice Earl Warren asked Rowley when it comes to seeing someone with a rifle, "Don't you think that if a man went to bed reasonably early and hadn't been drinking the night before, he would be more alert to see those things as a Secret Service agent than if they stayed up until 3, 4, or 5 o'clock in the morning, going to beatnik joints and doing some drinking along the way?"[108]

Rowley first tried to dodge the question and did not answer it, so Warren repeated, "I say, wouldn't an alert Secret Service man in this motorcade, who is supposed to observe such things, be more likely to

---

[105] Warren Commission Hearings and Exhibits, Volume XVIII, pp. 682, 685, 687, & 690
[106] Warren Commission Hearings and Exhibits, Volume V, p. 461
[107] Warren Commission Hearings and Exhibits, Volume XVIII, p. 746
[108] Warren Commission Hearings and Exhibits, Volume V, p. 459

observe something of that kind if he was free from any of the results of liquor or lack of sleep than he would otherwise?"

And Rowley replied, "Well, yes; he would be."

Warren also had Rowley read from the Secret Service manual, which strictly prohibits the consumption of alcohol, "including beer and wine, by members of the White House Detail and special agents cooperating with them, or by special agents on similar assignments, while they are in a travel status." All such agents "are considered to be subject to call for official duty at any time while they are in travel status . . . either during the day or night when they are off duty."[109]

The manual clearly reflects the seriousness of violating the prohibition against alcohol, stating, "Violation or slight disregard" of these regulations "at any time will be cause for removal from the service."

As noted earlier, Landis, Ready, and Hill, being assigned to the outside running boards of the Presidential follow-up car, would be the first to react in the event of any danger to the President. They all had to wake up early, get ready, and report for the 8 a.m. shift, just a few short hours after their all-night partying with Bennett.

Bennett's KGB colleague, Tim McIntyre, the fourth agent on the running boards, certainly did not need to be disabled. KGB officers McIntyre and Bennett were the agents that Roberts immediately assigned to "take over" Vice President Johnson after President Kennedy was shot in the head. That was when KGB officer Emory Roberts exclaimed, "They got him! They got him!"

Secret Service Chief Rowley wrote a letter to the Warren Commission stating, "The first duty of agents in the motorcade is to attempt to cover the President as closely as possible and practicable and to shield him by attempting to place themselves between the President and any source of danger . . . . Agents are instructed that it is not their responsibility to investigate or evaluate a present danger, but to consider any untoward

---

[109] Warren Commission Hearings and Exhibits, Volume XVIII, p. 665

circumstances as serious and to afford the President maximum protection at all times."[110]

The running board agents' Secret Service reports lay out in detail how they were unable to perform their "first duty" of affording the President "maximum protection at all times."

Special Agent Landis's report states that after he arrived at Dallas Love Field at 11:35 a.m., less than an hour before the assassination, he "walked to where the motorcade vehicles were parked." He then stood by the Presidential follow-up car and thought it would be funny to ask Special Agent Kinney, the agent who would be driving the car, where the follow-up car was. In Landis's own words, "I remember speaking to him and standing by the follow-up car and jokingly asking him if he could tell me where the follow-up car was."[111]

Landis also "walked over to Special Agent Win Lawson just to double check to see if I was still assigned to work the follow-up car as had previously been arranged." (Landis was clearly hoping against hope that he would not have to stand upright on an outside running board.)

When the Presidential follow-up car "started moving," Landis was standing "with my right leg on the running board and my left leg up and over and inside the follow-up car. I stayed in this position until we were leaving the airport area and remarked that, 'I might as well get all the way in,' and I did so." (Landis arbitrarily decided that President Kennedy could make do with only three running board agents protecting him on November 22, 1963.)

Landis wrote that after he climbed all the way into the Presidential follow-up car, Roberts told him to "get back on the outside running board 'just in case.'" As the highest-ranking Secret Service agent in the car, KGB officer Emory Roberts certainly did not want to be scrutinized for allowing Landis to sit inside the car during the assassination. Roberts knew, however, that Landis was in no shape to be on guard against a Presidential assassination.

---

[110] Warren Commission Hearings and Exhibits, Volume XVIII, p. 710
[111] Warren Commission Hearings and Exhibits, Volume XVIII, p. 751-752

In the agents' reports on the drinking incident, Landis admitted that he did not leave The Cellar, the all-night beatnik rendezvous, until "approximately 5:00 a.m."[112] But how much alcohol the agents actually consumed during their all night partying will never be known because the Secret Service' is the only source for that information.

Landis wrote that when the Presidential limousine and the follow-up car were turning left onto Elm Street to go past the Texas School Book Depository, which would be the only building on the President's right side, he "made a quick surveillance of a building which was to be on the President's right once the left turn was completed."

He described the Book Depository as a "modernistic type building," and he wrote that when the first shot was fired, it "sounded like the report of a high-powered rifle from behind me, over my right shoulder."[113] (Lee Harvey Oswald allegedly fired three shots from the sixth floor window of the Book Depository.)

Landis also wrote, "There was no question in my mind what it was," but Landis ignored the fact that Agents are specifically instructed that it is "not their responsibility to investigate or evaluate a present danger."

He stated that after definitively hearing the report of a high-powered rifle, "My first glance was at the President," and then, "I immediately returned my gaze over my right shoulder toward the modernistic building I had observed before."

His report states that it was just "a quick glance" at the Texas School Book Depository, and he "saw nothing." But he continued to violate the directive not to investigate or evaluate a present danger when, after seeing "nothing," he "immediately started scanning the crowd at the intersection from my right to my left."

Landis then "began to think that the sound was a firecracker," even though it "sounded like the report of a high-powered rifle,"

---

[112] Warren Commission Hearings and Exhibits, Volume XVIII, p. 687
[113] Warren Commission Hearings and Exhibits, Volume XVIII, p. 754

and there was "no question" in his mind as to what it was. A few seconds later, "the next shot was fired" and Landis "thought that maybe one of the cars in the motorcade had a blowout that echoed off the buildings," and Landis "looked at the right front tire of the President's car," at which point Landis witnessed President Kennedy being shot in the head.

Special Agent Landis's own report makes it clear that he was dazed and confused while the President was being assassinated. His report makes it clear that when he arrived at the Dallas airport less than an hour earlier, he was in no shape to perform his "first duty" of affording the President "maximum protection at all times," not only because of the consumption of alcohol just hours earlier, but also because of a definitive lack of sleep.

As noted earlier, KGB officer George Hickey arrived in Dallas the previous day on an Air Force plane transporting the Presidential limousine and the Secret Service follow-up car, and he admitted to being "an extra man" in the follow-up car. Another Secret Service report states that Hickey's KGB colleague, Glen Bennett, was with the "Protective Research Section" and only "temporarily assigned to the White House Detail."[114] Instead of having just two KGB officers on hand for the assassination, which would be Roberts and McIntyre, they were able to get Hickey and Bennett into the back seat and have four KGB officers in the follow-up car.

KGB officer Hickey wrote that Roberts instructed him to "take control of the AR-15 rifle" whenever he was riding "as an extra man" in the Presidential follow-up car.[115] The AR-15 rifle was the "automatic weapon" that Senator Yarborough saw "uncovered" after witnessing "all of the Secret Service men" responding "very slowly, with no more than a puzzled look."

Hickey wrote that it was not until "the end of the last report" that he "reached to the bottom of the car and picked up the AR-15 rifle, cocked and loaded it, and turned to the rear."

---

[114] Warren Commission Hearings and Exhibits, Volume XVIII, p. 783
[115] Warren Commission Hearings and Exhibits, Volume XVIII, p. 762

Bennett, who was only "temporarily assigned to the White House Detail," wrote in his "Protective Assignment" report that after seeing the last shot strike the President in the head, he "immediately hollered 'he's hit'" and then "reached for the AR-15 located on the floor of the rear seat. Special Agent Hickey had already picked-up the AR-15."[116]

But before seeing the last shot strike President Kennedy in the head and before saying anything, KGB officer Bennett watched silently as President Kennedy was shot in the back.

Bennett wrote that he "looked at the back of the President" and "saw the shot hit the President about four inches down from the right shoulder." Even though Bennett saw the President take a bullet in the back, Bennett sat there and said absolutely nothing. It was not until one of the assassins' bullets struck President Kennedy in the head that Bennett hollered, "He's hit!"

After five to eight seconds of gunfire, President Kennedy sustained what proved to be a fatal head wound, at which point KGB officers Hickey and Bennett realized the plan had come to fruition. Like KGB officer Roberts, they both had an instantaneous response. Hickey belatedly "picked up the AR-15 rifle" and "turned to the rear," and Bennett exclaimed, "He's hit!" and reached for the AR-15 rifle that Hickey was already holding. Roberts then twice instructed the lead car to drive to the hospital "at a safe speed," after which he turned to KGB officer McIntyre and exclaimed, "They got him! They got him!"

Hickey's report states that he is with the "White House garage,"[117] and McIntyre's report describes Hickey as "a driver."[118] Special Agent Kinney drove the Presidential follow-up car, while Special Agent Greer drove the President's limousine, and Texas State Highway Patrolmen were driving both the Vice President's

---

[116] Warren Commission Hearings and Exhibits, Volume XVIII, p. 760
[117] Warren Commission Hearings and Exhibits, Volume XVIII, p. 761
[118] Warren Commission Hearings and Exhibits, Volume XVIII, p. 746

car and the Vice Presidential follow-up car.[119] KGB officer Hickey, the "driver" with the "White House garage," had nothing to drive, which obviously made him an "extra man" in the follow-up car.

Hickey wrote that while President Kennedy was being treated at Parkland Hospital, Assistant Special Agent in Charge Roy Kellerman "told Agent Kinney and me to take the cars to the plane and stand by for orders." Hickey then drove the Presidential limousine to the airport.[120]

Hickey would have served no purpose in the Presidential follow-up car if President Kennedy had not been assassinated, but by tagging along as an "extra man," Hickey was conveniently on hand to drive the President's limousine back to the airport and thus have access to the crime scene.

The Warren Commission Report states, "After the Presidential car was returned to Washington on November 22, 1963, Secret Service agents found two bullet fragments in the front seat."[121]

"One fragment" was "found on the seat beside the driver," and the "other fragment" was "found along the right side of the front seat." The FBI "positively identified" both fragments as having been "fired" from the "rifle found in the Depository," the building from which Lee Harvey Oswald allegedly fired the shots. KGB officer Hickey had no problem whatsoever planting two bullet fragments that had at one time been fired from the rifle that would be "found in the Depository."

The reactions of Secret Service agents in the Presidential follow-up car, as detailed in the reports they wrote, clearly contradict what they were expected to do, especially the reactions of KGB officers Roberts, Bennett, McIntyre, and Hickey. The previously cited letter from Chief Rowley to the Warren Commission clearly explained that agents in the motorcade are instructed to "consider any untoward

---

[119] Warren Commission Hearings and Exhibits, Volume XVIII, pp. 800-801
[120] Warren Commission Hearings and Exhibits, Volume XVIII, p. 764
[121] Warren Commission Report, pp. 76 & 85

circumstances as serious" and "afford the President maximum protection at all times."

KGB officer Roberts, who was sitting in the prime position for witnessing the assassination and who was the highest-ranking agent in the follow-up car, stated very clearly that he sat and watched everything from the first shot to the last without saying a word until it was all over. As noted earlier, Special Agent John Ready, the agent closest in proximity to President Kennedy, was standing right next to Roberts on the right front running board while Roberts silently and patiently watched the Soviet KGB assassinate the President of the United States.

KGB officer Bennett's report states that at the sound of the first shot, he looked at the President and watched everything without saying or doing anything until it was all over.

McIntyre, the only KGB officer on a running board, wrote that the President's car was 200 yards from the underpass "when the first shot was fired," and "after the second shot" he "looked at the President and witnessed his being struck in the head by the third and last shot."[122]

McIntyre did not say what he was doing for five to eight seconds after "the first shot was fired," but a photo shown later in this chapter shows McIntyre focused across the Secret Service car on Special Agents Ready and Landis, two of the three running board agents that needed to be disabled.[123]

KGB officer Hickey reported that he stood up and turned his back to the President at the sound of the first shot, allegedly "in an attempt to identify it," and then after "two or three seconds" of looking toward the rear, he turned to look at the President and watched as the next two shots were fired.[124] Hickey picked up the AR-15 rifle only after a bullet struck President Kennedy in the

---

[122] Warren Commission Hearings and Exhibits, Volume XVIII, p. 747
[123] Warren Commission Hearings and Exhibits, Volume XVIII, p. 93
[124] Warren Commission Hearings and Exhibits, Volume XVIII, p. 762

head, more than five seconds and possibly as many as eight seconds after the first shot.

Special Agent Ready, who stood on the right front running board, wrote in his report that after hearing "what appeared to be firecrackers going off . . . . I immediately turned to my right rear trying to locate the source but was not able to determine the exact location."[125]

Ready also wrote that he "heard someone" inside the follow-up car say, "He's shot." (That would most likely be Bennett, the KGB officer in the back seat who exclaimed, "He's hit," or it could be Roberts, the KGB officer who turned around and exclaimed, "They got him! They got him!")

After hearing someone say that the President has been shot, Ready "left the follow-up car in the direction of the President's car," but he was "recalled" by Roberts "as the cars increased their speeds."

Ready, being closest in proximity to the President, should have been the very first agent to shield the President, but he made no mention of seeing President Kennedy get shot, and he was oblivious to the President being shot in the head until he heard someone say something. His ignorance of the President being shot would be due to "trying to locate the source" of "firecrackers" for five to eight seconds.

Ready was clearly suffering from the effects of alcohol and a lack of sleep when he spent five to eight seconds violating the directive not to "investigate or evaluate a present danger."

As noted earlier, Special Agent Landis was on the right rear running board behind Ready, and after hearing the first shot from "a high-powered rifle," he "immediately returned my gaze over my right shoulder toward the modernistic building I had observed before," and then he "started scanning the crowd at the intersection."

Like Ready, Landis was suffering from the effects of alcohol and a lack of sleep, which was more than obvious in his report. After his lackadaisical and listless behavior at the airport, now he's "gazing" at a building and "scanning" a crowd after the President has been shot.

---

[125] Warren Commission Hearings and Exhibits, Volume XVIII, p. 749

Landis then "began to think that the sound was a firecracker" before concluding that it might have actually been an echo from "a blowout."

Special Agent Clint Hill was standing on the left front running board next to Kinney, the driver, and Hill went into action only after seeing the President react to being shot. The facts bear out Hill's remarkably slow reaction time, as he, too, had engaged in the late-night drinking and partying.

Hill's report states that he heard "a noise similar to a firecracker" that "came from my right rear, and I immediately moved my head in that direction." When Hill moved his head "in that direction," his "eyes had to cross the Presidential automobile," and he "saw the President hunch forward and then slump to his left."[126]

Hill "jumped from the follow-up car and ran toward the Presidential automobile," after which he "jumped onto the left rear step of the Presidential automobile."

Hill, who was oblivious to the first shot, told the Warren Commission that he was not "up on" the limousine until after the last shot "removed a portion of the President's head."[127]

The Zapruder film, an actual film of the assassination that runs at approximately eighteen frames per second, clearly shows Hill's slow reaction to the gunfire. When the limousine emerges from behind a road sign at frame 225 of the film, President Kennedy can be seen already reacting to being shot, which means he was shot at some point prior to frame 225.

The photo on the next page (Warren Commission Exhibit 900) coincides with frame 255 of the Zapruder film.[128] Hill is clearly resting atop the car door and leaning into the car as the assassination continues to unfold. He obviously did not hear the

---

[126] Warren Commission Hearings and Exhibits, Volume XVIII, p. 742
[127] Warren Commission Hearings and Exhibits, Volume II, p. 138
[128] Warren Commission Report. P. 112

first shot and does not know at this point that the President has been shot.

Special Agent Clint Hill, standing on the left "front" running board, is clearly resting atop the car door and leaning into the car with his right leg crossed in front of his left as the assassination continues to unfold. Ready and Landis are standing on the right-side running board looking back after the first shot, while KGB officer Tim McIntyre, standing on the left "rear" running board, is focused across the car on Ready and Landis. Roberts is the KGB officer in the front passenger seat quietly watching the assassination unfold. More than three seconds after this photo was snapped, President Kennedy was shot in the head, after which Roberts turned to McIntyre and exclaimed, "They got him! They got him!" (Warren Commission Exhibit 900, Warren Commission Hearings, Volume XVIII, page 93)

The President does not begin to "slump to his left" until about frame 266 of the Zapruder film. When Hill finally sees the President hunching forward and slumping to his left, he suddenly realizes the President is being assassinated.

The fatal headshot occurred precisely at frame 313, five to eight seconds after the first shot. Another film taken during the assassination (the "Muchmore" film) clearly shows that Hill has not even passed the left front fender of the follow-up car.

Hill catches up to the now accelerating limousine by frame 333 of the Zapruder film, which means that after his slow reaction time, it took him less than two seconds to get to the limousine. He is not able to get up onto the rear step of the limousine until frame 382 due to the limo accelerating after President Kennedy was shot in the head.

He then climbs onto and across the trunk, forcing Jackie Kennedy back into her seat.

If the sound of the shot came from Hill's "right rear," there was no reason for him to move his head "in that direction." All Secret Service agents are expected to "consider any untoward circumstances as serious and to afford the President maximum protection at all times."

This frame from the "Muchmore" film shows President Kennedy being shot in the head after five to eight seconds of gunfire. Hill has just come off the running board and has not yet passed the left front fender of the Secret Service follow-up car.[129]

Secret Service policy clearly dictates that Hill, who was oblivious to the first shot, should have immediately jumped from the running board and ran toward the Presidential limousine instead of moving his head toward what he called "a noise similar to a firecracker." Secret Service agents are not supposed to look back thinking that they should, or somehow can, determine if someone has fired a rifle or simply set off a firecracker.

Hill went into action only because he saw the President "hunch forward and then slump to his left" while he was turning to look back toward the "firecracker" noise.

---

[129] https://www.youtube.com/watch?v=TGKTKKoT64k

With Special Agent Kinney focused on driving the car, and four agents being part and parcel to the plan to kill Kennedy, and three running board agents suffering from the effects of alcohol and a lack of sleep, it is no surprise that Senator Yarborough stated, "All of the Secret Service men seemed to me to respond very slowly, with no more than a puzzled look."[130]

Policy dictates that all the running board agents should have leaped from the running boards at the sound of the first shot, but for five to eight seconds Senator Yarborough, who was riding directly behind the Secret Service follow-up car and who knew with certainty that a rifle shot had been fired, observed a "lack of motion, excitement, or apparent visible knowledge by the Secret Service men that anything so dreadful was happening."

Like Hill, KGB officers Roberts and Bennett could clearly see the President "hunch forward and then slump to his left" while KGB officer Hickey stood looking toward the rear and KGB officer McIntyre stood on the left rear running board focused across the Secret Service car on Ready and Landis. The four KGB officers knew perfectly well what was happening when the gunfire began.

When the first shot sounded and Hickey "stood up and looked to my right and rear" with a what-was-that attitude, he clearly wanted to draw attention to himself so that the three running board agents would look to the rear "with no more than a puzzled look" while the President was being shot to death in front of the follow-up car. In taking no action to protect the President, the running board agents most definitely ignored the directive that "it is not their responsibility" to "investigate or evaluate a present danger."

Running board agents Landis, Ready, and Hill did not perform their "first duty" of protecting the President by attempting to "place themselves between the President and any source of danger," nor did they "consider any untoward circumstances as serious" and "afford the President maximum protection at all times," because Bennett took them out for drinking and late-night partying, which meant they

---

[130] Warren Commission Hearings and Exhibits, Volume VII, p. 440

were all the more susceptible to Hickey's suggestive movement to look to the rear while the President was being assassinated in front of the car.

The Moscow TASS News Agency's "International Services in English" went so far as to blatantly boast that "only a few hours" before the assassination, the plan to assassinate President Kennedy included having the Secret Service "virtually isolated by getting them thoroughly drunk . . . . Several bodyguards were drinking throughout the night . . . . As a result, the President's bodyguards were virtually unable to protect their chief in the morning."[131]

As noted earlier, Special Agents Landis, Ready, and Hill were in "travel status" and were strictly prohibited from consuming any alcohol, even when they were "off duty."[132] The Secret Service manual clearly states that even a "slight disregard" of these regulations "at any time will be cause for removal from the service."

Secret Service Chief James Rowley took no disciplinary action against the running board agents. He, instead, dismissed their actions, testifying to the Warren Commission that "their conduct had no bearing on the assassination."[133]

Landis and Hill claimed that they each had one "scotch" while at the Press Club, and Ready claimed he had "two cans of beer."[134] Regardless of the Agents' claims that they consumed very little alcohol, their judgment was so impaired that they went to an "all-night beatnik rendezvous" after the bar closed at nearly 3 a.m., not to mention they had been "on duty for 16 hours" when they first arrived at the Fort Worth hotel at "about 12:00 midnight."[135]

The idea that they were out all night for one scotch or two cans of beer is absurd. They were drunk, and they could not risk going

---

[131] National Archives Record Number 104-10404-10243
[132] Warren Commission Hearings and Exhibits, Volume XVIII, p. 665
[133] Warren Commission Hearings and Exhibits, Volume V, p. 453
[134] Warren Commission Hearings and Exhibits, Volume XVIII, pp. 685, 687, & 690
[135] Warren Commission Hearings and Exhibits, Volume XVIII, p. 682

back to the hotel reeking of alcohol, which explains why the three running board agents were agreeable to hanging out at an "all-night beatnik rendezvous," regardless of having to report for the 8 a.m. shift on November 22, 1963.

The KGB officers knew that if they could get the three running board agents out consuming alcohol until the bar finally closed, the agents would not only be drunk, but would also realize that they could not go back to the hotel until they sobered up a bit and let the stink of alcohol dissipate from their breath. Landis, as noted earlier, admitted he did not leave the all-night beatnik rendezvous, otherwise known as "The Cellar," until "approximately 5:00 a.m."

The reactions of the four Secret Service agents in the Vice Presidential Detail were very different from the reactions of agents in the Presidential follow-up car.

Special Agent in Charge Rufus Youngblood, who was riding with the Vice President, wrote that when he saw something wrong in the Presidential car, "I turned in my seat and with my left arm grasped and shoved the Vice President, at his right shoulder, down and toward Mrs. Johnson and Senator Yarborough. At the same time I shouted, 'Get down!'"

Youngblood then "stepped over into the back seat and sat on top of the Vice President," and according to Vice President Johnson, he was "on top of the Vice President before the second shot."[136]

The report of Vice President Johnson's driver, Texas Highway Patrolman Hurchel Jacks, similarly states that Youngblood "appeared to be shielding the Vice President with his own body" before Jacks "heard two more shots ring out."[137]

Youngblood, at that point, told Hurchel Jacks to "get out of there as fast as possible,"[138] which is a lot different than Roberts twice repeated instructions to drive to the hospital "at a safe speed."

---

[136] Warren Commission Hearings and Exhibits, Volume XVIII, p. 768
[137] Warren Commission Hearings and Exhibits, Volume XVIII, p. 801
[138] Warren Commission Hearings and Exhibits, Volume XVIII, p. 801

The Vice President's follow-up car was a Mercury four-door sedan and did not have outside running boards like the Presidential follow-up car, the "1955 Cadillac 9-passenger convertible specifically outfitted for use by the Secret Service."[139]

The three agents inside the Vice President's follow-up car had to take the time to reach for the door handle and then open the car door before stepping out of the moving car and running ahead to the Vice President's car, which obviously delayed their ability to reach the Vice President.[140]

Assistant Special Agent in Charge Thomas Johns wrote in his report, "I jumped from the security car and started running for the Vice President's car . . . . Before I reached the Vice President's car, a third shot had sounded and the entire motorcade then picked up speed and I was left on the street at this point."[141]

The report of Special Agent Warren Taylor states that after he heard the first shot, he "opened the door and prepared to get out of the car. In the instant that my left foot touched the ground, I heard two more bangs."[142]

The Vice Presidential follow-up car then "picked up speed and I pulled myself back into the car."

Special Agent Jerry Kivett, the third agent in the Vice Presidential follow-up car, wrote in his report that after the sound of the first shot, he was "looking in the direction of the noise, which was to my right rear . . . . I heard another report. Then there was no doubt in my mind what was happening. I looked toward the Vice Presidential car," and upon hearing the third shot, "I was getting out of the car to get to the Vice President's car and assist Youngblood."[143]

---

[139] Warren Commission Document 3 - Secret Service Report of 18 Dec 1963, p. 94
[140] Warren Commission Hearings and Exhibits, Volume XVIII, p. 777
[141] Warren Commission Hearings and Exhibits, Volume XVIII, p. 774
[142] Warren Commission Hearings and Exhibits, Volume XVIII, pp. 782-783
[143] Warren Commission Hearings and Exhibits, Volume XVIII, p. 778

After seeing "the Presidential car speed down the street," Kivett knew he "could not get to the Vice Presidential car," and he "fell back into the follow-up car."

The four agents assigned to protect the Vice President did not sit and think, "It sounds like firecrackers. I wonder where that noise is coming from," nor did the agents sit idly by and watch the entire assassination unfold. The four agents assigned to the Vice Presidential Detail did their job and moved to protect the Vice President, and three of the four did so at the sound of the first shot.

Secret Service agents assigned to the Vice President reacted quickly because they did not go out to a bar in the early morning hours of November 22 and then go to an "all-night beatnik rendezvous" to sober up and let the stink of alcohol dissipate from their breath.

KGB officers Roberts, Bennett, and McIntyre stated in their reports that they tried to locate the source of the shots after the shooting was over, but they said and did absolutely nothing while the shots were being fired. They did not even try to give the appearance of trying to locate the source of the shots.

The reports of KGB officers Roberts, Bennett, and McIntyre describe in detail how President John F. Kennedy was shot to death from the first shot to the last while they silently and patiently watched the entire assassination unfold.

KGB officer Hickey stood up and looked toward the rear, allegedly to "identify" the first shot, and then, in an attempt to either witness the assassination or see if they had already killed the President, he turned to look at the President, whereupon he saw, in his own words, that the second shot "missed" and "there didn't seem to be any impact against his head."[144]

Like the reports of his KGB colleagues, Hickey's report is a blatant admission that he watched to see if the assassination would be successful. His report, bemoaning that the second shot "missed" and "there didn't seem to be any impact against his head," perfectly

---

[144] Warren Commission Hearings and Exhibits, Volume XVIII, p. 762

complements Roberts' report in which Roberts exclaimed, "They got him! They got him!" after the third and final shot struck President Kennedy in the head.

KGB officer Emory Roberts wrote that at 1:15 p.m. Vice President Johnson "was informed by me that the President was dead."[145]

The "Secret Service" also insisted that President Kennedy's motorcade travel down Elm Street and go directly past the Texas School Book Depository when traveling through Dealey Plaza, overruling the Dallas Host Committee's plans for the Presidential motorcade.

Dallas Police Chief Jesse Curry testified to the Warren Commission, "We left the parade route up to the Host Committee. They chose the route, asking that we go down Main Street.... But had we proceeded on down Main Street, we could not have gotten onto Stemmons Expressway unless we had public works come in and remove some curbing and build some barricades over it."[146]

Curry testified that he met with the "Secret Service people," and they "suggested" that when the motorcade passed through Dealey Plaza, it could go over to "Elm Street" and drive past the Texas School Book Depository. It could then access the Stemmons Expressway without the City of Dallas removing a small section of curbing.

Curry testified that without "removing" the curbing, it was "necessary" to take the Secret Service's route to get to the Stemmons Expressway, adding that doing something with the curbing would be "disturbing" to "the regular flow of traffic," even though the Dallas Host Committee had no problem with it.

The motorcade was already "disturbing" to "the regular flow of traffic" through much of the city. Dallas Police Officer Joe Marshall Smith, with the "traffic division point control," told the Warren Commission that "nearly the whole traffic department"

---

[145] Warren Commission Hearings and Exhibits, Volume XVIII, p. 737
[146] Warren Commission Hearings and Exhibits, Volume IV, p. 169

was assigned "all along the motorcade route from the airport into downtown Dallas." Officers were told to "keep traffic out of the way when the motorcade was coming and keep an open and clear route."[147]

There was absolutely no "security" reason for the Secret Service to alter the Host Committee's designated parade route through Dealey Plaza. The Secret Service's job has nothing to do with limiting the lengths to which a city should go for a Presidential visit. Their job is security.

The Warren Commission asked Chief Curry, "Was there any consideration given prior to establishing the parade route to removing this curbing?"[148]

Curry replied, "No, sir; nothing was said about it at all. In fact, when they were choosing the routes for this parade, we left it entirely up to the Host Committee and to the Secret Service."

Curbing that blocked easy access to the Stemmons Expressway from Main St. The "Secret Service" prevented the City of Dallas from removing this curbing so that the motorcade would have to travel down Elm St. directly in front of the Texas School Book Depository.

In an interview with the FBI on the evening of November 22, 1963, President Kennedy's limousine driver, Secret Service Special Agent William Greer, stated that Secret Service drivers "have always been instructed to keep the motorcade moving at a considerable speed inasmuch as a moving car offers a much more difficult target than a vehicle traveling at a very slow speed."[149]

---

[147] Warren Commission Hearings and Exhibits, Volume VII, p. 533
[148] Warren Commission Hearings and Exhibits, Volume IV, p. 169
[149] ARRB Master Set of Medical Exhibits, MD 151, p. 9

In taking the "Secret Service" route through Dealey Plaza, President Kennedy's limousine and the entire, lengthy motorcade, consisting of at least seventeen cars and three buses, had to slow down, make the right turn onto Houston, travel one block, and then slowly turn left onto Elm to drive past the Texas School Book Depository.[150] Almost the entire motorcade was still back on Houston or Main Street when the assassins opened fire on the slow-moving limousine.

If the motorcade had continued straight down Main Street when passing through Dealey Plaza, it would have been moving at a considerably faster pace.

Other than the assassination plans being disturbed, it would not have disturbed anything for the Secret Service if the City of Dallas "public works" did something with the curbing so that the motorcade could follow the Dallas Host Committee's route. There is no legitimate reason why the Secret Service would not want the motorcade to continue down Main Street when traveling through Dealey Plaza.

To repeat, the Secret Service's job has nothing to do with limiting the lengths to which a city should go for the President's visit. Their job is security, and the claim that removing the curbing would disturb "the regular flow of traffic" was just an excuse for choosing the route on which President Kennedy would be assassinated.

The Host Committee consisted of Robert Cullum, President of the Dallas Chamber of Commerce; Sam Bloom of the Sam Bloom Agency, a public relations firm in Dallas; and Felix McKnight, Editor of the Dallas Times Herald.[151] They most certainly knew of the curb issue when they chose to have the Presidential motorcade go straight down Main Street. The Dallas Host Committee wanted something done with the curbing.

---

[150] Warren Commission Hearings and Exhibits, Volume XVII, p. 596
[151] Warren Commission Hearings and Exhibits, Volume XVII, pp. 608, 610, & 619

In a letter to the Warren Commission, Secret Service Chief James Rowley stated that on November 14 Secret Service Special Agents Lawson and Sorrels drove along the route on which President Kennedy would be assassinated, and on the following day, Lawson and Sorrels met with Curry in his office, where three "route possibilities" were discussed "from the airport to the Trade Mart."[152]

Rowley stated very clearly in his letter that when Lawson and Sorrels met with Curry, "Emphasis was placed on the route driven the preceding day from the airport to the Trade Mart," which means someone chose two specific "route possibilities" that were less inviting than the assassination route.

One can only wonder who was giving input to Lawson and Sorrels. The KGB officers clearly took charge of everything in order to bring about the assassination.

On November 14, Special Agent Lawson told the Dallas Police that "the announcement of the definite route would be made in the press by the Host Committee,"[153] and the Warren Commission reported that "representatives of the local Host Committee" were "advised by the Secret Service of the actual route" on November 18,"[154] which means the Secret Service overruled the Dallas Host Committee and made the definitive choice for the assassination route.

In 1984, the KGB officers admitted that killing President Kennedy was only the first step in a two-stage plan to take over the Presidency. They also planned to kill Kennedy's successor, President Lyndon Johnson, on October 31, 1964, three days before the 1964 Presidential election. Their objective was to have Senator Barry Goldwater, who was both a CIA officer and a KGB asset, elected to the Presidency. (Information on Members of Congress being in the CIA and Goldwater being a KGB asset is addressed later in this book.)

---

[152] Warren Commission Hearings and Exhibits, Volume XVIII, p. 716
[153] Warren Commission Document 81.1, p. 54
[154] Warren Commission Report, p. 32

But the plan to assassinate President Johnson went awry when Suffolk County Police arrested the KGB's intended patsy, a man named Robert Babcock.

Suffolk County detectives spotted Babcock parked along President Johnson's motorcade route with a telescopic rifle "on the seat beside him," and after searching his car, they found "a loaded 12-gauge shotgun" in his trunk.[155]

Babcock was parked "300 yards from the gate" of Republic Aviation Corporation in New York State and arrested "eight minutes" before President Johnson stepped from his plane on the company's airstrip.

President Johnson's motorcade had been "expected to make a number of stops along the motorcade route," but it made absolutely no stops after Babcock was found with the telescopic rifle and shotgun, which completely derailed the assassination plans.

President Johnson passed by the spot where Babcock was taken into custody "twenty minutes" after his arrest.

Suffolk County Police and the "Secret Service" questioned Robert Babcock, who "said first that he had been going on a hunting trip when he decided to stop and see the motorcade. He then said he had made a bet with barroom acquaintances that he could do what he did without being detected."

With their intended patsy prematurely apprehended and with no chance of assassinating President Johnson, the "Secret Service" wanted the incident to receive as little attention as possible, and Babcock was simply "charged with disorderly conduct and jailed for the night." The few details that are available ended up in a few paragraphs back on page 78 of the *New York Times* and on page 10 of the *Dallas Morning News* on November 1, 1964.

Babcock's "barroom acquaintances" undoubtedly knew that he intended to carry out their plans. Robert Babcock obviously thought he was going to come into some easy money from his

---

[155] Dallas Morning News, 11-1-64, p. 10 and New York Times, 11-1-64, p. 78

fellow bar patrons with a simplistic act when he parked "300 yards" from Republic Aviation.

There were no bullets in the telescopic rifle, which would have been conducive to persuading Babcock to take this action, but that would not be a problem for the KGB officers, and Robert Babcock would have found it impossible to understand how he could be in possession of the assassination weapon and why the loaded shotgun in his trunk made him look even guiltier.

The Suffolk County Police gave an alibi to a man who was not supposed to have one, a man who was intrinsic to a Presidential assassination, and in the process, they averted the assassination. The CIA/Secret Service was easily appeased because they knew their plans had gone awry. Where, when, why, and how Robert Babcock obtained the weapons, or if he owned them, was instantaneously of no significance, and the anonymous "barroom acquaintances" who "made a bet" with him remained anonymous while he was only "charged with disorderly conduct."

The 25th Amendment to the Constitution, providing for Presidential succession and the appointment of a new Vice President, did not become part of the Constitution until 1967.

There was no Vice President on Saturday, October 31, 1964.

The first person in line for the Presidency was John W. McCormack, a Representative from Massachusetts who had been elected Speaker of the House in January 1962 following the death of House Speaker Sam Rayburn. President Johnson's death would have catapulted Congressman McCormack into the Presidency on Saturday, October 31, 1964, after serving as Speaker of the House for less than three years.

The United States would be into the third day of a McCormack Presidency on Tuesday, November 3, 1964, when the American people voted in an election pitting the late President Lyndon Johnson against CIA officer and KGB asset Barry Goldwater.

With Johnson dead, the Southern states, including the electoral prizes of Texas and Florida, would definitely not be going to the liberal "Vice Presidential candidate," Hubert Humphrey, nor would the mountain states, where conservatism flourished in 1964.

As for the electoral prize of California, it already had one Republican Senator going into the 1964 election, and a second Republican Senator was elected in 1964. San Francisco, which hosted the Republican National Convention in 1964, had a Republican Mayor at the time and had nothing but Republican Mayors from 1912 to 1964, and California was conservative enough to elect staunch Goldwater supporter Ronald Reagan as its Governor in 1966.

Goldwater's running mate was Representative William Miller of New York, Chairman of the Republican National Committee. Going into the 1964 election, the electoral prize of New York had two Republican Senators and a Republican Governor, and more than half of New York's forty-one Congressional Representatives were Republicans.

Efforts to block Senator Barry Goldwater's election to the Presidency would be totally devoid of the political capital garnered by the late Presidents Kennedy and Johnson among liberals, moderates, independents, and conservatives. Even with fellow Southerner Lyndon Johnson alive and running as the incumbent President, the electoral prize of Florida gave 49 percent of its vote to Goldwater.

People who were determined to stop Goldwater from being elected to the Presidency would have to figure out who, if anyone, they were trying to elect as President.

Were they now trying to elect Johnson's running mate, Senator Hubert Humphrey, to the Presidency, or were they trying to elect President John W. McCormack to a four-year term?

Were they trying to elect President McCormack to a four-year term while electing Vice Presidential candidate Hubert Humphrey to the Office of Vice President?

Or were they trying to elect one of them to the Office of President while not electing anyone to the Office of Vice President?

Devout opponents of Barry Goldwater would have to tune in to the news, read the newspapers on Sunday and Monday, and try to find out from polling officials just who and what they were voting for as they futilely tried to prevent Goldwater from being elected President.

According to the Twentieth Amendment to the Constitution, if the Johnson-Humphrey ticket prevailed on election day with President Johnson dead, Vice Presidential candidate Hubert Humphrey would become the "Vice President-elect," while no one would be elected to the Presidency. Humphrey would then "become President" at the "beginning of the term of the President" on January 20, 1965, and the Vice Presidency, which had been vacant for fourteen months, would remain vacant for another four years.

John W. McCormack would relinquish the Presidency and most likely return to his position as Speaker of the House, where the Massachusetts Representative would again be first in line for the Presidency should anything happen to "President Humphrey."

With Johnson dead, few people would realize that their only choice would be to elect Hubert Humphrey to the Office of Vice President and that Vice President-elect Humphrey would "become President" at the "beginning of the term of the President."

A 1964 CIA memorandum states that the "Disinformation Department" of the KGB has "covert propaganda campaigns aimed at the creation of confusion and panic in Western countries."[156]

In the end, the confused 1964 election would pit a liberal Senator from Minnesota, who had done no campaigning for President and who, as the Vice Presidential candidate, had no running mate, against the well-traveled, high-profile Republican nominee, Senator Barry Goldwater, and his running mate, Representative William Miller of New York, Chairman of the Republican National Committee.

---

[156] National Archives Record Number 104-10428-10235

KGB officers inside the CIA would have easily realized their goal of having Barry Goldwater elected to the Presidency in 1964. Robert Babcock's story about a bet with "barroom acquaintances" would not have helped him any more than a letter to "President Goldwater" stating, as a very upset Lee Harvey Oswald once said, "I emphatically deny these charges."[157]

Once they knew their plan to kill President Johnson had gone awry, certain individuals in the "Secret Service" made sure that Robert Babcock was only "charged with disorderly conduct and jailed for the night."

Babcock's case makes it crystal clear that in 1964, a man could be paid money to sit along the Presidential motorcade route with a telescopic rifle on the seat beside him and a loaded shotgun in the trunk, and when discovered, the "Secret Service" would conduct no investigation, even though the Presidential election was three days away and the preceding President had been assassinated with a telescopic rifle less than a year earlier.

It was just two days after the Suffolk County Police discovered Robert Babcock that CIA Director John McCone's "Special Assistant" wrote a memorandum stating there was a "continuing problem" of the "legal status" of CIA officers who were "detailed" to the Secret Service. Suffolk County Police undoubtedly deferred to the CIA/Secret Service on what to do with Robert Babcock when they questioned him.

The KGB officers admitted that they began formulating plans to kill President Kennedy as soon as he took office in January 1961.

On December 8, 1961, the CIA had information that one of Cuban Premier Fidel Castro's "right-hand men," Emilio Aragones, was "attempting to enter the US" along with Aldo Margolles, Chief of Operations in the Cuban National Police, so that they could "meet with Castro agents and assassinate President Kennedy."[158]

---

[157] Warren Commission Document 962, p. 47
[158] National Archives Record Number 104-10308-10150

In early January 1962, the Secret Service was "investigating a plot against President Kennedy" involving the two Cubans, and a CIA memo in late January stated, "Margolles and Aragones are known to have generated plot to assassinate President of U.S."[159]

Two months later, CIA Deputy Director for Plans Richard Helms sent information to Secret Service Chief James Rowley detailing where Aragones and Margolles were residing in Cuba. Helms also told Rowley, "Any additional information received by this Agency will be promptly forwarded to the United States Secret Service."[160]

Raymond G. Rocca, Chief of Research and Analysis in the CIA's Counterintelligence division, wrote that a Communist Party cell leader in Guatemala told his compatriots in January 1962, "We need not preoccupy ourselves over the politics of President Kennedy because we know, according to prognostications, that he will die within the present year, 1962."[161] (The Communist Party cell leader obviously knew there were plans to assassinate President Kennedy.)

The KGB ultimately realized they would have to assassinate President Kennedy themselves, and it was made all the more easy by having four of the KGB officers inside the CIA "detailed" to the Secret Service during the President's Texas trip.

CIA officers functioning as Secret Service agents clearly supplement the CIA officers who are detailed to "the immediate office of the White House" and to "components associated intimately with the immediate office of the President."

As will be explained later in this book, it was just a matter of time before the entire Secret Service was comprised of nothing but CIA officers "detailed" to the Secret Service.

In 1981, the KGB officers again sought to catapult one of their assets, CIA officer George H. W. Bush, into the Presidency. CIA officers, who had been "detailed" to the "Secret Service," were tasked with making it happen when President Reagan left the Washington

---

[159] National Archives Record Numbers 104-10308-10147 & 104-10506-10026
[160] National Archives Record Number 104-10308-10145
[161] National Archives Record Number 104-10419-10269, p. 17

Hilton Hotel on March 30, 1981, a short sixty-nine days after CIA officer George Bush took office as Vice President. (George Bush being a career CIA officer is addressed extensively in another chapter.)

"When Reagan came out of the Hilton, the bulletproof Presidential limousine was not waiting directly in front of the hotel exit, as Secret Service practice usually requires. If it had been, Reagan would have had a straight-line walk of about eight feet from door to car. Instead, he had to walk diagonally down the sidewalk about twenty-five feet, bringing him around a curve and into the line of fire of accused assailant John W. Hinckley, Jr."[162]

"Television crew members at the Hilton said they had complained to the Secret Service about bystanders pushing into the area reserved for the press. One bystander, as it turned out, was the accused gunman."[163]

ABC News cameraman Henry M. Brown "said he had complained earlier to the Secret Service that members of the public had 'penetrated the police line,' creating crowded conditions in the press area and making it difficult to work. His complaint went unheeded, and Brown went on working. He was standing near the assailant when he started to fire."

"'He just opened up and kept squeezing the trigger,' Brown said."[164]

"The advance agent on the scene concluded that it would be counterproductive to set up an area restricted only to the press on the narrow, curving walk outside the hotel."

"Generally, agents want the armored limousine waiting in a direct line with the President's exit door as he moves from building to car. Such positioning shortens the period of vulnerability and makes it easier for agents to form a human shield as the public figure moves. In some cases, agents have had

---

[162] Washington Post, 4-1-81, p. 16
[163] Washington Post, 4-1-81, p. 16
[164] Washington Post, 3-31-81, p. 10

the car moved one foot or less to have it perfectly aligned with the exit.

"On Monday, though, Reagan's limousine was waiting about twenty to twenty-five feet down the driveway from the door. To reach the car, Reagan had to walk down the curving sidewalk. Around the curve, flush against the hotel wall, the assailant waited with his pistol."

By positioning the Presidential limousine down the driveway and leading Reagan past the intended assassin, the "Secret Service" chose the "route" for President Reagan's assassination, just like they chose the route for President Kennedy's assassination. How fitting that the *New York Times* reported, "It was the first time that a President had been injured in such an attempt since President Kennedy was shot and killed more than 17 years ago."[165]

When President Truman signed legislation making the Secret Service permanent in 1951, the *New York Times* reported: "'I am glad I have legal protection at last,' Mr. Truman laughingly observed."[166]

Truman's sense of humor was no longer apparent one month after President Kennedy was assassinated. As cited in Chapter 1, Truman wrote an article on December 22, 1963, titled "Limit CIA Role to Intelligence" in which he stated, "For some time I have been disturbed by the way the CIA has been diverted from its original assignment."[167]

---

[165] NYT, 3-31-81, p. 6
[166] New York Times, 7-17-51, p. 15
[167] Washington Post, 12-22-63, p. 11

Chapter 3: The Blatant Cover-Up of a Presidential Assassination

Assassinating the President of the United States and covering it up was a monumental achievement for the KGB. Covering up the wounds on President Kennedy's body is a prime example of how the CIA works.

The "official story" puts forth that President Kennedy was shot from behind and that there was a small entrance wound at the back of his head. It also puts forth that there was a large gaping wound at the front of his head. But a mountain of evidence clearly contradicts the official story.

Secret Service Special Agent Clint Hill, who climbed onto the back of the President's limousine within seconds of the fatal headshot, wrote in his official report on November 30, 1963: "As I lay over the top of the back seat, I noticed a portion of the President's head on the right rear side was missing and he was bleeding profusely. Part of his brain was gone. I saw a part of his skull with hair on it lying in the seat."[168]

Hill testified to the Warren Commission on March 9, 1964, "The second noise that I heard had removed a portion of the President's head," and he reiterated what was in his report, "The right rear portion of his head was missing. It was lying in the rear seat of the car. His brain was exposed. There was blood and bits of brain all over the entire rear portion of the car."[169]

Hill stated that the only wound he observed was the "large gaping wound in the right rear portion of the head."

---

[168] Warren Commission Hearings and Exhibits, Volume XVIII, p. 742
[169] Warren Commission Hearings and Exhibits, Volume II, pp. 138 & 141

Dr. Charles Carrico told the House Select Committee on Assassinations that when President Kennedy was being treated at Parkland Hospital, Dr. Ronald Jones and Dr. Malcolm Perry "took over the primary management" in the emergency room, where one of their objectives was to "assess how bad his head injury was."[170]

Dr. Ronald Jones testified to the Warren Commission that President Kennedy had "what appeared to be an exit wound in the posterior portion of the skull."[171]

Dr. Malcolm Perry wrote in his hospital report on November 22, 1963, that the President had sustained "a large wound of the right posterior cranium," and a few months later he testified that it was "a large avulsive wound on the right posterior cranium."[172]

Parkland Nurse Pat Hutton, who assisted from the moment President Kennedy was brought in from the car until he was placed in a coffin, wrote in her report on November 22, 1963, "Mr. Kennedy was bleeding profusely from a wound on the back of his head."

Her report states that a doctor asked her to "place a pressure dressing on the head wound," and she wrote, "This was of no use, however, because of the massive opening on the back of the head."[173]

The "summary" of medical reports from Parkland Hospital on November 22 states that Dr. Charles Carrico observed a head wound "in the occipital region of the skull . . . . Through the head wound, blood and brain were extruding."[174]

The occipital region of the skull, which was referred to more than once by the doctors, is located at the back of the head.

Dr. Robert McClelland testified to the Assassination Records Review Board in 1998 that when he closely examined President Kennedy's head, he could clearly see that a bullet "came out the back."[175] (The Assassination Records Review Board was established by Congress in the 1990s to bring forth all possible information and records related to President Kennedy's assassination.)

---

[170] House Select Committee on Assassinations, Volume VII, pp. 272-273
[171] Warren Commission Hearings and Exhibits, Volume VI, p. 56
[172] Warren Commission Hearings and Exhibits, Volume XVII, p. 6 & Volume III, p. 368
[173] Warren Commission Hearings and Exhibits, Volume XXI, p. 216
[174] Warren Commission Hearings and Exhibits, Volume XVII, p. 2
[175] ARRB Testimony of Charles Baxter, Ronald Coy Jones, Robert M. Mclelland, Malcom Perry, Paul C. Peters, 27 Aug 1998, pp. 72 & 100-101

Dr. McClelland also testified that while standing and holding a retractor, he had a "concentrated view" of the head, where the bullet "came out the back."

He testified that he observed the wound, which was "mostly really in the occipital part of the skull," for "an absolute minimum of five minutes" from a distance of "twelve to eighteen inches."[176]

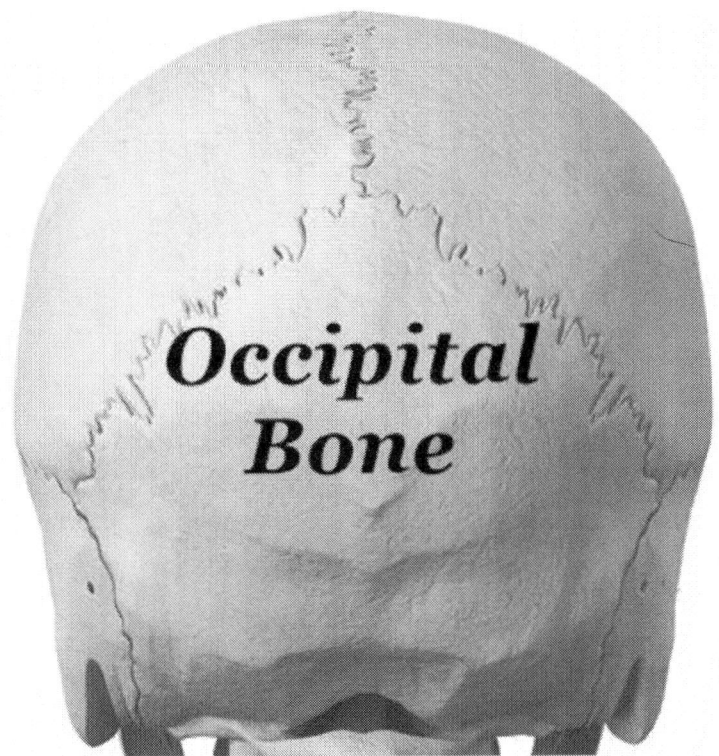

Rear View of Human Skull

"As I was looking at it, a fairly large portion of the cerebellum fell out of the skull. There was already some brain there, but during the tracheotomy more fell out and that was clearly cerebellum."

Dr. McClelland testified that he "could look down into the skull . . . . There was nothing in the area where the cerebellum usually sits. Most of it was probably gone when I first began to look down into the

---

[176] Ibid., pp. 28 & 72

wound, and then as I stood there, probably just maybe a minute after I came in, another large portion of it, which I thought – I remember thinking now, well, that's the rest of the cerebellum, oozed out into the table."[177]

Thirty-four years earlier, in 1964, Dr. McClelland testified to the Warren Commission, "As I took the position at the head of the table . . . I was in such a position that I could very closely examine the head wound, and I noted that the right posterior portion of the skull had been extremely blasted . . . . You could actually look down into the skull cavity itself and see that probably a third or so, at least, of the brain tissue, posterior cerebral tissue and some of the cerebellar tissue, had been blasted out."[178]

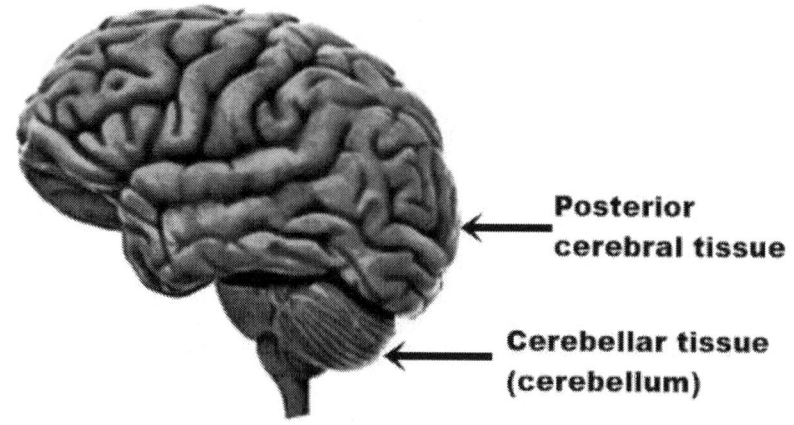

Dr. Paul Peters testified to the Assassination Records Review Board in 1998 that the wound "was pretty far posteriorly" and the bullet had "gone out through the occiput . . . . I walked around right and looked in his head. You could look directly into the cranial vault and see cerebral injury to the cerebral cortex and I thought at the

---

[177] ARRB Testimony of Charles Baxter, Ronald Coy Jones, Robert M. Mclelland, Malcom Perry, Paul C. Peters, 27 Aug 1998, pp. 43-44
[178] Warren Commission Hearings and Exhibits, Volume VI, p. 33

time to the cerebellum. So I know the hole was big enough to look into."[179]

In his Warren Commission testimony thirty-four years earlier, Dr. Peters stated that he observed "the large occipital wound," which he said was "a large wound of exit . . . . There appeared to be bone loss and brain loss in the area."[180]

Nurse Diana Bowron, who went out to the Presidential limousine to assist in bringing President Kennedy into the hospital, testified to the Warren Commission that while the President was lying across Mrs. Kennedy's knee, she "saw the condition" of "the back of his head," which she testified was "very bad." When a Warren Commission staff member asked for clarification on what she saw, she stated, "I just saw one large hole."[181]

Nurse Audrey Bell told the Assassination Records Review Board that "the right side of the President's head and the top of his head were intact," and she "had to ask Dr. Perry where the wound was." He then "turned the President's head slightly to the President's anatomical left so that she could see a right posterior head wound, which she described as occipital."[182]

FBI Agent James Sibert, who was present at President Kennedy's autopsy, submitted an affidavit to the House Select Committee on Assassinations in 1978 stating that "a large head wound" was located at the "back of the head," where a "section of the skull bone" was "missing."[183]

Edward Reed, a radiology technician on duty when the X-rays were taken at Bethesda Naval Hospital, told the House Select Committee on Assassinations that President Kennedy's head wound was "very large and located in the right hemisphere in the occipital region."[184]

Tom Robinson, a funeral home employee who witnessed most of President Kennedy's autopsy and embalmed his corpse afterwards,

---

[179] ARRB Testimony of Charles Baxter, Ronald Coy Jones, Robert M. Mclelland, Malcom Perry, Paul C. Peters, 27 Aug 1998, pp. 46, 51-52, & 56
[180] Warren Commission Hearings and Exhibits, Volume VI, p. 71
[181] Warren Commission Hearings and Exhibits, Volume VI, p. 136
[182] ARRB Master Set of Medical Exhibits, MD 184
[183] ARRB Master Set of Medical Exhibits, MD 46, p. 3
[184] ARRB Master Set of Medical Exhibits, MD 194

told the Assassination Records Review Board that he "saw the brain removed from President Kennedy's body," and "a large percentage of it was gone 'in the back.'" Robinson "described a large open head wound in the back of the President's head."[185]

Robinson told the House Select Committee on Assassinations that during the embalming, he found a wound in the President's right temple that was "very small," measuring "a quarter of an inch." Robinson stated that the wound could easily be "hidden by the hair."[186]

The first written reports from Dallas on November 22, 1963, stated, "He was shot at 12:30 p.m. today by an assassin who sent a rifle bullet crashing into his right temple," and a broadcast by the U.S. State Department's Voice of America stated, "A bullet struck his right temple while the Presidential motorcade was driving at the edge of downtown Dallas."[187]

Within seconds of the fatal headshot, Secret Service Agent Clint Hill observed the gaping exit wound at the back of President Kennedy's head, and witnesses all along the way observed the wound until his corpse was prepared for burial. Virtually none of these witnesses placed the massive exit wound at the top of the head, or on the side of the head, and certainly not at the front of the head.

The CIA, in an effort to dispel any idea that there was a conspiracy to kill President Kennedy, fabricated autopsy photos that place the massive exit wound at the "front" of President Kenney's head, and they enlisted the pathologists who performed the autopsy to participate in the cover up.

In 1972, Dr. John Lattimer examined the photographs and X-rays purportedly from President Kennedy's autopsy that are on file at the National Archives, and he testified to the Rockefeller Commission in 1975 that they show a "wound of entrance into the back of his skull" and a "large wound of exit on the front top of the President's head" where the bullet "exited on the front of the head, just above the forehead."[188]

---

[185] ARRB Master Set of Medical Exhibits, MD 180
[186] ARRB Master Set of Medical Exhibits, MD 63, p. 2
[187] Washington Post, 11-23-63, p. 1 and Warren Commission Document 1135, p. 13
[188] Rockefeller Commission Files: Testimony of John K. Lattimer, pp. 22 & 24

In February 1968, four years before Dr. Lattimer examined the autopsy material, Attorney General Ramsey Clark assembled a panel of physicians to examine the autopsy photographs and X-rays, after which the "Clark Panel" issued a report stating that a bullet entered President Kennedy's skull in the "occipital region" and produced a small wound measuring .23 inches by .59 inches. The bullet then "passed forward" to "explosively fracture the right frontal and parietal bones as it emerged from the head."[189]

In March 1979, the House Select Committee on Assassinations had their "Medical Panel" examine the autopsy photographs and listen to the testimony of President Kennedy's three pathologists, after which the Medical Panel concluded, "The bullet exited in the top front area of the skull."[190]

A 1967 Secret Service document states that the autopsy photographs and X-rays "were in the custody and the possession of the United States Secret Service" from November 22, 1963, until April 26, 1965, during which time the CIA easily substituted bogus autopsy photographs.[191]

Moving the massive exit wound to the front of the head was, however, a two-stage process.

The CIA first used fabricated autopsy photos to support the pathologists' 1964 autopsy report, which says absolutely nothing about the front of the head. It states that there was a "small occipital wound" at the back of President Kennedy's head and that the bullet left a massive exit wound on the "right" side of the head, as opposed to the "front" of the head.[192]

In January 1967, the Justice Department had President Kennedy's three pathologists "examine the X-rays and photographs for the purpose of determining whether they are consistent with the autopsy report." The Justice Department also prepared a document for the pathologists to sign stating that the autopsy X-rays and photographs show "a small wound" in the "back of the head" and a "massive" wound located on the "right side of the head," which

---

[189] ARRB Master Set of Medical Exhibits, MD 59
[190] House Select Committee on Assassinations, Volume VII, p. 176
[191] ARRB Master Set of Medical Exhibits, MD 122, p. 2
[192] Warren Commission Hearings and Exhibits, Volume XVI, pp. 981 & 983

"corroborates" the pathologists' obviously fabricated autopsy report.[193]

The three pathologists, all of whom were military officers, dutifully signed the Justice Department document.

The following year, 1968, autopsy photographs were fabricated to move the massive exit wound to the front of the head. The "Clark Panel" then examined them and confirmed that they show a small entrance wound at the back of the head and a massive exit wound at the front of the head, thus firming up the "official" position that President Kennedy was shot from behind.

Concerning President Kennedy's throat wound, Parkland Hospital doctors were adamant that it was a wound of entry. Dr. Paul Peters testified to the Warren Commission, "We saw the wound of entry in the throat."[194]

Dr. Robert McClelland testified, "The wound in the neck, the anterior part of the neck, was an entrance wound."[195]

Dr. Charles Carrico, who used a "laryngoscope" to look down into President Kennedy's throat, told the House Select Committee on Assassinations, "There was some injury to the trachea behind it," and the bullet "must have been going front to back."[196]

Dr. Marion Jenkins wrote up a report at 4:30 p.m. on November 22 stating that Doctors Baxter, Perry, and McClelland "began a tracheotomy and started the insertion of a right chest tube" because President Kennedy had sustained "obvious tracheal and chest damage."[197]

Additionally, Dr. Malcolm Perry, who performed the tracheotomy, testified to the Assassination Records Review Board in 1998 that the neck wound "looked like an entrance wound and the bullet appeared to be coming at him."

Thirty-five years earlier, at a press conference on the day of the assassination, Dr. Perry stated, "There was an entrance wound in the

---

[193] ARRB Master Set of Medical Exhibits, MD 14 & MD 32
[194] Warren Commission Hearings and Exhibits, Volume VI, p. 71
[195] Warren Commission Hearings and Exhibits, Volume VI, p. 35
[196] House Select Committee on Assassinations, Volume VII, pp. 300 & 270
[197] Warren Commission Hearings and Exhibits, Volume XX, p. 252

neck," and the bullet "appeared to be coming at him."[198]

The "official" version of the throat wound maintains that it was an "exit" wound for a bullet that allegedly struck President Kennedy in the back of the neck, which completely contradicts the Parkland Hospital doctors' absolute knowledge that it was an entrance wound and the bullet "must have been going front to back."

It also contradicts the eyewitnesses who saw the bullet wound located considerably farther down on President Kennedy's back.

Secret Service Special Agent Clint Hill, who had been summoned to the morgue to witness "the damage of the gunshot wounds," wrote in his report that he "observed a wound about six inches down from the neckline on the back just to the right of the spinal column."[199]

Hill told the Warren Commission the same thing, testifying, "I saw an opening in the back, about six inches below the neckline to the right-hand side of the spinal column."[200]

Even the lead pathologist, James Humes, first acknowledged that the wound was "below the shoulders." FBI Agents Sibert and O'Neill wrote in their report that during the autopsy, Dr. Humes "located an opening which appeared to be a bullet hole, which was below the shoulders." Humes probed the wound with his finger, and "it was determined that the trajectory of the missile entering at this point had entered at a downward position of 45 to 60 degrees."[201]

And one of the KGB officers in the Presidential follow-up car, Special Agent Glen Bennett, wrote in his report on November 22 that after the first shot, he heard another shot and "saw the shot hit the President about four inches down from the right shoulder."[202] Bennett wrote that it was four inches down from the "shoulder," not four inches down from the neck.

When Humes, the lead pathologist, testified to the Warren Commission, he totally contradicted what he and the FBI Agents saw during the autopsy. Humes claimed the wound in the front of the

---

[198] ARRB Testimony of Charles Baxter, Ronald Coy Jones, Robert M. Mclelland, Malcom Perry, Paul C. Peters, 27 Aug 1998, pp. 52-53 and ARRB Master Set of Medical Exhibits, MD 41, p. 5
[199] Warren Commission Hearings and Exhibits, Volume XVIII, pp. 727 & 744-745
[200] Warren Commission Hearings and Exhibits, Volume II, p. 143
[201] ARRB Master Set of Medical Exhibits, MD 151, p. 6
[202] Warren Commission Hearings and Exhibits, Volume XVIII, p. 760

neck is "physically lower" than an alleged "point of entrance" in the back of the neck. The autopsy report that Humes signed similarly states that a bullet "traversed the soft tissues . . . of the neck . . . and made its exit through the anterior surface [front] of the neck."[203]

Originally, after lead pathologist James J. Humes acknowledged there was a back wound "below the shoulders," the throat wound was being explained away as an exit wound for a bullet "fragment" from an alleged rear headshot.

In the Warren Commission's Executive Session on January 27, 1964, the Commission's General Counsel, Lee Rankin, stated, "We have an explanation there in the autopsy that probably a fragment came out the front of the neck."[204]

Rankin continued, "It seems quite apparent now, since we have the picture of where the bullet entered in the back, that the bullet entered below the shoulder blade to the right of the backbone, which is below the place where the picture shows the bullet came out in the neckband of the shirt in front."

Rankin repeated that according to the autopsy report, there were "bullet fragments" from an alleged rear headshot, one of which "came out in part through the neck."

Rankin, who had "the picture of where the bullet entered in the back," could clearly see that President Kennedy's back wound was "below the shoulder blade," and he could see that the back wound was below President Kennedy's throat wound.

The public never saw the autopsy report on which Rankin based his statements, and the CIA saw to it that this Warren Commission Executive Session would remain classified for quite some time. The National Archives sent a letter to the CIA in 1974 concerning the transcript of the "executive session of January 27, 1964," stating, "The Central Intelligence Agency requested us to withhold this transcript from research in a letter of December 22, 1972."[205]

The media were also touting the story that a bullet fragment caused the throat wound. A *Washington Post* story on December 18, 1963, twenty-six days after the assassination, stated that the "as yet

---

[203] Warren Commission Hearings and Exhibits, Volume II, p. 368 & Volume XVI, p. 983
[204] Warren Commission Executive Session, Jan 27, 1964, pp. 193-194
[205] National Archives Record Number 104-10413-10091

unofficial report of pathologists" says a bullet "fragment" from an alleged rear head shot had been "deflected" and had "passed out the front of the throat."[206]

Since the official story was that he had been shot from behind and everyone could see the back wound was lower down on the back, the only possible way to explain away the throat wound was to claim it was an exit wound for a bullet fragment.

The "official" autopsy report would not be released to the public as a Warren Commission exhibit until ten months after the assassination, by which time people would accept the new version of a bullet striking President Kennedy in the back of the neck. The throat wound would then be easily explained away as an exit wound, and the fragment story would be ancient history.

The "Secret Service" finally gave an autopsy report to the FBI on December 23, 1963,[207] more than a month after the assassination, and on the same day, the "Secret Service" gave an entirely different autopsy report to the Warren Commission. Lee Rankin was apparently looking at this other version of the autopsy report during the Warren Commission's Executive Session in January when he said it had "an explanation" that "probably a fragment came out the front of the neck."

The autopsy report that was given to the FBI eventually became the "official" autopsy report. It states that a bullet entered "above the scapula,"[208] otherwise known as the shoulder blade, which directly contradicts the autopsy report stating that a bullet "entered below the shoulder blade."

The only bullet in evidence, Warren Commission Exhibit 399, was found on a stretcher at around 1 o'clock by an engineer at Parkland Hospital. The bullet had been "lodged under the edge of the mat" and rolled out when the engineer pushed the stretcher against a wall.[209]

The Warren Commission Report clearly states that the bullet was "positively identified" as having been "fired" from the "rifle found in

---

[206] Washington Post, 12-18-63, p. 3
[207] National Archives Record Number 124-10369-10022, p. 105
[208] Warren Commission Hearings and Exhibits, Volume XVI, p. 983
[209] Warren Commission Hearings and Exhibits, Volume VI, pp. 129-130

the Depository," as were the two bullet fragments that the "Secret Service" found in the front seat of the Presidential limousine.[210]

It appears that the bullet had been spotted earlier. In 1967, the *New York Times* reported on an interview with O. P. Wright, chief of security at Parkland Hospital. Wright recounted that a bullet "had dislodged after a stretcher had been moved and it was lying on the floor."[211]

"Mr. Wright said that for more than half an hour Secret Service men 'didn't seem interested in coming in and looking at the bullet in the position it was in' . . . . His efforts to get a Federal agent to take the bullet finally led to a matter-of-fact acceptance without questioning or additional investigation, Mr. Wright said."

If the bullet had actually been "dislodged," the unwanted help from the Parkland Hospital security chief was interfering with plans for a cover-up. If he was mistaken and it had not been "dislodged," then it was planted there to factor into the story of President Kennedy's wounds. Either way, it was undoubtedly very important that the "Secret Service" ignore the security chief's attempts to call their attention to the bullet on the floor. A "Federal agent" obviously took the bullet in order to get Mr. Wright to stop talking about it.

There would, of course, be no need to worry about the bullet lying around on the floor after someone "lodged" it "under the edge of a mat."

FBI Agents Sibert and O'Neill wrote that they had specific instructions from the FBI to attend President Kennedy's autopsy and "obtain bullets reportedly in the President's body." They also wrote that the pathologists who conducted the autopsy "were at a loss to explain why they could find no bullets."[212]

The pathologists allegedly could not find any bullets or bullet fragments in the President's body that could be connected to the "rifle found in the Depository." But a bullet in "almost perfect condition"[213] had been "lodged" under a mat at Parkland Hospital, and it was "positively identified" as having been fired from the "rifle

---

[210] Warren Commission Report, pp. 76 & 85
[211] New York Times, 6-29-67, p. 18
[212] ARRB Master Set of Medical Exhibits, MD 151, pp. 3 & 6
[213] New York Times, 8-27-72, p. 1

found in the Depository," as were the two bullet fragments that the "Secret Service" found in the front seat of the Presidential limousine.

In an Executive Session of the Warren Commission on December 16, 1963, Warren Commission member John J. McCloy stated, "This bullet business leaves me confused," to which Chief Justice Earl Warren replied, "It's totally inconclusive."[214]

Senator Richard Russell then said, "They couldn't find where one bullet came out, that struck the President, and yet they found a bullet in the stretcher." (The story that a bullet "came out" the front of President Kennedy's throat had not yet been fabricated, which is why Senator Russell complained that the pathologists supposedly "couldn't find where one bullet came out.")

The evidence is overwhelming that President Kennedy was shot twice from the front in addition to being shot lower down on his back. But when the CIA assassinates the President of the United States, a coverup is inevitable.

---

[214] Warren Commission Executive Session, Dec 16, 1963, p. 12

Chapter 4: KGB Asset and Future President George H. W. Bush

{Part 1 – The Bright Hope on the Political Horizon}

CIA officer George Bush, under the auspices of his KGB handlers, violated the Constitution when he became a Member of Congress in January 1967. Article I, section 6, of the Constitution states: "No Person holding any Office under the United States shall be a Member of either House during his Continuance in Office."

The men and women of the CIA are not CIA agents. They are "CIA officers," and officers of the United States Central Intelligence Agency clearly "hold office under the United States." They are Constitutionally prohibited from being Members of Congress while they are in the CIA.

There have been CIA officers in Congress in violation of the Constitution since the early 1950s.

Over the years, CIA officers in Congress, both Democrats and Republicans, have risen through the ranks to become some of the most powerful and influential Members of Congress. They have ranged across the political spectrum from the far left to the far right, as both groups were easy to exploit while CIA officers established themselves in government, supporting liberal and conservative causes and bringing about egregious bipartisan corruption.

CIA officers in Congress are literally spearheading the quest to control the government. They are vanguards for renegade CIA operations inside the United States. They are themselves renegade CIA officers by sheer token of the fact that they are violating the Constitution.

As noted in Chapter 1, CIA officers are required to fill out intelligence reports every day. CIA officers in Congress regularly fill out intelligence reports on other Members of Congress.

But none of this is about politics. This is about virulently corrupt elements of the CIA destroying our Constitution and corrupting our government far beyond what anyone could imagine. It is about corruption, murder, intrigue, and assassinating our elected officials.

George Bush, while still acting under the auspices of his KGB handlers, held a variety of "official" and "nonofficial" covers before being appointed to be Director of the CIA in 1975 and then elected to the Vice Presidency in 1980. After the KGB was exposed in 1984, Bush and his CIA colleagues took up the mantle and began their own quest to control the government, and Bush was elected to the Presidency in 1988.

Bush's KGB handlers were constantly touting him for the "Vice Presidency" with the ultimate goal of assassinating the President to catapult Bush into the "Presidency."

When Bush lost the Republican nomination to Ronald Reagan in 1980, Reagan's advisers "heavily pressured" him to choose Bush as a running mate, and President Reagan was shot sixty-nine days after he and Bush took the oath of office. The KGB infiltration was exposed less than three years after they failed to catapult Bush into the Presidency.

The KGB officers had Bush enter the political arena for the first time in 1964 when he ran for the U.S. Senate in Texas, while they had another one of their "assets," CIA officer and Senator Barry Goldwater, running for President.

Bush's Senate campaign culminated at a Republican rally on October 31, 1964 in San Antonio, Texas, where fellow CIA officer and Republican Presidential nominee Barry Goldwater was the main speaker.

Three days before CIA officers Bush and Goldwater would go down to defeat in their respective races, Barry Goldwater "singled out" Bush "as a bright hope on the political horizon."[215]

---

[215] Dallas Morning News, 11-1-64, p. 9

KGB asset George Bush was then targeted for either the Presidency or the Vice Presidency in the next seven Presidential elections, all of which is detailed in this chapter.

Two years after losing his 1964 Senate race, CIA officer George Bush was elected to Congress as a Representative from Houston. He took the oath of office to become a Member of Congress on January 3, 1967.

His meteoric rise began on June 5, 1968, seven months before his first Congressional term would expire. On that day, a *Washington Post* headline read: "Young Texas Congressman Bush Gets Nixon Look As Running Mate."[216]

Evans and Novak, well-known syndicated columnists for decades, wrote that prominent Evangelist Billy Graham told Richard Nixon that he should choose freshman Congressman George Bush as his 1968 running mate.

Evans and Novak called it "an unusual suggestion" and said it "violates all the rules for picking running mates," because Bush "has neither a national reputation nor a bloc of delegates to offer Nixon."

They went on to state, "Nevertheless, Billy Graham's suggestion was by no means the last Nixon heard of Bush. A quiet Bush-for-Vice President campaign has developed in business and Congressional circles. What's more, Nixon himself definitely is interested and is considering Bush as a possibility . . . . Moreover, the Texas business establishment is beating the drums for Bush. In one New York meeting with contributors, Nixon received a Bush sales pitch from a Texas industrialist. Another Texas businessman has fired off appeals for Bush to key Nixon supporters, including board chairman George Champion of Chase Manhattan.

"The latest talk about Bush heard by Nixon came last weekend in Atlanta from Rep. Fletcher Thompson of Georgia, a freshman Congressman elected with Bush. Informing Nixon of wide interest in a Nixon-Bush ticket by younger Republican Congressmen, Thompson told Nixon that the combination's appeal would cross

---
[216] Washington Post, 6-5-68, p. 21

sectional lines . . . . Nixon was interested . . . . There is at least a chance, long shot though it is, that George Bush is the one."

The CIA enlisted "Evangelist Billy Graham" as an asset more than a year before Graham initiated the "Bush for Vice President" campaign. One month after it was exposed that the CIA channels money through foundations in a money laundering operation, a *Time* magazine article stated that the CIA had financed Billy Graham's trip to Latin America, and the *New York Times* quoted Graham as saying he would "'try to find out' if the CIA had funded the trip without his knowledge."[217]

As noted in Chapter 1, the CIA has been channeling huge sums of money to "a wide spectrum of youth, student, academic, research, journalist, business, legal and labor organizations" in the United States since the 1950s,[218] and if the CIA could use the money laundering foundations to finance its 10-year LSD program, they could certainly use it to finance Billy Graham's travels.

In November 1968, five months after the KGB's first attempt to have Bush chosen for the Vice Presidential spot failed, Bush was re-elected to Congress.

Less than halfway through his second term, he was again being targeted for the United States Senate, and it soon became clear that a mere Senate seat would not be enough for CIA officer George Bush.

President Richard Nixon's Chief of Staff, H. R. Haldeman, who kept a diary of what took place in the Nixon White House, wrote that on December 16, 1969, people at the White House were concerned about "losing at least a couple" of the 1970 Senate races, including "George Bush in Texas."[219]

---

[217] New York Times, 3-25-67, p. 1
[218] New York Times, 2-19-67, p. 1
[219] The Haldeman Diaries, p. 116 (*G.P. Putnam's Sons, 1994*)

Ten months later, there was a concerted effort inside the White House to bolster Bush's prospects in his Senate race and in the next two Presidential elections.

On October 27, 1970, one week before CIA officer George Bush would go down to defeat in his second run at the United States Senate, the *Washington Post* reported: "President Nixon is going to Texas in hopes of finding his running mate for 1972 and the Republican Presidential candidate for 1976 . . . . That seems far-fetched, but it is the firm conviction of men 'intimately' involved in White House political operations that 46-year-old Rep. George Bush of Houston will be that man, if he can, with the President's help, win his close Senate race next week."[220]

The *Post* detailed the unhappiness with Nixon's Vice President, Spiro Agnew, and noted five possible replacements, adding, "Within this group, Bush is the standout; so much so that Mr. Nixon considered him for Vice President in 1968 when he was just a freshman Congressman."

In advancing George Bush's continuing meteoric rise, the article said several positive things about Bush and then added: "His appeal would be more than regional . . . . But his biggest political asset and his greatest attraction to Mr. Nixon is simply the fact that he is a Texan with a chance to carry that vital state.

"It is impossible to exaggerate the importance of Texas to 1972 Republican plans . . . . And that is why, strange as it sounds, Wednesday's Presidential visit to Texas may without exaggeration be called a milestone in the next two Presidential elections."

As noted in Chapter 1, CIA officers at the White House are "associated intimately" with the "immediate office of the President," which accounts for men "intimately involved in White House political operations" pushing the idea that Nixon would choose Bush as his 1972 running mate. CIA officers with "official covers" at the White House are there to gather intelligence and, when possible, advance the CIA's agenda. This was the second time in the space of

---

[220] Washington Post, 10-27-70, p. 19

three years that CIA officer George H. W. Bush was touted for the Vice Presidency, and it was the first time that he was touted for the Presidency.

Bush's loss of his second Senate bid in 1970 derailed efforts to get him onto the 1972 Presidential ticket, but in a prime example of CIA officers using their influence to advance their colleagues up through the ranks, CIA officer George Bush's "political" career made significant leaps during the Nixon and Ford Administrations.

On December 11, 1970, a short thirty-eight days after Bush lost his second Senate bid, President Nixon announced the appointment of Congressman George Bush to be the United States Ambassador to the United Nations.[221]

CIA officer George Bush, ostensibly nothing more than a former oilman who lost Senate races in 1964 and 1970 and served four years in Congress in violation of the Constitution, now had an "official cover" with the State Department as U.N. Ambassador, also known as a "diplomatic cover."

A *New York Times* editorial was highly critical of it, stating: "There seems to be nothing in his record that qualifies him for this highly important position. The chief of the American mission at the United Nations should be either an outstanding diplomat or someone of demonstrated national stature who has ready access to the President. Mr. Bush is a novice in diplomacy . . . . He is unknown nationally.[222]

"In fact, the choice of Mr. Bush is only the latest oddity in a bizarre chapter that began with the newspaper report of the imminent appointment to the United Nations post of Daniel P. Moynihan, the President's counselor on urban problems. That was a surprise to the present ambassador, Charles W. Yost, a distinguished career diplomat who had acceded to Mr. Nixon's request two years ago to serve 'for the duration.'" (Like

---

[221] New York Times, 12-12-70, p. 3
[222] New York Times, 12-12-70, p. 30

Republicans George Bush and Barry Goldwater, future Democratic Senator Daniel Patrick Moynihan was a CIA officer and a KGB asset, which is addressed later in this book.)

But replacing U.N. Ambassador Charles Yost, the "distinguished career diplomat" who agreed to serve "for the duration," was not President Nixon's idea. It was Bush's idea.

Two days before the appointment, Nixon Chief of Staff H. R. Haldeman wrote that Nixon "definitely wanted to bring Bush into the White House on a general basis" and "called Bush in and gave him the pitch on taking a White House job."

But George Bush, the two-term Congressman who had just lost his second Senate bid a few weeks earlier, was "clearly disappointed" that the President of the United States was now offering him a job at the White House "because he had been hoping for the UN spot."[223]

Haldeman wrote that Bush told Nixon "what he'd like to do at the UN in the way of really being an advocate for the President, not only at the UN, but in the overall New York community." Bush "made such a good pitch" that Nixon was persuaded to give him the UN post. Nixon "decided this was, in fact, a better use of Bush than having him at the White House. This really does work out better because it gives Bush a more prestigious appointment and a seat in the Cabinet."

The CIA clearly has influence in the right places, and one month after losing his second consecutive Senate race, Nixon "definitely wanted" to give Bush a "White House job." CIA officer George Bush then persuaded the President of the United States that instead of giving him a lowly White House job, he should give him "a more prestigious appointment and a seat in the Cabinet."

Bush could now more easily gather intelligence on Nixon and the inner workings of Nixon's Cabinet, more so than if he were shuttered in an office somewhere in the White House. As noted in Chapter 1, a CIA officer's job, whether using an "official cover" or a "nonofficial cover," is to gather intelligence and conduct secretive operations.

---

[223] The Haldeman Diaries, p. 217 (*G.P. Putnam's Sons, 1994*)

KGB efforts to get Bush into the Vice Presidency picked up again in 1974 and 1975, and Bush, himself, knew precisely what buttons to push as he worked in conjunction with his KGB handlers and other CIA officers at the White House. CIA officers will use a person's trust to advance the CIA's agenda.

The "prestigious appointment" to Nixon's Cabinet came to an end two years later when Bush's KGB handlers wanted to reignite his political standing among Republicans. Advancing Bush's political standing was critical to getting him into the Vice Presidency at some point so that they could assassinate the President and catapult Bush into the Presidency.

On November 27, 1972, Nixon's Chief of Staff, H. R. Haldeman, wrote that certain people at the Republican National Committee wanted "a full-time professional"[224] to replace the current RNC Chairman, Robert Dole, who had to devote his time to serving as a U.S. Senator.

Two weeks later, the *New York Times* reported, "Senator Robert Dole announced that he was resigning as Republican National Committee Chairman and that George Bush, United States Representative to the United Nations, had been chosen to replace him . . . . Until today, Senator Dole has maintained that he wanted to stay on and had Mr. Nixon's support to do so."[225]

But even though Dole publicly maintained that he still had Nixon's support to stay on as RNC Chairman, Nixon had given him the bad news thirteen days earlier. Haldeman wrote that Nixon met with Dole on November 28, 1972, and told him that he was replacing him, and Nixon "did mention George Bush as a possibility for the job."[226]

Dole responded by telling Nixon, "Well, if I came here for the hanging, I at least want to say a word in my own defense."

---

[224] The Haldeman Diaries, pp. 544-545 (*G.P. Putnam's Sons, 1994*)
[225] New York Times, 12-12-72, p. 1
[226] The Haldeman Diaries, pp. 544-545 (*G.P. Putnam's Sons, 1994*)

On the following day, November 29, two short days after Haldeman wrote that certain people at the Republican National Committee wanted to replace Dole, Nixon had already "told Bush that he's his choice, and that's set."

In 1968, certain people "in business and Congressional circles" were promoting Bush as Nixon's running mate, and in 1970, certain people at the White House were pushing to have Nixon choose Bush as his 1972 running mate while promoting Bush as "the Republican Presidential candidate for 1976."

Certain people at the White House also persuaded Nixon to give Bush "a White House job" in 1970, which Bush turned down only to persuade Nixon to give him "a more prestigious appointment and a seat in the Cabinet," all of which means certain people at the White House had to be involved in promoting Bush as a particularly ideal choice for RNC Chairman in 1972.

Bush's KGB handlers obviously had proxies where they needed them.

On May 10, 1973, as clouds of the Watergate scandal formed heavily over the nation and threatened to bring down the Nixon Presidency, RNC Chairman George Bush was one of "two special envoys from President Nixon" who attended the President's Cabinet meeting.[227] (As noted in Chapter 1, the "Watergate scandal" originated in June 1972 when operatives in the Nixon re-election campaign broke into the Watergate Hotel in Washington, D.C.)

Unlike his previous position, which had him attending Presidential Cabinet meetings with his "official cover" as U.N. Ambassador, Bush was now using his "nonofficial cover" as RNC Chairman to gather intelligence on what was said in the President's Cabinet meeting.

After the meeting, Bush flew to New York to attend the semiannual Conference of Republican Governors, where he proclaimed, "I'll be darned if we are going to let the ugliness of Watergate obscure the positive record of the President," which is

---

[227] New York Times, 5-11-73, p. 17

rather ironic because the KGB officers who were handling Bush orchestrated the entire "Watergate scandal" to sabotage Nixon's re-election bid. (With no hope of getting Bush onto the Republican ticket in 1972, the KGB officers were planning to get a CIA officer in Congress onto the Democratic ticket in 1972, more of which is explained later in this book.)

On October 10, 1973, five months after Bush's "ugliness of Watergate" comment, Vice President Spiro Agnew resigned after pleading no contest to a charge of failure to pay income taxes. President Nixon then "began his search" for a new Vice President and met with "Congressional leaders of both parties and with George Bush, chairman of the Republican National Committee."[228]

CIA officer George Bush now had direct input into the Presidential decision-making process while gathering intelligence on Nixon's Vice Presidential search.

Nixon chose House Republican Leader Gerald Ford for the Vice Presidency on October 12, 1973, and ten months later, as the Watergate scandal heated up, Bush's CIA colleague, Senator and KGB asset Barry Goldwater, helped advance the KGB's agenda.

Goldwater told a gathering of his fellow Republican Senators that President Nixon had consistently lied during the Watergate scandal, and CIA officer Barry Goldwater proclaimed, "There are only so many lies you can take, and now there has been one too many. Nixon should get his ass out of the White House -- today!"[229]

Nixon, facing impeachment for his role in the Watergate cover-up, resigned from the Presidency three days later, thus catapulting Vice President Ford into the Presidency, which meant Ford would need to appoint a new Vice President.

---

[228] New York Times, 10-11-73, p. 1
[229] https://www.politico.com/story/2007/02/when-the-gop-torpedoed-nixon-002680

Senator and CIA officer Barry Goldwater gave his "personal endorsement" to CIA officer George Bush for the Vice Presidential spot.[230]

In addition to Goldwater's endorsement, Congressman Barber Conable, chairman of the Republican Policy Committee, touted Bush for the Vice Presidency.[231] There were also "former colleagues" in the House of Representatives who were promoting Bush for the Vice Presidency,[232] which is not unlike the 1968 effort in "Congressional circles" to have Nixon choose freshman Congressman George Bush as a running mate. This was the third time in a short five years that CIA officer George Bush, who had served two terms in Congress in violation of the Constitution, was being widely promoted as the man who should be Vice President.

Bush, while still using his nonofficial cover as RNC Chairman, met with "Vice President Ford" on August 8, 1974, the day before Nixon resigned, and he met with "President Ford" after Nixon resigned on August 9, 1974.[233] He met with President Ford again two days later, which is when KGB asset Barry Goldwater "personally endorsed" Bush to be Ford's Vice President.

President Ford chose Nelson Rockefeller for the Vice Presidency, which still worked out well for the KGB, as it left their asset, George Bush, available for the position of CIA Director, a position from which he could springboard into higher office.

But there had to be a buffer between Bush's very partisan political job with the RNC and his appointment to be CIA Director. CIA Directors must be confirmed by the Senate, and Senate Democrats would never confirm the chairman of the Republican National Committee as CIA Director.

So, just a few weeks after Bush and Ford had their series of meetings, Ford appointed Bush to be Chief of the U.S. Liaison Office

---

[230] New York Times, 8-12-74, p. 14
[231] New York Times, 8-12-74, p. 1
[232] New York Times, 8-10-74, p. 1
[233] New York Times, 8-10-74, p. 3

in Peking, China. The United States had no diplomatic relations with China at the time but did have a Liaison Office, and Bush, as a career CIA officer, was again given an "official cover" with the State Department, or more precisely, a "diplomatic cover."

The *New York Times* reported, "Explaining the selection of Mr. Bush for the Peking post, a high White House official said, 'George Bush was a strong and viable candidate to be Ford's Vice-President until the last minute. He is somebody the President holds in high regard. His appointment, therefore, is a signal to the Chinese that the new United States envoy is somebody who has the President's ear.'"[234]

Fourteen months later, on November 3, 1975, one year before the 1976 Presidential election, President Ford announced he was nominating KGB asset George Bush to be Director of the Central Intelligence Agency.[235]

Ford also touted Bush as a possible 1976 running mate.

On November 12, 1975, *Washington Post* columnist George Will headlined his column "George Bush: Political Ambitions" and wrote: "When nominated to be Director of the Central Intelligence Agency, George Bush said he did not think that being Director would forever prevent him from seeking political office. Obviously, he hopes it will not, and his hope was stroked by President Ford's declaration that Bush is not excluded from consideration as his 1976 running mate.

"At the CIA he would be the wrong kind of guy at the wrong place at the worst possible time . . . . The CIA is under a cloud of dark suspicion based on proven misdeeds. The suspicion is that the CIA is a threat to civil liberties, and perhaps to tranquility, because it is insubordinate or otherwise immune to proper control.

---

[234] New York Times, 9-5-74, p. 1
[235] Washington Post, 11-4-75, p. 1

"The problem with Bush is less that he has a political past than that he so obviously and avidly wants to have a political future."[236]

A *Washington Post* editorial on November 18 was also critical of Bush and the idea that he should be Director of the CIA, first quoting from the Rockefeller report: "In the final analysis, the proper functioning of the Agency must depend in large part on the character of the Director of Central Intelligence. The best assurance against misuse of the Agency lies in the appointment to that position of persons with the judgment, courage, and independence to resist improper pressure and importuning, whether from the White House, within the Agency or elsewhere."[237]

The editorial then stated, "Mr. Ford, however, has rejected this advice. In nominating George Bush, a pleasant and able Republican politician currently serving as ambassador in Peking, he has selected a man who, for all of his qualities, would be on very few lists of 'persons with the judgment, courage, and independence to resist improper pressure and importuning.'

"He apparently would like to be Vice President, a post which is almost entirely the President's to bestow or withhold. On the basis of his record as ambassador to the U.N., there are doubtless a great many jobs in government which he could do very well, but brief service as Director of Central Intelligence is not among them.

"We mean no offense to Mr. Bush, but we fail to see why the Senate would wish to confirm him, or why, for that matter, he would want the job."

Bush's stint as special envoy to China did serve as the necessary buffer between his partisan political position with the RNC and his appointment to be CIA Director. But Democrats on the Senate Armed Services Committee still saw Bush's political aspirations as a roadblock to approving his nomination, thus Bush faced "the prospect of an 8 to 8 deadlock."[238]

---

[236] Washington Post, 11-12-75, p. 27
[237] Washington Post, 11-18-75, p. 26
[238] Washington Post, 12-19-75, p. 1

So, Bush took it upon himself to meet with President Ford three times on December 17, 1975, the day before the Senate Armed Services Committee was to vote on his nomination.

On December 18, the President submitted a letter to the Senate Armed Services Committee Chairman "just before the Committee met to vote on the Bush nomination." Ford stated that he would "no longer consider Bush as a Vice Presidential running mate." The Committee then voted twelve to four to approve Bush's nomination, dashing the hopes of Bush's KGB handlers that he would be elected to the Vice Presidency in 1976.[239]

George Bush in one of his three meetings with President Ford on December 17, 1975, one day before the Senate Armed Services Committee would vote on his nomination to be CIA Director. (Source: Gerald R. Ford Library)

And just as Bush had persuaded President Nixon to give him a job already held by a "distinguished career diplomat" so that he could have "a more prestigious appointment and a seat in the Cabinet," it was Bush who, in his three meetings with President Ford, persuaded him on the best way to get his CIA nomination approved. Ford's letter to the Committee states that "Bush urged that his name be eliminated from consideration" as Ford's 1976

---

[239] Washington Post, 12-19-75, p. 1

running mate, obviously so that he could get the top spot at the CIA.[240]

Ford's consideration of Bush as a 1976 running mate was the fourth time in less than eight years that Bush was promoted as a possible Vice Presidential running mate.

Five months before Bush's nomination to be CIA Director, the Rockefeller Report stated that there are no "outsiders" in "top-level management" at the CIA. In other executive branch agencies, the "chief officer" and "top-level assistants" are "appointed from the outside," but "no such infusion occurs in the CIA,"[241] which means KGB asset George Bush was a high-ranking CIA official five years earlier when he was a Member of Congress. (As will be seen later in this book, other Members of Congress have similarly held high-ranking positions in the CIA while they were in Congress.)

Former CIA Director William Colby wrote a book stating that President Ford fired him in 1975 and replaced him with George Bush because of Colby's "determination not 'to stonewall' Congressional and executive branch investigations of CIA wrongdoing."[242]

It soon became evident that Bush, unlike Colby, was a vanguard for CIA corruption.

In September 1976, less than eight months after being confirmed by the Senate, CIA Director George Bush addressed a gathering of retired intelligence officers and boasted that the CIA had "weathered the storm"[243] of Congressional and Executive Branch investigations, which would be the Senate Church Committee and President Ford's "Commission on CIA Activities Within the United States."

Bush also told his audience of retired intelligence officers that investigating the CIA's illicit activities inside the United States was tantamount to "campaigning against strong intelligence," and he

---

[240] Ibid.
[241] Rockefeller Report, pp. 83 & 85
[242] Washington Post, 3-15-78, p. 1
[243] Washington Post, 9-19-76, section C, p. 6

boldly proclaimed that the CIA had no need to "ferret out corruption."[244]

A CIA memorandum from 1978 stated that the "leadership" of the CIA "had easy access to those in power in and out of Government," and it referred to the CIA's "aura of political clout" in the United States.[245]

Bush, like many renegade CIA officers, clearly had "easy access to those in power" from the time he was elected to Congress in 1966 until he ended his reign as CIA Director in January 1977, and the KGB-infused CIA most definitely had the "political clout" to get Bush into the various high-profile positions in the Nixon and Ford Administrations.

After resigning as CIA Director in January 1977, Bush, working in conjunction with his KGB handlers, significantly ramped up his role in the CIA's quest to control the government.

Bush began "running for President" in 1977, which included "a two-year grass-roots effort that followed the Carter model all the way to the winning of the Iowa precinct caucuses."[246] (Democratic President Jimmy Carter, elected in 1976, was also a CIA officer being handled by the KGB. Carter was the only CIA officer that the KGB managed to get into the Presidency before they were exposed in 1984. More on Carter being a CIA officer along with Senators and Congressmen from both parties is addressed later in this book.)

Bush lost the Republican nomination to Ronald Reagan in 1980, after which "the Presidential nominee's advisers heavily pressured him" to choose Bush as a Vice Presidential running mate.[247] Reagan's "advisers" included his campaign chairman, William J. Casey, a high-ranking CIA official who became

---

[244] Washington Post, 9-17-76, p. 10 and Arizona Republic, 9-17-76, pp. 16 & 19
[245] National Archives Record Number 104-10404-10361
[246] Washington Post, 3-31-81, p. 11
[247] Washington Post, 4-1-81, p. 16

Reagan's CIA Director after the election. As will be seen, Casey was intrinsic to the CIA takeover of the United States government.

With Nixon, Ford, and Reagan each considering Bush for the Vice Presidency, it is clear that no Republican could run for President without being pushed to choose CIA officer George Bush as a running mate.

Newsweek reported in July 1980 that former President Gerald Ford was being promoted as Reagan's running mate and that Ford, not Bush, was everyone's favorite for the Vice Presidential spot. In the end, according to *Newsweek*, it was a choice between former President Ford and former CIA Director George Bush.

But Ford, of course, being a former President, turned down Reagan's offer to be his running mate. *Newsweek* noted how unlikely it was that a former President would end up becoming a Vice Presidential candidate, stating it would be "a political morass and a Constitutional nightmare . . . . In retrospect, the entire scheme seemed doomed from the start, and the wonder was that it went as far as it did."[248]

Newsweek also reported that the prospect of a "former Chief Executive" taking "second place on the ticket" had been "rejected by Ford himself on numerous occasions."

The *Washington Post* likewise reported that Reagan chose Bush "only after the draft Jerry Ford effort fizzled," which is when Casey "heavily pressured" Reagan to choose Bush.

By manipulating the situation so that Reagan anxiously awaited Ford's acceptance of the number two spot up until the last minute, Casey and his CIA cohorts kept Reagan from making serious offers to other potential candidates. With one of the two supposedly best choices for a running mate continuing to reject the offer, Reagan, in reality, had only one choice for the Vice Presidential spot: CIA officer and KGB asset George Bush.

The previously cited *Washington Post* article recalling that Bush was "running for President" by 1977 and that Reagan's advisers

---

[248] Newsweek: July 28, 1980 issue

"heavily pressured him" to choose Bush was on March 31, 1981, because one day earlier, sixty-nine days after Bush finally became Vice President of the United States, President Reagan was shot as he was leaving the Washington Hilton Hotel.

Bush immediately "cut short" a trip to Texas and returned to the White House to "take charge of the crisis in the government and to assume the responsibilities of the Presidency if President Reagan's injuries prevented him from serving in office."[249]

As noted in Chapter 2, CIA officers "detailed" to the "Secret Service" gave the would-be assassin, John Hinckley, access to President Reagan.

According to the *Washington Post*, if the Secret Service had parked the Presidential limousine where it should have been parked outside the Washington Hilton Hotel, "Reagan would have had a straight-line walk of about eight feet from door to car."[250]

Instead, Reagan's limousine "was waiting about twenty to twenty-five feet down the driveway from the door." In order to get to the limousine, Reagan had to "walk down the curving sidewalk."

"Around the curve, flush against the hotel wall, the assailant waited with his pistol." ("Come this way, Mr. President, your limo is down here.")

"Generally, agents want the armored limousine waiting in a direct line with the President's exit door as he moves from building to car. Such positioning shortens the period of vulnerability and makes it easier for agents to form a human shield as the public figure moves. In some cases, agents have had the car moved one foot or less to have it perfectly aligned with the exit."

"Television crew members at the Hilton said they had complained to the Secret Service about bystanders pushing into the area reserved for the press. One bystander, as it turned out,

---

[249] Washington Post, 4-1-81, p. 16
[250] Washington Post, 4-1-81, p. 16

was the accused gunman." ("Don't worry about the bystanders. We know what we're doing.")

Henry Brown, an ABC television cameraman, "had complained earlier to the Secret Service that members of the public had 'penetrated the police line,' creating crowded conditions in the press area and making it difficult to work . . . . His complaint went unheeded, and Brown went on working. He was standing near the assailant when he started to fire."[251]

"'He just opened up and kept squeezing the trigger,' Brown said."

"A Secret Service official said the advance agent on the scene concluded that it would be counterproductive to set up an area restricted only to the press on the narrow, curving walk outside the hotel." (It would clearly be counterproductive to the assassination plans.)

On April 4, 1981, the *Washington Post* reported: "The bullets that struck President Reagan and two of the three other persons wounded in Monday's assassination attempt were positively identified yesterday by the FBI as 'Devastators,'" which are "expensive, customized .22 caliber cartridges designed to explode upon impact with the force of slugs fired from much more powerful handguns."[252]

Besides the CIA's "designated officers of the Secret Service" being intrinsic to the attempt to kill President Reagan, the intended assassin, John Hinckley, was traveling in the same cities with his CIA/Secret Service handlers in October 1980, and Hinckley had made off-and-on stays in Washington, D.C. dating back to September 1980, six months prior to the attempted assassination.

The *Washington Post* reported that Hinckley "was in Chicago, Dayton, and Nashville last October" at the same time President Carter "was in those cities for campaign appearances," and Hinckley stayed at the "Capital Hilton Hotel September 27 and 28 and at the

---

[251] WP, 3-31-81, p. 10
[252] Washington Post, 4-4-81, p. 1

Quality Inn on Capitol Hill October 17-19, February 10 and 11, and February 16 and 17."[253]

The *Post* went on to state, "There is no evidence to indicate that these visits were tied either to the attack on Reagan or to any plan directed at former President Carter," and no evidence "that he was stalking Reagan or any other political figure," but "many of Hinckley's travels are otherwise unexplained."

The KGB officers obviously kept Hinckley close by while grooming him for the assassination, which they did by instilling him with a maniacal desire to impress teenage actress Jodie Foster by assassinating Reagan. Before setting off to kill Reagan, Hinckley wrote a letter to Foster stating that he was performing "this historical deed to gain your respect and love."[254] It was well-established in 1981 that Hinckley thought he was going to impress Jody Foster by killing the President.

The *Washington Post* reported that Hinckley bought "what is apparently his first gun sometime in early September at a pawnshop in Lubbock, Texas,"[255] after which he was staying at a hotel just three blocks from the White House in late September and then traveling in the same cities as President Carter and his "Secret Service" handlers in October.

Regardless of the "not guilty by reason of insanity" verdict, information in the *Washington Post* on April 5, 1981, clearly shows why Hinckley was chosen to kill Reagan. The *Post* reported that Hinckley joined the National Socialist Party of America in the spring of 1978, marched in a Nazi parade in St. Louis, and studied *Mein Kampf* in college. The National Socialist Party said Hinckley had been "expelled" because "he was too violence-prone."[256]

CIA operatives, specifically KGB officers inside the CIA, had no trouble manipulating the violent deranged psychotic into thinking

---

[253] Washington Post, 5-6-81, pp. 1-2
[254] http://time.com/4426013/know-about-john-hinckley-jr/
[255] Washington Post, 4-5-81, p. 18
[256] Ibid.

he would impress a teenage actress by killing President Reagan. With KGB asset George Bush finally in the Vice Presidency, Hinckley's KGB handlers easily provided him with access to the President of the United States.

In the three weeks following Hinckley's failed attempt on March 30, 1981, there were a substantial number of arrests of people who had been incited to try and kill President Reagan.

On Saturday, April 11, twelve days after Hinckley "opened up and kept squeezing the trigger," a Philadelphia man was arrested in Hatboro, Pennsylvania, for threatening to kill President Reagan. He was charged with assaulting "two Hatboro police officers" and "a Secret Service agent" who came to his apartment, and he was to be charged in U.S. District Court "with threatening to kill the President and with assaulting the Secret Service agent." This arrest brought "to at least 10 the number of people taken into custody this week for threatening Reagan's life."[257]

Six days later, on Friday, April 17, 1981, a Virginia man was arrested after he "telephoned the Secret Service in Richmond and told agents he was 'going to shoot President Reagan.' Neither Secret Service agents nor the court papers revealed a motive for the alleged threat." The *Washington Post* reported this arrest was "one of 16 the agency has made across the nation since the March 30 shooting of Reagan and three other men in Washington."[258]

The KGB officers undoubtedly manipulated drug addicts, psychotics, and malcontents in their quest to put their asset, CIA officer George Bush, into the Oval Office, but they were unable to pull off another assassination attempt. Another threat, however, did materialize on September 2, 1981, five months and three days after Hinckley shot Reagan, but like the earlier slew of threats, it failed to actually become an attempted assassination.

On September 2, 1981, police arrested 27-year-old Isom Joseph Dean in Towson, Maryland when they "found three scope-equipped

---

[257] Washington Post, 4-13-81, p. 18
[258] Washington Post, 4-23-81, p. 43

rifles, an M-18 semiautomatic rifle, a handgun, and a pair of high-powered binoculars" in the car he was driving.

"Police spokesman E. Jay Miller quoted Dean as telling arresting officers, 'You're lucky. If I hadn't had to stop for gas in Towson, you would not have gotten me. I would have killed the President' . . . . Secret Service agents said Dean told them he intended to kill the President and 'planned to sit around and wait until the opportunity presented itself because the President always has to come out' . . . . Charged with threatening to assassinate the President, Dean was ordered held without bond."[259]

It was never disclosed where, how, or when Dean obtained "three scope-equipped rifles, an M-18 semiautomatic rifle, a handgun, and a pair of high-powered binoculars," just as it was never disclosed that John Hinckley had considerable help in his effort to assassinate President Reagan.

There is something seriously wrong when a man who cannot legally distinguish between right and wrong can stand outside a hotel with a gun and plenty of Secret Service agents nearby and then "open up" on the President as walks to his limousine, which had been purposely parked down the driveway to lead the President passed his assailant. And to think that George Bush said that there was no need to "ferret out corruption" in the CIA back in 1976.

The KGB officers failed to get Bush chosen as a Vice Presidential running mate on four separate occasions over an eight-year period, and after finally getting Bush into the Vice Presidency, they failed to catapult him into the Presidency. But things were still going their way. Besides having Bush as Vice President, veteran Senators and Congressmen from both parties were in the CIA and being handled by the KGB, and the KGB wielded substantial control within the CIA. The ramifications seemed almost limitless, and the KGB-initiated quest to control

---

[259] Washington Post, 9-3-81, p. 4

the United States government was rolling along just fine for the time being.

{Part 2 - The CIA, Bush's Friends, and A Threat to Kill President Kennedy}

CIA records disclose that George Bush was an old friend of a CIA asset named George DeMohrenschildt dating back to the 1940s and lasting until DeMohrenschildt was killed in 1977. DeMohrenschildt wrote a personal letter to CIA Director George Bush on September 5, 1976, in which DeMohrenschildt complained about federal operatives harassing him, pleading with Bush, "Maybe you will be able to bring a solution into the hopeless situation I find myself in."[260]

The CIA's file on the letter states, "According to a note from the Director, he had first met DeMohrenschildt in the early 40s . . . . The Director had not heard from him in many years until the letter arrived. The Director responded to DeMohrenschildt's letter."[261]

In Bush's reply on September 28, 1976, he told DeMohrenschildt that his "staff" had determined that "Federal authorities" had no interest in him "in recent years."[262]

But in earlier years, the CIA was extremely interested in George Bush's old friend, because DeMohrenschildt was also a close friend of President Kennedy's accused assassin, Lee Harvey Oswald.

DeMohrenschildt was also a "source" for "what is now the Domestic Collection Division" of the CIA "in the late 1950s and early 60s."[263]

(When CIA Director William Colby testified in 1975, he pointed out that the CIA had "changed the name" of the "Domestic

---

[260] National Archives Record Number 104-10414-10143
[261] National Archives Record Number 104-10414-10144
[262] National Archives Record Number 104-10414-10134
[263] National Archives Record Number 104-10414-10019

Operations Division."[264] They obviously "changed the name" to the "Domestic Collection Division.")

DeMohrenschildt's friendship with Oswald began immediately after Oswald returned from Russia in the summer of 1962 while DeMohrenschildt was working as a CIA asset. Oswald even listed DeMohrenschildt as a reference when he applied for work in Dallas on October 4 and on October 10, 1963, and DeMohrenschildt was listed in Oswald's personal address book.[265]

When CIA Director George Bush wrote his 1976 "note" about not having heard from DeMohrenschildt "in many years," he also stated that DeMohrenschildt "surfaced when Oswald shot to prominence. He knew Oswald before the assassination of President Kennedy."[266]

DeMohrenschildt testified to the Warren Commission in 1964 about his relationship with Oswald, but he made no mention of his friendship with CIA officer and then Senatorial candidate George Bush, nor did DeMohrenschildt say anything about being a CIA asset.

Regarding DeMohrenschildt's friendship with Oswald, a CIA document in December 1963 refers to "an incoming State Department telegram" and states, "It appears from information in the telegram that the DeMohrenschildts were well acquainted with the Oswalds."[267]

According to a March 1964 CIA memorandum, "The DeMohrenschildts were among the first to befriend the Oswald family when they came back to the United States," and George DeMohrenschildt's son-in-law "said that he knew no one who had

---

[264] National Archives Record Number 157-10011-10025, p. 9
[265] Warren Commission Hearings and Exhibits, Volume XX, p. 3, FBI Files on George DeMohrenschildt, Batch 23, p. 43, and Warren Commission Hearings and Exhibits, Volume XVI, p. 48
[266] National Archives Record Number 104-10414-10142
[267] National Archives Record Number 104-10434-10226

more influence over Lee Oswald than George DeMohrenschildt."[268]

Six months before President Kennedy was assassinated, a CIA memorandum of May 9, 1963, states that the files of the CIA's Records Identification Division "revealed several references on subject, also known as George S. DeMohrenschildt."[269]

George Bush's old friend was also "the object of observation"[270] by the CIA "after President Kennedy's assassination," which included "opening and photographing the contents" of his mail.[271]

In 1964, CIA Deputy Director for Plans Richard Helms sent a memorandum to the Warren Commission stating that "shortly after" the assassination, DeMohrenschildt and his wife were "among the guests attending a cocktail party in Haiti.

"When the guests were told that Lee Harvey Oswald had been arrested, Mrs. DeMohrenschildt turned to her husband and said, 'Don't we know someone by that name? Yes, now I remember. He used to come to our house regularly and you gave him money.'"[272]

Helms's memorandum clearly states that Bush's old friend DeMohrenschildt, a CIA asset, was financing Lee Harvey Oswald after Oswald's return from Russia.

Gaeton Fonzi, an investigator for the House Select Committee on Assassinations in the 1970s, wrote that DeMohrenschildt had been "a consultant for various Texas oil companies" dating back to the late 1940s,[273] and as noted earlier, CIA officer George Bush used a "nonofficial cover" in the oil business. Bush formed Bush-Overby Oil Development in 1951, and he was the co-founder of Zapata Petroleum Corporation in 1953.[274]

Like all CIA officers with "nonofficial covers," Bush lived ostensibly as a normal, everyday working American and refrained

---

[268] National Archives Record Number 104-10418-10270
[269] National Archives Record Number 104-10436-10014, p. 7
[270] National Archives Record Numbers 104-10414-10019
[271] National Archives Record Numbers 104-10414-10144
[272] National Archives Record Number 104-10408-10070
[273] National Archives Record Number 104-10404-10057, p. 41
[274] George Bush Presidential Library "Series: Zapata Oil Files"

from telling anyone that he was a CIA officer gathering intelligence and conducting secretive operations inside the United States.

On December 2, 1976, Senator Gary Hart of the Senate Church Committee told the CIA he wanted "access to every piece of paper on DeMohrenschildt," pursuant to the Senate Church Committee's investigation of the Kennedy assassination.[275]

The CIA's Legislative Counsel, George Cary, told a Church Committee staffer that the CIA had "run into some snags" and asked "if there was any way that we could answer some questions" rather than allowing the staffer to search through the CIA's files on DeMohrenschildt. The CIA obviously did not want Senator Hart to have its information on DeMohrenschildt.

Cary's information on his dealings with Senator Hart ended up on CIA Director George Bush's desk a few days later.

In response, Bush wrote a memo on December 8, 1976, stating, "Please note references to George DeMohrenschildt. I have known him for many years. I recently asked for some Agency info on him. Now I see Hart is interested in him." Bush also asked if DeMohrenschildt is "suspected of being involved in any way in the Kennedy assassination matter."[276]

Two days before CIA Director George Bush noted that he "recently" asked for "Agency info" on DeMohrenschildt, a CIA memorandum of December 6, 1976, stated that the CIA was in the process of gathering all available information on DeMohrenschildt, which included searching the CIA's Directorate of Operations files and the Domestic Collection Division files. The CIA also checked the "Interagency Source Register" to see if other U.S. agencies had anything on him.[277]

George DeMohrenschildt was killed by a "shotgun wound in the head" on March 29, 1977, three months after Bush requested that

---

[275] National Archives Record Number 104-10322-10243, p. 8
[276] Ibid., p. 3
[277] National Archives Record Number 104-10414-10025

the CIA compile all of its information on him and six months after DeMohrenschildt's personal letter to Bush requesting help with his "hopeless situation." The shotgun wound was allegedly "self-inflicted."[278]

When Bush replied to DeMohrenschildt in September 1976 and told him there was no federal interest in him at all, Bush stated, "I hope this letter has been of some comfort to you."

DeMohrenschildt had another noteworthy friend besides George Bush and Lee Harvey Oswald. DeMohrenschildt was also friends with one of the KGB officers inside the CIA, J. Walton Moore, who worked out of the CIA's Dallas Field Office.

In 1964, Moore documented that he had "known George DeMohrenschildt and his wife since 1957," adding that it was in 1957 when he made his "initial contact" with DeMohrenschildt.[279]

CIA records also contain a personal letter that Moore wrote to DeMohrenschildt on January 7, 1964, forty-six days after President Kennedy's assassination. In the letter, Moore thanked DeMohrenschildt for a Christmas card, and in closing his letter to George Bush's old friend, Moore told DeMohrenschildt, "We are looking forward to your return to Dallas."[280]

Moore's personal letter to DeMohrenschildt would not be in the CIA's files unless Moore, the KGB officer, was one of DeMohrenschildt's CIA handlers in the early 1960s, which means KGB officer J. Walton Moore was also one of Lee Harvey Oswald's handlers.

Back in May 1976, four months before DeMohrenschildt notified CIA Director George Bush of his "hopeless situation," KGB officer J. Walton Moore documented that a "research writer from Reader's Digest" had contacted him about a book he was writing on "the Kennedy assassination."[281]

---

[278] National Archives Record Number 104-10414-10019
[279] National Archives Record Number 104-10414-10145, p. 13
[280] National Archives Record Number 104-10414-10028
[281] National Archives Record Number 104-10414-10145, p. 25

The writer had already spoken to George DeMohrenschildt and wanted Moore to tell him about his "association with Lee Harvey Oswald and George DeMohrenschildt."

Moore also documented that in July 1976, a man writing "a book on the Kennedy assassination" contacted him at home because he knew Moore to be "a friend of George DeMohrenschildt" and wanted to know if Moore "had ever met Lee Harvey Oswald."[282]

Moore and his KGB colleagues obviously saw DeMohrenschildt as a loose end that needed to be tied up, and CIA operations targeting DeMohrenschildt were so intense by September 1976 that he sought help from his old friend, CIA Director George Bush.

Moore sent a memo to CIA Headquarters on March 18, 1977, stating that a journalist in Dallas wanted to interview him "concerning his knowledge and connection with George DeMohrenschildt."[283]

It was obvious at that point that the KGB had to get rid of George DeMohrenschildt, who could clearly link them to President Kennedy's assassination.

DeMohrenschildt died eleven days later from the allegedly "self-inflicted" shotgun blast to the head.

On April 1, 1977, three days after DeMohrenschildt's "suicide," Moore wrote to another KGB officer in the CIA, the CIA's Domestic Operations Chief, stating, "DeMohrenschildt's death is getting a lot of play in the local press. So far my name hasn't surfaced, but it may be just a matter of time before my association with DeMohrenschildt comes out."[284]

Three days later, Moore sent newspaper clippings on DeMohrenschildt to the Domestic Operations Chief with a

---

[282] National Archives Record Number 104-10414-10145, p. 24
[283] National Archives Record Number 104-10400-10137, p. 2
[284] National Archives Record Number 104-10414-10015

notation that reads, "I think interest in the DeMohrenschildt story is dying down in Dallas."[285]

One of the clippings from the *Dallas Times Herald* stated that DeMohrenschildt was writing a manuscript concerning Oswald and the Kennedy assassination.

The manuscript, titled, "I'm A Patsy, I'm A Patsy," was turned over to the House Select Committee on Assassinations, which stated that DeMohrenschildt was still writing it "at the time of his death in March 1977."

The Committee included all 246 pages of the manuscript in their report, and the first words of DeMohrenschildt's manuscript are: "'I'm a patsy! I'm a patsy!' These last words of my friend, Lee Harvey Oswald, still ring in my ears and make me think of the terrible injustice inflicted on the memory of this 'supposed assassin.'"[286]

Toward the end of the still uncompleted manuscript, DeMohrenschildt wrote, "I cannot say that I was never a CIA agent." (The CIA defines an "agent" as "a person who acts in our behalf, at our instigation and in consonance with our direction."[287])

After DeMohrenschildt was killed on March 29, 1977, three months after CIA Director George Bush asked if DeMohrenschildt was "suspected of being involved in any way in the Kennedy assassination matter," Congressman Richardson Preyer, a member of the House Select Committee on Assassinations, stated, "He was a crucial witness for us based on the new information he had. He was intimately involved with Oswald."[288]

Congressman Preyer obviously did not know about DeMohrenschildt's decades-long relationship with Bush, who had been replaced as CIA Director two months earlier. But while Bush was still functioning as CIA Director, he and CIA Legislative Counsel George Cary took a special interest in Congressman Preyer.

---

[285] National Archives Record Number 104-10414-10014
[286] House Select Committee on Assassinations, Volume XII, pp. 69, 70, & 314
[287] National Archives Record Number 104-10408-10241
[288] National Archives Record Number 104-10414-10027

On November 28, 1976, fifty-three days before President-elect Carter would assume the Presidency and appoint a new CIA Director, Bush wrote a memo to Cary stating, "I note that Richardson Preyer of N.C. is to be head of the Kennedy part. I know him very well indeed. He is one of my closest friends in the House. If it would be useful to chat with him, taking you with me, I will be glad to do this before I leave CIA."[289]

Bush's memo makes it clear that when CIA officers become Members of Congress in violation of the Constitution, they make "friends" that will help them head off Congressional investigations into CIA corruption. Top ranking CIA officials will gladly head over to Capitol Hill to prevent Congress from doing anything about CIA corruption. As noted in Chapter 1, CIA officers conducted "intensive behind-the-scenes opposition" on Capitol Hill to block Congressional oversight of the CIA back in 1956.

On November 22, 1963, thirteen years before Bush sought to interfere with the House Select Committee's investigation of President Kennedy's assassination, Bush used his nonofficial cover as a Houston oilman to insert himself into the immediate aftermath of President Kennedy's assassination.

FBI Special Agent Graham Kitchel wrote a memorandum stating that at 1:45 p.m. on November 22, 1963, one hour and fifteen minutes after President Kennedy was assassinated, "George H. W. Bush," a resident of "Houston," called the FBI from Tyler, Texas and "wanted to furnish hearsay that he recalled hearing in recent weeks."[290]

Bush told the FBI that the "day and source" of the hearsay were "unknown," and Bush alleged that a man named James Parrott "has been talking of killing the President when he comes to Houston."

---

[289] National Archives Record Number 104-10322-10246
[290] FBI File 62-2115-6, Referenced in Warren Commission Document 14, "FBI Kitchel Report of 25 Nov 1963 re: Phone call Details," p. 7

When Bush called the FBI, he identified himself as "President of the Zapata Off-shore Drilling Company" in Houston and said that Parrott is "possibly a student at the University of Houston." He also gave the names and phone numbers of two people who, according to Bush, "would be able to furnish additional information regarding the identity of Parrott."

Why didn't George Bush tell the FBI that he was the son of former Senator Prescott Bush and that he was a candidate for the Republican nomination for Senator in Texas?

Did George Bush simply refrain from citing these credentials as a believable person when he furnished information on someone who had threatened to kill the President of the United States, a President who had just been assassinated?

Why were the "day and source" of what Bush allegedly overheard "unknown," and if Bush had "in recent weeks" overheard that James Parrott "has been talking of killing the President when he comes to Houston," then why didn't Bush provide that information to federal authorities before the President came to Houston on November 21?

Wouldn't a candidate for the United States Senate have a responsibility to report his knowledge that someone "has been talking of killing the President?"

Why did Bush wait until after the President went to Dallas and after he was assassinated on November 22 to furnish information about a threat to kill the President of the United States?

When Bush inserted himself into the aftermath of the assassination, he told the FBI that he was "proceeding to Dallas" and "would remain in the Dallas-Sheraton Hotel" and then "return to his residence on 11-23-63."

The Dallas-Sheraton Hotel is where the "Secret Service" had set up shop for President Kennedy's Dallas visit.[291]

---

[291] Warren Commission Hearings and Exhibits, Volume XVII, p. 625

```
UNITED STATES GOVERNMENT
Memorandum

TO      : SAC, HOUSTON                    DATE: 11-22-63

FROM    : SA GRAHAM W. KITCHEL

SUBJECT : UNKNOWN SUBJECT;
          ASSASSINATION OF PRESIDENT
          JOHN F. KENNEDY

        At 1:45 p.m. Mr. GEORGE H. W. BUSH, President
of the Zapata Off-shore Drilling Company, Houston, Texas,
residence 5525 Briar, Houston, telephonically furnished
the following information to writer by long distance
telephone call from Tyler, Texas.

        BUSH stated that he wanted to be kept confidential
but wanted to furnish hearsay that he recalled hearing in
recent weeks, the day and source unknown. He stated that
one JAMES PARROTT has been talking of killing the President
when he comes to Houston.

        BUSH stated that PARROTT is possibly a student
at the University of Houston and is active in political
matters in this area. He stated that he felt Mrs. PAWLEY,
telephone number SU 2-5239, or ARLINE SMITH, telephone
number JA 9-9194 of the Harris County Republican Party
Headquarters would be able to furnish additional informa-
tion regarding the identity of PARROTT.

        BUSH stated that he was proceeding to Dallas, Texas,
would remain in the Sheraton-Dallas Hotel and return to his
residence on 11-23-63. His office telephone number is
CA 2-0395.
```

One week after George Bush called the FBI and then traveled to the Dallas-Sheraton Hotel, FBI Director J. Edgar Hoover sent a memorandum to the State Department's Bureau of Intelligence and Research stating that information concerning the "Assassination of President John F. Kennedy" had been "orally furnished to Mr. George Bush of the Central Intelligence Agency."[292]

The Assassination Records Review Board, which was established by Congress in 1992 to declassify records related to President Kennedy's assassination, inquired with the CIA

---

[292] Final Report of the Assassinations Records Review Board, p. 108

concerning Hoover's 1963 memorandum and his identification of "George Bush of the Central Intelligence Agency."

The CIA claimed it had "no association with George Herbert Walker Bush during the time frame referenced," and they supplied the Review Board with "records" to support their claim.

But CIA officers are assigned pseudonyms when they join the CIA, and all CIA "records" concerning Bush would refer to him not as "George Herbert Walker Bush," but would instead refer to him by his CIA pseudonym.

When CIA officer Philip Agee wrote a book about his career in the CIA, he stated that the CIA's "Records Branch" assigned him a "pseudonym" when he joined the CIA. Agee stated that it was "the secret name that I'll use for the next thirty years on every piece of internal Agency correspondence: dispatches, cables, reports, everything I write. It will be the name by which I'll be known in promotions, fitness reports, and other personnel actions."[293]

Bush, with a "nonofficial cover" as a private citizen in the oil business, used his real name when he called the FBI, identifying himself as "President of the Zapata Off-shore Drilling Company," but Bush obviously displayed his CIA credentials when he went to the Dallas-Sheraton Hotel.

When FBI Director J. Edgar Hoover notified the State Department's Bureau of Intelligence and Research that "George Bush of the Central Intelligence Agency" had been "orally furnished" with information on the assassination, it was not "internal Agency correspondence." J. Edgar Hoover simply identified Bush by his real name, the name Bush used when he called the FBI, not the name by which Bush is known on CIA "records."

It is patently absurd to think the CIA would acknowledge that the 41st President of the United States was a CIA employee running for the United States Senate back in 1963 and that he was "orally furnished" with information on the "Assassination of President John F. Kennedy."

---

[293] Inside The Company; CIA Diary, p. 133 (*Bantam Books, 1975*)

The CIA maintains covers for CIA officers, and Bush was supposed to be nothing more than a Houston oilman running for the Senate when President Kennedy was assassinated. The CIA was allegedly unable to provide any information concerning the "George Bush of the Central Intelligence Agency" in FBI Director J. Edgar Hoover's memorandum.

Like all CIA officers in Congress, George Bush used his CIA pseudonym on every intelligence report he wrote, including his intelligence reports on Members of Congress.

The FBI's subsequent investigation of James Parrott determined that he had nothing to do with President Kennedy's assassination and that there was no evidence of him threatening to kill President Kennedy. And far from being a "student at the University of Houston," Parrott was a 24-year-old "self-employed" sign painter who lived with his mother and had a seventh-grade education.[294]

Bush's claim that James Parrott had been talking about "killing the President" was just a pretext for going to the Dallas-Sheraton Hotel, where he obviously met with his CIA colleagues and inserted himself into the aftermath of President Kennedy's assassination.

Barbara Bush, George Bush's wife, wrote in her memoirs that when President Kennedy was assassinated, she and George were in Tyler, Texas "in the middle of a several-city swing" pursuant to George's bid for the U.S. Senate.

She was at the "beauty parlor" when she heard on the radio that President Kennedy had been shot, and after George picked her up, they "went right to the airport," which means George was off doing his CIA stuff and notifying the FBI while his wife was at the beauty parlor.[295]

Mrs. Bush, however, said nothing about George going to the Dallas-Sheraton Hotel after they landed in Dallas.

---

[294] Warren Commission Document 14, p. 7-8
[295] Barbara Bush: A Memoir, p. 59 (*Charles Scribner's Sons, 1994*)

Concerning George H. W. Bush and Billy Graham, who suggested Nixon choose freshman Congressman George Bush as his running mate in 1968, I personally witnessed a conversation between Bush and Graham after the KGB was exposed in 1984. Graham brought up one name after another of CIA officers that both he and Bush had known, and Bush identified each one as having been a KGB officer.

Billy Graham was also acquainted with the family of John Hinckley, who shot President Reagan on behalf of the KGB when they were trying to catapult George Bush into the Presidency.

On April 17, 1981, eighteen days after Hinckley shot the President, President Reagan wrote in his diary that he "talked by phone with Billy Graham" and that Graham "knows the family of the young man who did the shooting."[296]

Graham was not the only person acquainted with the Hinckley family.

On March 31, 1981, the day after Hinckley shot Reagan, the *Houston Post* reported that according to George H. W. Bush's son, Neil Bush, "The Bush family knew the Hinckley family because of the large political contributions they made to the Vice President's campaigns."[297]

Sharon Bush, Neil's wife, was quoted as saying, "From what I know and have heard," the Hinckleys "have given a lot of money to the Bush campaign."

{Part 3 – The Aftermath of Exposing The KGB}

CIA officers like George Bush have been thriving for years in an egregiously corrupted CIA. After the KGB was exposed in 1984, renegade CIA officers immediately filled a power vacuum in the hierarchy of corruption. They were shielded in the CIA hierarchy and at all levels of the CIA, and they were intent on maintaining the grip on power that the KGB had established over the course of 37 years.

---

[296] The Reagan Diaries, p. 13 (*HarperCollins Publishers 2007*)
[297] Houston Post, 3-31-81, pp. 1 & 7

They would keep the American public in the dark about the KGB infiltration that had been exposed and make sure that CIA officers in Congress continued doing their part in the quest to control the government.

Toward that end, they were intent on having Vice President George H. W. Bush, the highest-ranking CIA officer in government, succeed Ronald Reagan as President as they picked up where the KGB left off in the quest to control the United States government.

Meanwhile, renegade CIA officers in the CIA's "Democratic faction" were hoping to have their CIA colleague, former Senator and Vice President Walter Mondale, elected to the Presidency in 1984. Mondale was Vice President under fellow CIA officer Jimmy Carter from 1977 to 1981.

The American public, of course, was none the wiser in 1984 concerning the KGB infiltration and the surreptitious efforts to control the government, but everyone in the 98th Congress knew of the CIA officers in their ranks. None were willing to break the silence about Article I, section 6, of the U.S. Constitution being secretly violated.

In 1984, Members of Congress were more interested in their own political futures, the forthcoming campaigns, and in getting re-elected, while CIA officers in Congress were intent on building up the corruption that they had established in conjunction with their KGB handlers over the course of three decades.

President Ronald Reagan, with his re-election looming in 1984, had no intention of sacrificing Vice President and CIA officer George Bush on the altar of Constitutionality, and Democrats were not going to expose anything because many of the renegade CIA officers in Congress were long-term members of the Democratic Party.

CIA officer Walter Mondale went on to become the Democratic nominee for President in 1984, and he chose another CIA officer, Congresswoman Geraldine Ferraro, as his running mate.

The 1984 campaigns were the first campaigns in which Bush, Mondale, Ferraro, and the rest of their CIA colleagues in the political arena were not being handled by KGB officers. Renegade CIA officers were no longer working in conjunction with their KGB handlers. The CIA officers themselves were now in charge of the ongoing quest to control the United States government, and their ranks would swell in the ensuing years as CIA officers continued to violate the United States Constitution by becoming Members of Congress.

Three days before he lost his 1964 Senate bid, George H. W. Bush, whose CIA work invariably connected him to President Kennedy's assassination, was CIA officer Barry Goldwater's "bright hope on the political horizon." Bush was then targeted for the Presidency or the Vice Presidency in the next seven Presidential elections from 1968 through 1992.

First, there was an orchestrated, widespread push in business and Congressional circles to get President Nixon to choose freshman Congressman Bush as his 1968 running mate. Then, there was the 1970 push inside the White House to get Bush onto the ballot as Nixon's 1972 running mate and as the 1976 Republican Presidential nominee.

There was even an effort to get Bush into the Vice Presidency when Ford needed a Vice President in 1974, and there was an effort in 1975 to have Ford choose Bush as his 1976 running mate.

Bush was finally elected to the Vice Presidency in 1980. He ran and won re-election to the Vice Presidency in 1984. He was elected President of the United States in 1988 but lost his bid to be re-elected in 1992.

CIA officers were not going to let the "bright hope" fade just because their progenitors, the KGB officers handling Bush, had gone to prison. The CIA's vast domestic operations and the KGB's systematic corruption of both the CIA and the government provided the CIA with a platform for initiating its own quest to control the United States government.

When renegade CIA officers followed in the footsteps of the KGB, they not only sought to have Bush succeed Reagan as President, but also sought to conceal the means by which Bush had come to power.

George H. W. Bush, however, had risen through the ranks as a result of KGB efforts. Renegade CIA officers wanted "assets" of their own to eventually be elected to the Presidency, more of which is addressed later in this book.

Chapter 5: How to Kill Members of Congress and How to Empower the CIA

A 1964 CIA memorandum on Soviet "Executive Action" states that beginning in 1953, the Soviet Union's "executive action component" was assigned to "carry out 'special action tasks' such as sabotage and political murders."

The memorandum goes on to say that one of the KGB's "main target areas" for "political murders" is the United States, and it states, "Soviet intelligence is doubtlessly involved in incidents that never become officially recognized as executive action, such as assassinations which are recorded as accidents" or "suicide."[298]

After going to prison in 1984, some of the KGB officers admitted that during their quest to control the government, their KGB colleagues inside the CIA killed thirteen Members of Congress in the space of twenty-six years from 1957 to 1983, with twelve of those deaths recorded as "accidents" and "suicides."

CIA officer and KGB "asset" George Bush was elected to the Presidency four years after the KBG admitted to killing Members of Congress. Renegade CIA officers then began their own "executive action" program, using four separate "accidents" to kill four Members of Congress in less than two years.

During the first eight years of the KGB's killing campaign, they killed five Members of Congress in addition to assassinating President Kennedy. Three of the deaths came by way of traffic "accidents" spaced out over the years 1957, 1959, and 1965.

---

[298] National Archives Record Number 104-10428-10235, pp. 4 & 9

Significant details tie the three traffic "accidents" together and show why, after the 1965 "accident," the KGB officers ceased to use this method of assassination and opted for airplane "accidents" as their preferred method for killing Members of Congress.

In the 1965 "accident," a state trooper had Congressman T. Ashton Thompson pull over onto the apron of a highway in North Carolina on July 1, 1965.

"As Mr. Thompson got out of the car, a truck veered onto the apron. It struck the Congressman, crushing him against his car and then hurling him over it.[299]

"Mr. Thompson and his family were returning to Louisiana for the Fourth of July weekend . . . . The impact sent the Congressman's car crashing into the rear of the patrol car."

The Congressman's wife, his son, and his daughter, "were taken to a hospital for treatment of shock and bruises . . . . The truck overturned about fifty yards away," after which the truck driver was "taken to a hospital with internal injuries."

Four months later, in November 1965, the Interstate Commerce Commission (ICC) issued a report recommending "a review of physical standards for truck drivers."

The ICC report stated that the truck driver's eyes were examined in August and "cataracts existed in both of the driver's eyes."[300]

It also stated the truck driver's physician said he was "being treated for asthma and high blood pressure," and it went on to say that the truck driver "had been exceeding the ICC limit on maximum hours of service" when he killed Congressman Thompson.

The truck driver supposedly experienced "vision impairment" and a "loss of control" of his "tractor-trailer" while the

---

[299] New York Times, 7-2-65, p. 15
[300] New York Times, 11-19-65, p. 29

Congressman was "talking to a state trooper who had stopped him for alleged speeding."

High blood pressure is something that a hospital would invariably determine when treating a man with internal injuries, and they would certainly need to know if he suffered from asthma.

And having just killed a Member of Congress in a traffic "accident" would have instantaneously qualified the truck driver for an eye examination on July 1, 1965, but the Federal report from a Federal agency said the alleged eye examination that found cataracts on both eyes was in August, and it was allegedly his physician who said the truck driver suffered from asthma and high blood pressure, not the hospital report.

A significant factor in the cover story is that the truck driver was "exceeding the ICC limit on maximum hours of service," which would mean the "sickly" truck driver with cataracts on both eyes had been driving too long and had a "need for sleep" when he killed the Congressman with his tractor-trailer.

The entire cover story includes the premise that people who were affected by Congressman Thompson's death were surprised to learn, at least a month later, that the truck driver who killed him had cataracts on both of his eyes. It also includes the premise that the truck driver offered no explanation for how he happened to "accidentally" kill a Member of Congress, which would explain why his eyes were not examined for a month, if they were examined at all.

According to the cover story, the truck driver either suddenly developed extremely poor vision in both eyes and then, by sheer coincidence, killed a Congressman with his tractor-trailer, or he had been driving around for some time with extremely poor vision but did not get into an accident until Congressman Thompson was pulled over onto the apron of a highway, after which the truck driver veered off the highway and headed straight for the Congressman.

An alleged "need for sleep" also factored into the traffic "accident" preceding Congressman Thompson's murder.

"Early" on November 4, 1959, Congressman Charles Boyle was killed when his car "smashed into an elevated train pillar" in Chicago. Police said the Congressman had "apparently fallen asleep at the wheel or had been cut off by another car."[301]

The "accident" was early enough on November 4 to be front page news in the afternoon edition of the *Chicago Tribune* on that day,[302] and the fact is that if another driver did not "cut off" Congressman Boyle and kill him by running him into a train pillar, it would appear that the Congressman was simply in need of sleep and thus had "apparently fallen asleep at the wheel."

Congressman Boyle's "need for sleep" was no different than that of the "sickly" truck driver, who had supposedly exceeded "the ICC limit on maximum hours of service" and had a "need for sleep" when he ran down Congressman Thompson with his tractor-trailer.

The KGB officers must have seen the problem with continuing to put forth premises like: "Congressman Boyle wasn't murdered. He just didn't get enough sleep," and "Congressman Thompson wasn't murdered. The sickly truck driver with cataracts on both of his eyes who killed him with his tractor-trailer just didn't get enough sleep."

In the 1957 traffic "accident," which marked the beginning of the KGB's "executive action," Congressman Henderson Lanham was "killed instantly" when a switch engine (a train engine used to switch train cars) struck his car while he was "enroute to a speaking engagement before a PTA group" in Rome, Georgia on November 10, 1957.[303]

In the space of eight years, three Congressmen were killed by way of a train engine, an elevated train pillar, and a tractor-trailer, and when this book was published in 2019, these were the only traffic "accidents" in which Members of Congress died since 1951.

---

[301] New York Times, 11-5-59, p. 27
[302] Chicago Tribune, afternoon edition, 11-4-59, p. 1
[303] Atlanta Constitution, 11-12-57, p. 1

The first killing in 1957 seemed overtly accidental, but it was quite easy for the KGB officers to kill Congressman Lanham as he drove across the railroad tracks while on his way to the PTA meeting.

Killing a Congressman with a switch engine as he drives across railroad tracks is a one-time event, just as the "need for sleep" killings could not be extended beyond two.

The KGB was definitely stretching it with the 1965 story about an allegedly asthmatic truck driver with high blood pressure and cataracts on both eyes exceeding the ICC limit on maximum hours of service. By supposedly going without sleep and exhausting himself and suffering "vision impairment," the allegedly asthmatic truck driver with high blood pressure and cataracts on both eyes gained the dubious distinction of being the last man to assassinate a Member of Congress with a traffic "accident."

Culpability did not seem to be a problem in the 1957 "accident," and even the 1959 "accident" would not yet be pushing the envelope, but the string of three traffic "accidents" and the circumstances involved, culminating in the 1965 "accident," had to be raising the specter of responsibility and believability.

After the KGB killed Congressman Thompson with a tractor-trailer, the KGB's next Congressional target was Senator Robert F. Kennedy. The KGB officers used a radical Arab nationalist named Sirhan Sirhan and a CIA "double agent" to assassinate Senator Kennedy on June 5, 1968. More on Senator Kennedy's assassination is addressed later in this book.

In 1972, airplane "accidents" became the KGB's principal method for killing Members of Congress, as they were an easy and more acceptable alternative to the obviously suspicious traffic "accidents."

In less than four years, five Congressmen were killed in airplane "accidents," and another Congressman was killed with a shotgun in an alleged "suicide." The KGB admitted to culpability in these six deaths, just as they admitted to killing seven other Members of Congress over the course of twenty-six years.

The first in the KGB's series of airplane "accidents" was on October 16, 1972, when a plane carrying House Majority Leader Hale Boggs and Congressman Nick Begich disappeared in the Alaska wilderness while Boggs was making a campaign appearance for Begich.

"Campaign workers" were fully responsible for causing Boggs to miss a "commercial flight," and the trip itself was completely unnecessary for Majority Leader Hale Boggs during the busy campaign season.

The campaign workers "let him sleep a few extra hours, passing up a commercial flight to Juneau and chartering the plane flown by Jonz, owner of Pan-Alaska Airways.

"Ironically, it was a campaign trip Begich and Boggs probably did not have to make. Begich polled 37,900 votes to 16,500 for his two Republican opponents in the August Alaska primary election. Most political observers believe he would have no trouble in his re-election bid."[304]

The chartered plane that was used for a "campaign trip" that the two Congressmen "did not have to make" has never been found, and both Congressmen are "presumed dead."

As for "campaign workers" being party to killing Members of Congress, Chapter 1 clearly shows that CIA officers can be put into position anywhere, and nothing could be easier than becoming a "campaign worker."

Campaign workers would also be useful in keeping Boggs up late with questions so that they would have an excuse to "let him sleep a few extra hours" and pass up a "commercial flight." They could then put him on the privately owned Pan-Alaska Airways for the fatal trip.

There is no way to determine if the KGB used their prescribed method of "sabotage" in "political murders" on this occasion, but they clearly revived the "need for sleep" factor.

---

[304] Washington Post, 10-20-72, p. 3

A short fifty-three days after Congressmen Boggs and Begich were killed, Congressman George Collins became the KGB's next flying fatality while he was returning to Chicago on a commercial flight on December 8, 1972.

The Boeing 737 with Congressman Collins onboard was "descending near 71st and Lawndale when it plunged to the ground, smashed through a row of one-story houses and burst into flames."[305]

The pilot, Captain Wendell Lewis Whitehouse, had "about 18,000 hours of flying time," including 2,435 hours in a Boeing 737.[306]

But on the flight that killed Congressman Collins, Captain Whitehouse "failed to maintain flying speed" during his "final approach" to Midway airport.[307] The NTSB report cites a "rapid deterioration of air speed" and the pilot's failure to "apply effective corrective action." The report also cites the pilot's "failure to exercise positive flight management earlier during the approach."[308]

As noted earlier, the KGB's "political murders" were sometimes recorded as "suicide." Less than six months after killing three Members of Congress in airplane "accidents," the KGB used an alleged "suicide" by shotgun to snuff out a Member of Congress.

Congressman William O. Mills was shot to death, allegedly by his own hand, on May 24, 1973. He was found with "a single 12-gauge shotgun wound in the left side of his chest . . . . The automatic gun and a single spent shell were at his side."

Congressman Mills, "a Republican whose 1971 special election was aided by an unreported cash transfer of $25,000 from the Nixon campaign committee, was found shot to death and the authorities called his death an apparent suicide . . . . Mr. Mills had left at least

---

[305] New York Times, 12-9-72, pp. 1 & 70
[306] http://libraryonline.erau.edu/online-full-text/ntsb/aircraft-accident-reports/AAR73-16.pdf
[307] NTSB Identification: DCA73A0003
https://www.ntsb.gov/_layouts/ntsb.aviation/brief.aspx?ev_id=66703&key=0
[308] http://libraryonline.erau.edu/online-full-text/ntsb/aircraft-accident-reports/AAR73-16.pdf

seven notes, including one found on his body . . . . One official said that in one of the notes, Mr. Mills said that 'he had done nothing wrong but said he couldn't prove it, and so there was no other way out.'"[309]

"Mr. Mills was reported to have had no serious domestic or personal problems."

"Three of his Congressional aides, including his former campaign treasurer," were killed in "an automobile accident in 1972."

The Congressman's death "followed by five days the disclosure by the General Accounting Office that Mr. Mills' 1971 campaign was aided by an unreported cash transfer from the Finance Committee to Re-elect the President."

There had been an "unreported cash transfer of $25,000" from a political committee to the Congressman's campaign in a "special election" two years earlier, and therefore, the Congressman, whose campaign treasurer had already been killed, allegedly killed himself with a "12-gauge shotgun" and "left at least seven suicide notes," one in which he allegedly stated he "had done nothing wrong but said he couldn't prove it, and so there was no other way out."

Congressman Mills' "special election" in 1971 was held to fill the seat of Congressman Rogers Morton, who had resigned to become President Nixon's Interior Secretary. Morton told newsmen that the $25,000 transfer to the Mills campaign back in 1971 was "perfectly proper and above-board."[310]

After killing four Members of Congress in seven months, the KGB waited twenty-one months for their next "political murder."

Congressman Jerry Pettis met his fate on February 14, 1975, when the private plane he was piloting crashed.

The National Transportation Safety Board said the 58-year-old Pettis was "a veteran pilot with 18,250 hours of flying time,

---

[309] New York Times, 5-25-73, pp. 1 & 17
[310] New York Times, 5-25-73, pp. 1 & 17

including 700 in the type of small plane he was flying at the time of the crash."

The NTSB "listed the probable cause of the crash as Pettis's continued flight into adverse weather conditions . . . . Pettis had been adequately briefed on the weather before his flight."[311]

CIA officers would have no problem feeding inaccurate weather information to Congressman Pettis when he was "briefed on the weather before his flight," which would explain his "continued flight into adverse weather conditions."

On August 3, 1976, eighteen months after Pettis's death, KGB officers inside the CIA killed Missouri Congressman Jerry L. Litton, "who was winning the Democratic nomination for the U.S. Senate."

Congressman Litton and his entire family died after they boarded a plane and it "plummeted into a field shortly after taking off." They were "on their way to Kansas City for a victory celebration."[312]

The NTSB "said its investigation showed a broken crankshaft in the left engine caused the engine to fail on take-off," but the plane was clearly taking off and landing with a functioning crankshaft prior to the Congressman's flight.

The official NTSB report states that "shortly after" the Congressman's plane "took off," the crankshaft in the left engine "broke" with a "pre-existing fatigue crack" being the alleged cause of the break.[313] But again, the plane was clearly taking off and landing prior to Congressman Litton and his family boarding the plane.

There is no reason to think the KGB did not use their prescribed method of "sabotage" to kill Congressman Litton and his family. It was no coincidence that they got onto a plane with a crankshaft that would break shortly after takeoff.

After the KGB killed Congressmen Boggs, Begich, Collins, Mills, Pettis, and Litton in less than four years, Intelligence Oversight Committees were in place in both the House and the Senate, which

---

[311] Washington Post, 9-13-75, p. 10
[312] Washington Post, 8-11-76, p. 15
[313] National Transportation Safety Board Report AAR77-04, dated 16 JUL 77, pp. 13 & 14 http://libraryonline.erau.edu/online-full-text/ntsb/aircraft-accident-reports/AAR77-04.pdf

resulted in a thirteen-year lull in plane crashes that killed Members of Congress.

The next plane to go down with a Member of Congress on board did not crash. A Soviet fighter jet shot it down after it flew into Soviet airspace in a KGB-orchestrated intelligence operation in which the plane would supposedly probe the Soviet Union's radar defense system.

Congressman Lawrence McDonald, a CIA officer in Congress, was a passenger on Korean Air Lines Flight 007 when the pilot took it hundreds of miles off course and flew near a Soviet island near Siberia on September 1, 1983. The Soviet island was "part of the Soviet Far Eastern military network, with air bases, radar stations, and other tracking installations."[314]

A Soviet fighter jet intercepted Flight "Double-O-Seven" and destroyed it with a missile.

Afterwards, Korean Air Lines officials in New York "contended that the airliner could not have strayed off course into Soviet airspace because of what they called 'sophisticated' navigational equipment on board.

"'Since we skirt this area here very closely,' said Ralph Strafaci, the district sales manager, 'the equipment we have on board is very important and very technical. It's a very difficult thing for that aircraft to stray.'"[315] (More on the CIA's Flight "Double-O-Seven" intelligence operation is addressed in another chapter.)

Congressman McDonald was the last Member of Congress to die at the hands of the KGB before they were exposed in 1984.

Five years after the KGB was exposed, the thirteen-year lull in plane crashes came to an abrupt end when CIA officer George H. W. Bush became President. With one of their own in the Oval Office, renegade CIA officers disposed of four Members of Congress in less than two years using four separate plane crashes.

---

[314] New York Times, 9-2-83, p. 4
[315] Ibid.

Renegade CIA officers initiated their killing campaign less than seven months into the Bush Presidency on August 7, 1989, when they killed Congressman Mickey Leland.

Congressman Leland's "accident" took place in Ethiopia, and after a six-day search, the plane was found on a "mountainside" in a "remote region of Western Ethiopia."[316]

Ethiopia's Civil Aviation Authority reported that, after "improper flight preparation," the pilots caused the fatal crash by "pushing too far and flying into an area of rain and fog at a low altitude." With no explanation for the pilots' actions, Ethiopia's Civil Aviation Authority speculated that Congressman Leland's pilots may have been "pressured" to "fly in bad weather" by a "tight flight schedule."[317]

On August 13, 1989, the day that the wreckage of Congressman Leland's plane was found, a plane carrying Congressman Larkin Smith of Mississippi crashed.

Officials investigating the crash said the pilot "appeared nervous and even ran the aircraft off the taxiway shortly before takeoff.... The Cessna 177 later veered east from its planned flight path before hitting a 70-foot pine tree in the Desoto National Forest."[318]

Jorge Prellezo, the regional director of the National Transportation Safety Board, stated that people who saw Congressman Smith's pilot before takeoff "said he appeared nervous, like he was concerned about the flight."

William Dowden, a Southeast Aviation employee who watched the plane "both during and after takeoff," stated that the pilot "taxied straight out off the ramp area onto the grass," and then "made a 180-degree turn and taxied slowly out to the runway.... The taxiways are lit up with blue lights and what happened struck us as being highly unusual."[319]

---

[316] New York Times, 8-14-89, p. 1
[317] Sarasota Herald-Tribune, 8-25-90, p. 5A,
https://news.google.com/newspapers?nid=1755&dat=19900825&id=t-obAAAAIBAJ&sjid=u3oEAAAAIBAJ&pg=2361,5313857&hl=en
[318] New York Times, 8-17-89, section 2, p. 10
[319] New York Times, 8-17-89, section 2, p. 10

NTSB investigators "wanted to know why the pilot told controllers that he would follow the established route along US 49 but instead flew about nine miles to the east over the Desoto National Forest."

Two years after the deaths of Congressmen Leland and Smith, Senator John Heinz died when his plane was destroyed by another aircraft, not unlike how the KGB disposed of Congressman McDonald when his plane was destroyed by another aircraft in 1983.

On April 4, 1991, a helicopter collided with Senator Heinz' plane after making two completely unnecessary and pointless attempts to inspect the plane's landing gear.

NTSB documents show that the pilot of Senator Heinz' plane, a Piper Aerostar PA60, had "three hours of experience as pilot-in-command" on a Piper PA60 and had "problems on a previous flight."[320]

The incident began after Senator Heinz' inexperienced pilot radioed that he did not know if his "nose gear" was "locked" in the down position because the "light on the instrument panel did not illuminate" to indicate that the nose gear was locked.[321]

The airport control tower then alerted airport personnel to a "possible emergency."

One of the pilots on a nearby helicopter told the control tower that he had observed the "Aerostar" that "went past us," adding that it "looks like the gear is down."

Senator Heinz' pilot heard the helicopter pilot's transmission and told the control tower, "I can tell it's down, but I don't know if it's locked."

The control tower then told Senator Heinz' pilot to make "a low-altitude pass by the control tower" so that they could observe the nose gear. The helicopter pilot, who had coincidentally taken off just before Senator Heinz's plane passed by, told the control

---

[320] Washington Post, 7-4-91, p. 4
[321] https://www.ntsb.gov/safety/safety-recs/recletters/A91_91_93.pdf

tower that he would be willing to "take a real close look" at the plane's nose gear.[322]

Senator Heinz' pilot then flew past the control tower and was told, "Gear looks down; it appears to be normal . . . . I've got a helicopter north of the airport. He said he could take a look at it if you like."

The helicopter then flew toward the plane, making one pass on the "left side" and a "second pass" on the "right side." The helicopter's first officer told Senator Heinz' pilot, "Everything looks good," and Senator Heinz' pilot radioed that he would "start to turn in" to land the plane.

The "rotor of the helicopter" then struck the "underside" of Senator Heinz' plane.

According to the NTSB, the "nose gear locking mechanism" on a Piper Aerostar is "concealed," and there was "no reason" for the helicopter to do a "closer" inspection, as "it would have been virtually impossible" to visually determine that the nose gear was "locked."

What's more, the NTSB could not find anything wrong with the plane, and pilots who had previously flown that particular Aerostar had no problems with the nose gear indicator light. There was no explanation for why it was not working when Senator Heinz' inexperienced pilot was attempting to land the plane, and there is certainly no explanation for why the helicopter pilot, after making two passes and radioing that "everything looks good," remained close enough to Senator Heinz' plane for the "rotor of the helicopter" to strike the "underside" of the plane.

"Several experienced Piper PA60 pilots said in interviews with NTSB investigators that if the gear was observed to be down, it would automatically be locked." After it was determined that the plane "did not have landing gear problems, as its pilot first believed," it was "cleared for landing" before colliding with the helicopter.[323]

---

[322] Washington Post, 4-24-91, p. 5 and https://www.ntsb.gov/safety/safety-recs/recletters/A91_91_93.pdf
[323] Washington Post, 4-24-91, p. 5

One day after Senator Heinz was killed, former Senator John Tower became the fourth victim of renegade CIA officers during the Administration of President George H. W. Bush.

The *New York Times* described Tower as "one of the most influential and knowledgeable lawmakers" on "national security issues."[324] He served as Vice Chairman of the Senate Church Committee that investigated the CIA in 1975, and he retired from Congress in 1985. The CIA killed Tower while he was serving as Chairman of the President's Intelligence Advisory Board, which oversees the CIA.

The crash that killed Senator Tower was attributed to mechanical failure, which is how the KGB officers killed Congressman Jerry Litton and his entire family fifteen years earlier. The NTSB said that "failure of a severely worn part in the plane's propeller control unit caused the aircraft to spin out of control."[325]

Either someone replaced a perfectly good part in the "propeller control unit" with a "severely worn part" prior to Senator Tower's flight, or, for some reason, a "severely worn part" in the "propeller control unit" did not cause the plane to "spin out of control" until, by sheer coincidence, Senator Tower was aboard the plane.

The KGB officers killed one Member of Congress with an airplane "accident" ten years before they began to robustly pursue the airplane slaughters. Congressman Clem Miller's plane crashed on October 7, 1962, "in bad weather in a mountainous section of northern California . . . . This was the first private plane flight Mr. Miller had made in this campaign."[326]

As noted earlier, the KGB used a "12-gauge shotgun" to snuff out Congressman William O. Mills in an alleged "suicide" in 1973, less than two years after he had been elected in a "special election" to fill a vacancy in Congress. But Congressman Mills was not the

---

[324] New York Times, 4-6-91, p. 26
[325] New York Times, 4-29-92, section D, p. 24
[326] New York Times, 10-9-62, p. 30

first Member of Congress that the KGB eliminated by way of "suicide."

On June 19, 1960, KGB officers inside the CIA killed 39-year-old Congressman Douglas H. Elliott, and his death, too, was alleged to be a suicide. Congressman Elliott had taken office less than two months earlier after winning a "special election" to fill a vacancy in Congress.

His body was found "near a lakefront cabin" that he owned in Pennsylvania. The corpse was located "near the exhaust pipe of a new small car. A deerskin was draped over his head and the end of the pipe . . . . A coroner ruled that he had died of 'carbon-monoxide poisoning, self-administered'. . . . Friends and associates were unable to provide a clue that might explain his suicide."[327]

Douglas H. Elliott served four years in the Pennsylvania state senate before his "special election" and his brief fifty-five days in Congress proved to be fatal.

Before the KGB began killing Members of Congress in 1957, a legitimate traffic accident in 1951 would serve as a model for murder. Senator Virgil Chapman died on March 8, 1951, after his car collided with a tractor-trailer at 3:20 a.m. in Washington, D.C. while the Senator was trying to make a left turn.[328]

Senator Chapman's death at 3:20 a.m. can clearly be attributed to a "need for sleep," and a study in how to kill Members of Congress would account for the need for sleep factor in the traffic "accidents" of 1959 and 1965. It would also account for three Congressmen dying in "accidents" that did not involve a collision with another car, which is how tens of thousands of people die every year. As noted earlier, the three Congressmen died by way of a train engine, an elevated train pillar, and a tractor-trailer.

Besides the thirteen Members of Congress that the KGB killed, the four Members of Congress that renegade CIA officers killed, and the one Member of Congress who died in a genuine traffic accident, there

---

[327] New York Times, 6-20-60, p. 14
[328] Greencastle, Indiana Newspaper "The Daily Banner" and Hopewell, Virginia Newspaper "The Hopewell News," both articles on March 8, 1951, pg. 1.

were only three other Members of Congress who died from unnatural causes from 1951 to 1991. Senators Hunt and East, who were both in failing health and had announced that they would not seek re-election, committed suicide in 1954 and 1986, respectively, and Congressman Leo Ryan was shot and killed at a South American airport in 1978.

Besides using Senator Chapman's 1951 traffic accident as a model for murder, the KGB officers apparently used Senator Hunt's 1954 suicide as a model for murder. After using traffic "accidents" to kill Congressmen in 1957 and 1959, they used a "suicide" to kill a Congressman in 1960 as they carried out their third "political murder" in the United States.

In the traffic "accidents" of 1957, 1959, and 1965 – the traffic "accidents" involving a train engine, an elevated train pillar, and a tractor-trailer – the Congressman was the only one killed, which is another sign of the KGB's carefully orchestrated "accidents."

The KGB also had a precedent for the flying fatalities. The Rockefeller Commission documented that the CIA had sanctioned using an airplane "accident" to kill Cuban leaders in 1960. There had been "an exchange of cables concerning the possibility of an accident for an aircraft carrying Raoul Castro and several other high officials of the Cuban government."[329]

A CIA officer in Cuba notified CIA Headquarters that he had an "agent" who would be piloting the plane with the Cuban officials on board, and CIA Headquarters cabled back that "it was considering the possibility of a fatal accident and asked whether the pilot would be interested."

Someone at CIA Headquarters quickly decided against the plan within an hour of the first cable sanctioning the idea, but KGB officers inside the CIA employed this type of "fatal accident" when killing a Member of Congress two years later. And with Members of Congress having to travel by plane on a regular basis, the KGB

---

[329] Rockefeller Commission Files: National Archives Record Numbers 178-10002-10206, 178-10004-10051, & 178-10004-10050

eventually got around to using airplane "accidents" on a regular basis, as did their CIA successors.

As noted earlier, two out of four consecutive flying fatalities came by way of an aircraft that the Member of Congress was not on board. Congressman McDonald was killed when a Soviet fighter jet destroyed his plane with a missile in 1983, and Senator Heinz was killed when a helicopter destroyed his plane in 1991.

The helicopter pilot who crashed into Senator Heinz' plane is not unlike the train engineer who crashed his "switch engine" into a Congressman's car in 1957 and not unlike the truck driver who ran down a Congressman with his tractor-trailer eight years later in 1965. They are no different from the Soviet fighter pilot who, just before shooting down Congressman McDonald's plane in 1983, was told by the Soviet ground station, "Take aim at the target."[330]

The KGB officers who went to prison in 1984 said that they "can't remember" the names of all thirteen Members of Congress that their colleagues had killed, but they did name Senator Kennedy in 1968, Congressmen Boggs and Begich in 1972, and Congressman McDonald in 1983 as Members of Congress that the KGB killed, and they recounted each year in which the KGB had killed a Member of Congress, including having killed a total of three Congressmen during a fifty-three day period in 1972.

I was able to get the information on the seventeen Members of Congress that the CIA killed to FBI Director Louis Freeh in the mid-1990s, including details of the sixteen "accidents" and "suicides."

The FBI did investigate, and FBI Director Louis Freeh told me in person at FBI Headquarters that all seventeen deaths are now categorized as homicides. He also told me that he could not say anything beyond the fact that the FBI has them categorized as homicides, which obviously means the FBI knows the CIA killed all seventeen Members of Congress.

Senator John Ashcroft introduced himself to me while I was at FBI Headquarters, and he feigned profound concern about the CIA

---

[330] New York Times, 9-2-83, p. 4

killing Members of Congress. Knowing that he would not be there unless the CIA wanted him there, I asked him directly if he was in the CIA, and he confirmed that he was.

I informed him that he was blatantly violating Article I, section 6 of the Constitution, which I quoted for him, and I informed him that I knew he was not there to help. It is a simple fact that the CIA never wants to help. CIA officers will do or say anything to interfere with exposing CIA corruption.

The CIA killed Ashcroft's opponent in the 2000 Senate race in a failed bid to keep Ashcroft from losing his Senate seat. (Details of that "Executive Action" are cited in another chapter.)

Ashcroft went on to have an "official cover" as Attorney General of the United States in violation of the National Security Act of 1947, which prohibits the CIA from having "law enforcement powers."[331]

The Central Intelligence Agency Act of 1949 appears to be at the root of providing the CIA with the ability to kill Members of Congress and perpetrate other nefarious acts inside the United States. Two years after the CIA was created under the National Security Act of 1947, Congress passed the Central Intelligence Agency Act, which made the CIA a much more powerful entity and marked the beginning of the government losing control. It is abundantly clear that Members of Congress had no idea what was in the 1949 legislation when they voted on it.

The *New York Times* reported that on Friday, March 4, 1949, "The House Rules Committee cleared a super-secret measure legalizing the work of the Central Intelligence Agency," adding that the work of the CIA had been previously "accomplished under Executive Order . . . . The super-secret measure gives legal backing to the work of the Central Intelligence Agency . . . . Members of the

---

[331] National Security Act, section 104d
https://www.dni.gov/index.php/ic-legal-reference-book/national-security-act-of-1947
(Also archived from the CIA's own website at the link below)
https://web.archive.org/web/20180606172154/https://www.cia.gov/library/readingroom/docs/1947-07-26.pdf

Armed Services Committee have said that the spy bill is so vital and so confidential that almost nothing can be told of its aims."[332]

On Sunday, March 6, Congressman Clarence Brown of the House Rules Committee said "he was 'confident' that Congress would not put through secret legislation to hurt the nation, but only for its benefit . . . . Without much explanation, the measure gives the CIA authority to hire secretly and spend money freely, and without strings, in carrying on its activities."[333]

The *New York Times* reported that on Monday, March 7, just three short days after the "super-secret measure" made it out of the House Rules Committee, the House approved the legislation 348 to 4 "in an atmosphere of defense secrecy . . . . The vote was taken with the Members generally knowing little about how new authority proposed for the Central Intelligence Agency would be used."[334]

The House Armed Services Committee "bluntly" told the House of Representatives that "this program could not be discussed openly . . . . House rules were suspended to take up the bill under conditions permitting no amendments and requiring a two thirds vote for passage. Members yielded readily. Few questions were asked."

"The House and Senate Armed Services Committee both held secret hearings on the bill and told Members of Congress that full details could not be discussed in debate." Debate in the House was "limited to twenty minutes for and twenty minutes against" the legislation.[335]

The House of Representatives debated the Central Intelligence Agency Act for no more than forty minutes and essentially had no idea what it said. Four years later, the CIA began putting LSD into the food of unsuspecting Americans and soon got around to opening and reading U.S. mail, carrying out massive operations targeting Americans, conducting intelligence operations targeting the White

---

[332] New York Times, 3-5-49, p. 7
[333] New York Times, 3-7-49, p. 2
[334] New York Times, 3-8-49, p. 3
[335] New York Times, 3-5-49, p. 7 and 6-8-49, p. 15

House, killing Members of Congress, and having CIA officers elected to Congress in violation of the Constitution.

The Senate unanimously passed the new legislation that would "maintain the utmost in secrecy for all aspects of the Central Intelligence Agency, including all of its activities, personnel and expenditures . . . . The measure was described by its principal sponsor, Senator Millard Tydings of Maryland, as granting to the agency a degree of secrecy for its operations, even from Congress, that had no parallel in peacetime."[336]

"The bill gives immunity to the CIA from every ordinary form of Congressional supervision and restraint . . . . It authorizes the agency's director to disburse the money 'made available' to him 'without regard to the provisions of law and regulations relating to the expenditures of government funds.'[337]

"The measure lets the Central Intelligence Agency do its hiring and spending in a secrecy not allowed to other government agencies . . . and authorizes the Central Intelligence Agency to assign its agents to schools, industrial organizations, labor unions, and other groups in this country," supposedly "for training."

On June 20, 1949, "President Truman signed a bill setting up statutory operating authority for the super-secret Central Intelligence Agency."[338]

The National Security Act that Truman signed into law in 1947 was apparently not really a law. The alleged "statutory operating authority" that "gives legal backing" to the CIA appears to be an excuse for the new legislation as Congress began to relinquish control while setting the stage for the CIA to take control.

If the new legislation was meant to "legalize" the work of the CIA, then was the CIA operating "illegally" with no "statutory operating authority" prior to 1949, or did the CIA need special laws passed that allowed them to secretly commit egregious

---

[336] New York Times, 5-28-49, p. 5
[337] New York Times, 6-8-49, p. 15
[338] New York Times, 6-21-49, p. 16

crimes inside the United States with impunity, all in the name of national security?

The 1949 news article about Truman signing the bill into law reiterated that it authorizes the CIA to "assign its agents to schools, industrial organizations, labor unions, and other groups in this country," supposedly "for training."

The "Commission on *CIA Activities Within the United States*" revealed that the CIA established an "Office of Training" in 1951 and that it "has long worked closely with the Directorate of Operations to train agents in the special skills necessary for clandestine operations."[339]

But the Commission focused only on *CIA Activities Within the United States*, which means the CIA would conduct "clandestine operations" inside the United States under the guise of "training" CIA officers, and CIA officers could certainly use "schools, industrial organizations, labor unions, and other groups in this country" for cover when they target U.S. citizens with "clandestine operations."

As noted earlier, no one would think of normal, everyday, working Americans as spies gathering intelligence and conducting secretive operations targeting other Americans. Using the guise of "training" is just another excuse for allowing the CIA to run rampant inside the United States. In 1984, a CIA officer stated that she remembered me from a few years earlier when she had been undergoing her "training."

The Senate Church Committee stated that the purpose of the Central Intelligence Agency Act was to "improve" the way the CIA was administered by "strengthening the powers of the Director."[340]

But back on February 7, 1947, four months before the CIA was created under the National Security Act, President Truman's Secretary of State, George Marshall, a five-star General and Army Chief of Staff in World War II, warned President Truman that "the powers of the proposed agency seem almost unlimited and need

---

[339] Rockefeller Report, p. 92
[340] Church Committee: Book VI, p. 253

clarification." General Marshall was reported to have "severe doubts about plans to create the Central Intelligence Agency."[341]

Dean Acheson, Truman's Under Secretary of State in 1947, who succeeded Marshall as Secretary of State in 1949, acknowledged that he "advised President Truman when the CIA was created that neither the President, the National Security Council, 'nor anyone else would be in a position to know what it was doing or to control it.'"[342]

A *New York Times* article about the CIA in April 1966 stated, "In 1949, the agency's cloak of secrecy was firmly buttoned up against inquiry by the standing committees of Congress." It also stated that in the Central Intelligence Agency Act of 1949, Congress directed that "the CIA Director should be responsible for guarding secrets," which apparently means the CIA will do whatever it sees fit while guarding the secrets of profound criminal activity and corruption that took root early on and continued to grow.[343]

Even the Congressional Intelligence Oversight Committees, which Congress finally established in the mid-1970s, were kept in the dark. The CIA, in fact, made it clear that the CIA itself would make the rules on Intelligence Oversight.

The CIA General Counsel, who is expected to "find legal techniques" that would "facilitate" CIA activities, sent a letter to the recently established House Intelligence Oversight Committee on December 16, 1977. The General Counsel made reference to the National Security Act of 1947 and the Central Intelligence Agency Act of 1949, stating, "Both statutes, in my view, evidence a recognition that there are circumstances under which the withholding of certain information relating to intelligence activities is justified, if indeed it is not affirmatively required."[344]

---

[341] New York Times, 7-29-73, p. 21
[342] New York Times, 12-26-70, p. 17
[343] New York Times, 4-25-66, p. 20
[344] Rockefeller Report, p. 87 and NARA Record Number: 104-10427-10040
https://www.cia.gov/readingroom/docs/CIA-RDP81M00980R001600030007-5.pdf

The CIA General Counsel essentially told the House Intelligence Committee, "Sorry, but we are required by law to decide when our 'intelligence activities' are actually none of your business, thus rendering your Intelligence Oversight absolutely meaningless. You and everyone else in Congress will continue to pay us with the tax dollars of your constituents, and you will continue to use American tax dollars to finance everything we do."

The aforementioned *New York Times* article in April 1966 about the CIA's "cloak of secrecy" also stated that the legislation of 1947 and 1949 is "not the only basis for the agency's operations. Under that legislation, the National Security Council is permitted to issue directives to the CIA Director, and it is under such secret directives, often proposed by the Director himself, that the agency engages in many of its activities."

The National Security Council obviously used "such secret directives" when it established the CIA's "national policies in 1952 through 1954." Those policies were established during the Truman and Eisenhower Administrations, the two Administrations that carried the CIA through its first thirteen years of existence.

The Senate Church Committee stated that "spying on Americans" is "an illegal act under the terms of the law that created the CIA,"[345] which would be the National Security Act of 1947, but the Senators on the Church Committee knew that the Central Intelligence Agency Act of 1949 with the CIA's new "statutory operating authority" changed things dramatically.

Far beyond "spying on Americans," the CIA conducts massive domestic operations, kills Members of Congress, and commits all manner of egregious crimes inside the United States with impunity.

The Church Committee's statement about "spying on Americans" being "illegal" under the 1947 legislation is a transparent attempt to gloss over its knowledge that the CIA seemingly has no restrictions on running rampant domestically, courtesy of the new 1949 "terms of

---

[345] Church Committee: Book I, p. 550

law" and the "national policies established by the National Security Council in 1952 through 1954."[346]

The Senate Church Committee confirmed that CIA officials and CIA officers do not care if anyone has "authorized" their actions. The Church Committee Report states, "Formal procedures may be disregarded by either high Administration officials or officers in the CIA . . . . Authorization procedures have not always been clear and tidy, nor have they always been followed. Prior to 1955, there were few formal procedures."[347]

KGB officers inside the CIA began killing Members of Congress two years after "formal" authorization procedures went into effect in 1955. The KGB officers simply engaged in activities on their own and "disregarded" any and all "authorization procedures," which is exactly what renegade CIA officers do when they kill Members of Congress and commit other crimes.

The Church Committee Report explains that in an "expansion" of the "doctrine of plausible denial," CIA officers arbitrarily decide to keep "their superiors" in the dark about corrupt activities,[348] which means disregarding formal procedures and authorization procedures is a standard practice that allows higher ranking CIA officials to shirk responsibility and deny knowledge of anything. But the Rockefeller Commission stated that "virtually all" of the corrupt activities in its report "were known to top management."[349]

"Plausible denials" are nothing but "cover stories" designed to say, "This is plausible because no one can prove we are lying. Everyone will have to trust us and believe what we say because they cannot prove otherwise."

As noted in Chapter 1, former CIA Director Allen Dulles wrote a book in 1963 in which he stated, "Espionage is not tainted with

---

[346] New York Times, 2-24-67, p. 1
[347] Church Committee: Interim Report, p. 10
[348] Church Committee: Interim Report, p. 11
[349] Rockefeller Report, p. 85

any legality," which would mean ranking CIA officials and CIA field officers can rationalize breaking any law they choose as they carry out corrupt and criminal activities inside the United States.

President Eisenhower, who appointed Allen Dulles to be Director of the CIA, did not publicly express his views on "espionage," but he did express his views on "legality" in 1964 when he stated that "any law passed by Congress should be assumed to be constitutional until the Supreme Court rules otherwise." Prior to that, Eisenhower responded to a reporter's question about the constitutionality of the 1964 civil rights law by saying, "I wouldn't know about that."[350]

By elaborating and putting forth the assumed constitutionality of all laws, Eisenhower effectively said that no law is tainted with "legality" unless the Supreme Court decides it is, and since the American public did not know the laws governing the CIA (even the Members of Congress who passed them in 1949 did not know what they were), no one could challenge the constitutionality of those laws.

Recall that President Ford's *Commission on CIA Activities Within the United States* addressed legal challenges to the CIA's domestic activity, stating, "Practically all of the CIA's operations are covered by secrecy . . . . Few potential challengers are even aware of activities that might otherwise be contested; nor can such activities be easily discovered."[351]

---

[350] WP, 7-11-64, p. 6
[351] Rockefeller Report, p. 78

Chapter 6: The Big Picture

In November 1964, one year after KGB officers inside the CIA assassinated President Kennedy, Dr. Stefan T. Possony, Director of International Political Studies at the Hoover Institution on War, Revolution and Peace, who had served in U.S. intelligence agencies for eighteen years, prepared a report for a Congressional subcommittee in which he put forth that "Russian spy schools know all about the CIA's use of lie detectors in personnel screening and could be presumed to have no trouble at all training infiltrators to outwit the machine."[352]

Dr. Possony stated, "There is some ground to believe that Communist agents still are operating in American intelligence organizations and perhaps there are more of them than ever."

Less than eight months after Dr. Possony's declaration about Communists "operating in American intelligence organizations," KGB officers inside the CIA killed their fifth Member of Congress by running him down with a tractor-trailer.

Back on September 29, 1952, the Director of the CIA, General Walter Bedell Smith, testified at Senate hearings and stated, "I believe there are Communists in my own organization."[353]

When General Smith was asked if he knew who they were, he testified, "I do not. I wish I did. I do everything I can to detect

---

[352] New York Times, 11-24-64, P. 14
[353] New York Times, 9-30-52, pp. 1 & 4

them. I believe they are so adroit and adept that they have infiltrated practically every security agency of the government."

President Ford's Commission on CIA Activities Within the United States documented that in 1966 and 1967, CIA Counterintelligence Chief James Angleton and the President's Foreign Intelligence Advisory Board were focused on "the general problem of KGB agents in the U.S. and the specific problem of penetration of our intelligence services."[354]

In early 1984, I exposed 497 KGB officers that were operating inside the CIA, but the exposure of the KGB officers was never made public. I also exposed more than 800 double agents (i.e., American CIA officers who knowingly and willingly worked for the KGB).

I had been trying to expose the KGB infiltration and the double agents for seven years, and while I was at the CIA's Chicago field office in 1984, at my behest a CIA officer contacted two former CIA deputy directors, Admiral Bobby Ray Inman and Frank Carlucci, both of whom I had previously met while trying to expose the KGB infiltration. We also contacted former CIA Director William Colby.

After I identified several KGB officers who had infiltrated the CIA, someone mentioned the name J. Walton Moore, and I identified Moore as a KGB officer. I suggested contacting him and telling him that we had discovered there were KGB officers inside the CIA and that we "need his help" in exposing them. Admiral Inman did as I suggested, and Moore, who was unaware that he had been identified as a KGB officer, sent back a list of every KGB officer inside the CIA, claiming it was a list of people who would be "helpful" in exposing any KGB infiltration. That, in a nutshell, is how the KGB officers were ultimately exposed. What led up to me being at the CIA's Chicago field office on that day is explained later in this book.

I detected the KGB infiltration when I had contact with the CIA as a private citizen in the Spring of 1977 during the Carter Administration, but as noted in Chapter 4, President Carter was in

---

[354] National Archives Record Number 178-10002-10078: Rockefeller Commission Files; Interview With Wheaton B. Byers, PFIAB, 3/12/75

the CIA and being handled by the KGB, which meant the KGB had nothing to fear during the Carter Administration. Some of the CIA field officers with whom I interacted filed intelligence reports about the KGB infiltration, but it yielded no results because the KGB officers had seniority over the CIA field officers who filed the reports, and the KGB exercised control in the highest offices of government.

After Ronald Reagan became President in 1981, Vice President George Bush and the egregiously corrupted CIA hierarchy acted as vanguards for the KGB infiltration. CIA Director William Casey even tried to interfere when we were in the process of exposing the KGB infiltration in 1984, but we circumvented his interference and succeeded without his help.

Prior to 1980, there were 500 KGB officers inside the CIA, but two were killed in 1980 and another was killed in 1982.

As noted in Chapter 2, Congress held secret closed-door hearings following the exposure of the KGB infiltration, and every member of the 98th Congress was present at the hearings. I testified at those hearings, and every Member of Congress was made acutely aware that I had exposed KGB infiltration of the CIA.

I also spent time at the White House and met with President Reagan a number of times. On various occasions I met with Secretary of Defense Caspar Weinberger at the Pentagon, and I met more than once with Secretary of State George Schultz, National Security Advisor Robert McFarlane, CIA Director William Casey, and other people on Reagan's national security team.

The CIA hierarchy had become very corrupted by 1984, and the CIA was rife with corruption. The corruption had taken root in the early 1950s and continued to grow through seven Presidential Administrations, from Eisenhower to Reagan, mainly because of KGB machinations and opportunistic CIA officers who thrived on the corruption.

After the KGB was exposed, renegade CIA officers built up the corruption and strengthened their foothold inside the CIA during the five remaining years of the Reagan Administration, during which time they became more corrupt and more entrenched, a process that has continued unabated during six Presidential administrations from George H. W. Bush to Joe Biden.

KGB officers had been handling CIA officers targeted for political office for more than thirty years. Over the years, some of the most powerful Members of Congress were KGB-controlled CIA officers. They ranged across the political spectrum from the far left to the far right as the KGB played both ends against the middle.

The bipartisan corruption in Congress took root in the early 1950s and continued to grow, seemingly proportionate to the corruption in the CIA. When the KGB was exposed in 1984, bipartisan corruption was well entrenched in the Executive Branch and the Legislative Branch, leaving renegade CIA officers free to do as they please.

As noted earlier in this book, CIA officers in Congress are violating Article I, section 6 of the Constitution, which states: "No Person holding any Office under the United States shall be a Member of either House during his Continuance in Office."

The men and women of the CIA are not CIA agents. They are "CIA officers," and officers of the United States Central Intelligence Agency clearly "hold office under the United States," which means in no uncertain terms that they are Constitutionally prohibited from being Members of Congress while they are in the CIA.

Chuck Schumer is one of the CIA officers who was being handled by the KGB. A partial list of renegade CIA officers who were elected to the Senate includes former Senators Barry Goldwater, Daniel Patrick Moynihan, Walter Mondale, Edward Kennedy, Barbara Mikulski, Claiborne Pell, Chris Dodd, and Thomas Eagleton.

CIA officers who became Members of the House of Representatives are Leon Panetta, George H. W. Bush, Dick Cheney, Geraldine Ferraro, Edwin Forsythe, and Lawrence McDonald.

Thirteen of these CIA officers were Members of Congress in 1984 while George Bush, who had previously served two terms in Congress in violation of the Constitution, held the Office of Vice President.

There were other CIA officers in Congress from both parties whose names I do not recall, and there have been more CIA officers elected to Congress since 1984. To repeat, this is only a partial list.

Members of Congress most certainly do not know that their Congressional colleagues are filling out intelligence reports on them. Federal employees and government officials likewise do not know that CIA officers with "official covers" are gathering intelligence on them.

The KGB was especially focused on controlling the Congressional Intelligence Oversight Committees, which were established by Congress in the mid-1970s. By 1984, CIA officers under KGB control held the two ranking positions on the Senate Intelligence Oversight Committee. Republican Senator Barry Goldwater was the Committee Chairman and Democratic Senator Daniel Patrick Moynihan was Vice Chairman. There were several CIA officers on both the House and Senate Intelligence Oversight Committees and on other key committees in Congress.

Former Senator John Ashcroft and former Senator John Kerry are renegade CIA officers who were elected to the Senate after the KGB was exposed.

Republican John Ashcroft went on to have an "official cover" as Attorney General under President George W. Bush, and Democrat John Kerry went on to have "official covers" as President Obama's Secretary of State and President Biden's Climate Czar. Both Kerry and Ashcroft were KGB assets prior to the KGB being exposed.

The Congressional hierarchy tried to justify the Constitutional violation in 1984 by maintaining that CIA officers in Congress would simply treat their Congressional positions separately from their CIA positions. Adding to the ill-conceived logic is the fact that all CIA officers are identified on CIA records by pseudonyms, the names assigned to them when they join the CIA.

CIA officers in Congress use their CIA pseudonyms when they fill out intelligence reports on other Members of Congress.

CIA officer Chuck Schumer, elected to the position of Senate Democratic Leader in November 2016, took it upon himself to warn President-elect Trump about taking on the "intelligence community." In discussing Trump during an interview in January 2017, Schumer blatantly stated, "You take on the intelligence community, they have six ways from Sunday at getting back at you."[355]

Schumer ominously warned that the intelligence community is "very upset with how he has treated them and talked about them."

The CIA's vast domestic operations and the KGB's systematic corruption of both the CIA and the government paved the way for the massive corruption that the CIA perpetuated after the KGB was exposed.

In 1984, Congressman Leon Panetta was eavesdropping and gathering intelligence when I was speaking with some other Members of Congress about my efforts to expose the corruption. When I detected that Congressman Panetta was eavesdropping, he admitted to being in the CIA.

Panetta later came to see me in Chicago and tried to get me to throw in with him and become party to the corruption instead of fighting against it. Panetta, who held a high-ranking position in the CIA, made it clear that he had taken it upon himself to use both his CIA position and his position in Congress to act as a vanguard for sustaining the corruption.

Not only did I refuse to throw in with him, but I also pointed out that he was wretchedly corrupt and that he was violating Article I, section 6, of the U.S. Constitution by being a CIA officer in Congress. Panetta insisted that he was not corrupt and that the CIA had not been corrupted. He eventually admitted that, as an officer of the

---

[355] https://nypost.com/2017/01/11/schumer-predicted-intelligence-officials-would-get-back-at-trump/

United States Central Intelligence Agency, he held Office under the United States and was violating the United States Constitution.

Less than nine years later, Panetta continued climbing the covert ladder of success into positions where he could more effectively facilitate the CIA's quest to control the government. As soon as Bill Clinton assumed the Presidency in January 1991, Panetta resigned from Congress to adopt an "official cover" as President Clinton's Director of the Office of Management and Budget (OMB), where CIA officer Leon Panetta would be, according to the White House website, "essential to the President's ability to plan and implement his priorities."[356]

Panetta went on to adopt an "official cover" as President Clinton's Chief of Staff in July 1994, and he held that position until November 1996. As noted in Chapter 1, CIA officers infiltrate "the immediate office of the White House" and "components associated intimately with the immediate office of the President."[357]

Renegade CIA officer Leon Panetta also held the positions of CIA Director and Secretary of Defense under President Obama.

Recall that a CIA memorandum from March 1978 stated that CIA officers have "easy access to those in power in and out of Government," and the CIA officer who wrote it stated that the CIA has an "influential position" in "our country." The memorandum boldly proclaimed that the CIA is "politically influential" in the United States because it is "the U.S. Government's covert arm."[358]

Like CIA officer George H. W. Bush, CIA officer Leon Panetta climbed the covert ladder of success with "easy access to those in power" while endearing himself to the right people for decades.

Until the KGB officers went to prison in early 1984, CIA officers under KGB control had been targeted for the Oval Office in every Presidential race from 1964 to 1984.

---

[356] https://www.whitehouse.gov/omb
[357] CIA "Family Jewels," June 25, 2007 Release, p. 105
[358] National Archives Record Number 104-10404-10361

The one and only CIA officer that the KGB officers managed to get into the nation's highest office was Democrat Jimmy Carter, who was elected President of the United States in 1976. Carter's Vice President, former Senator Walter Mondale, was also a CIA officer. Carter and Mondale had no inkling that their CIA colleagues were Soviet KGB officers who had assumed the identities of deceased Americans. It was during the Carter Administration that a CIA memo referred to the CIA's "aura of political clout" and to the CIA being "politically influential" in the United States.

Details contained herein on the KGB's intentions and what they did to corrupt the United States government came directly from the KGB officers in 1984. Some of what I know about their intentions and actions was obtained from 1977 through 1984 while I was trying to expose the KGB, and it was all reaffirmed in 1984, which is when I found out much more about their intentions and actions during the several decades that they functioned inside the CIA.

Besides their effort to kill President Reagan, the KGB had plans to assassinate four other U.S. Presidents with the intention of getting a CIA officer into the Oval Office, but only one of their assassination plans came to fruition.

By their own admission, KGB officers inside the CIA assassinated President John F. Kennedy on November 22, 1963. The assassination was carried out by two KGB officers inside the CIA and a CIA "double agent," who knowingly and willingly worked for the KGB.

As noted in Chapter 2, killing President Kennedy was the first step in the KGB's plan to have one of their assets, Senator and CIA officer Barry Goldwater, elected to the Presidency. The second step was killing President Kennedy's successor, President Lyndon Johnson, on Saturday, October 31, 1964, three days before the Presidential election.

But Suffolk County Police unwittingly foiled the CIA's first attempt to control the Presidency when they discovered Robert Babcock, the man who had been set up to be President Johnson's accused assassin, parked along the motorcade route with a telescopic rifle on the seat beside him and a loaded shotgun in the trunk.

The main reason for wanting CIA officer Barry Goldwater in the Office of President was that he would be the KGB's foremost asset in exacerbating the very tense racial situation of the 1960s. Toward that end they had Goldwater, who had voted for civil rights legislation in 1957 and 1960, aligning himself with Southern Democrats in support of segregation in 1963, details of which are contained herein.

Goldwater's newfound support for segregation was well established by the Spring of 1964. The *New York Times*, reporting on an 18,000-strong Goldwater rally at Madison Square Garden in May 1964, stated, "The Negro choir that had been hired to sing The Battle Hymn of the Republic had to overcome a rebellion in its ranks," with one singer stating, "I can't help feeling strange here tonight because I know how Senator Goldwater stands on civil rights."[359]

Another singer, who "had to sing baritone" because of "desertions," complained, "It's like singing for the Ku Klux Klan."

The KGB envisioned that the assassinations of Presidents Kennedy and Johnson in less than a year, followed by Goldwater's election to the Presidency, would seem like nothing less than a conspiracy to seize power and support segregation at the crucial juncture of 1964. They also envisioned using the long tentacles of the CIA to stir up violent political and racial turmoil in the wake of "segregationist" Barry Goldwater seizing power.

The fact that the United States had been embroiled in a civil war over the rights of African-Americans 100 years earlier was undoubtedly not lost on the KGB officers. KGB officers inside the CIA were very focused on promoting racial violence and rioting during the 1960s, hence, the assassination of President Kennedy in 1963 and the intended assassination of President Johnson in

---

[359] NYT Article, May 13, 1964 titled, "Goldwater Fills Rally At Garden" http://www.nytimes.com/1964/05/13/goldwater-fills-rally-at-garden.html?_r=0

1964, which was to be followed three days later by the election of KGB asset and CIA officer Barry Goldwater to the Presidency.

As will be seen later in this book, President Ford's "Commission on *CIA Activities Within the United States*" admitted that the CIA was behind massive rioting across the United States from 1963 to 1968.

Not only did they kill President Kennedy and intend to kill Presidents Johnson and Reagan in the ongoing effort to put a CIA officer into the Oval Office, but the KGB officers also had plans to assassinate President Nixon in 1972 and President Ford in 1975, each time with the goal of putting a KGB-controlled CIA officer into the Oval Office.

They intended to kill Nixon in April 1972 so that Vice President Spiro Agnew, who was under investigation, would become President. They had no doubts that Agnew would lose the 1972 Presidential election to the Democratic nominee, who was supposed to choose Senator and CIA officer Thomas Eagleton as his running mate. They would then kill the newly elected Democratic President to catapult Vice President Eagleton into the Presidency.

When the plan to kill Nixon failed, which is addressed later in this book, they, by their own admission, orchestrated the Watergate break-in to discredit Nixon but still failed to prevent his re-election. They also failed to get Senator Eagleton onto the Democratic ticket with Presidential nominee George McGovern, who first chose Eagleton to be his running mate but was forced to choose a different running mate a few weeks later.

The KGB officers were grooming CIA officer Jimmy Carter, the former Governor of Georgia, to run for President when they tried to assassinate President Gerald Ford in September 1975. The KGB had no belief in the democratic process, and the hope was that Carter's election would be facilitated by assassinating Ford fourteen months before the election, which would have catapulted the relatively unpopular Vice President Nelson Rockefeller into the Presidency.

But the democratic process worked in 1976 to get a CIA officer elected to the Presidency, as Carter narrowly defeated President Ford in 1976, whereas the KGB efforts to take over the Presidency by way of assassination consistently failed.

A 1961 CIA study on "Soviet Strategic Executive Action" states that the KGB endeavored to "remove the threat to Soviet interests posed by certain members of Western governments, sometimes arranging for the dismissal of such persons from public office, at other times even having them 'eliminated' physically."[360]

KGB officers inside the CIA were not about to pass up the opportunity to "physically eliminate" Members of Congress and American Presidents during the Cold War, especially when their objective was to control Congress and the Presidency.

Renegade CIA officers, likewise, will try to remove or eliminate anyone who threatens their "interests," as they, too, are intent on controlling Congress and the Presidency.

Besides killing Members of Congress, renegade CIA officers will use CIA officers with "official covers" when going after a Presidential candidate or a sitting President, just as their KGB progenitors did when they orchestrated the Watergate scandal.

Leon Jaworski, the "Special Watergate Prosecutor" who forced President Nixon to resign for his role in the Watergate cover up, testified in 1984 that he was in the CIA and that the "Watergate scandal" was a CIA-orchestrated effort to derail Nixon's re-election bid in 1972. Jaworski had an "official cover" as "Special Watergate Prosecutor," an "official" position to "cover" the fact that he was carrying out the CIA's agenda.

Robert Mueller, who investigated the alleged "collusion" between Donald Trump's 2016 Presidential campaign and Russia, is likewise a CIA officer who had an "official cover" as Special Counsel. Mueller previously had an "official cover" as FBI Director from 2001 to 2013.

---

[360] National Archives Record Number 104-10412-10153

The CIA sent FBI Director Robert Mueller to see me after first sending James Comey while I was assisting the FBI with some federal investigations in 2013.

Comey admitted that he came to see me on behalf of the CIA, and Mueller admitted that he is in the CIA.

In 2017, CIA officer Robert Mueller was appointed Special Counsel to investigate the alleged "collusion" between Donald Trump's 2016 Presidential campaign and Russia, a claim that originated with the CIA while CIA "asset" James Comey was Director of the FBI.

Mueller was unable to find any evidence that the Trump campaign "conspired or coordinated" with Russia, but the CIA's intention all along was to discredit Trump, and Mueller made a slew of allegations against people associated with Trump that had nothing to do with the fabricated claim that Trump "colluded" with Russia.

The "Russia collusion" claim is addressed in detail later in this book along with documented evidence that the CIA was behind it all.

Comey's successor, Christopher Wray, is a CIA officer with an "official cover" as FBI Director. I met Wray in earlier years while trying to expose the corruption in the CIA. He admitted to being in the CIA and to being an intricate part of CIA plans to control the government. The CIA seems to get a kick out of flaunting its "there's nothing you can do about it" attitude.

The CIA's "Republican faction" obviously got Trump to appoint Wray to the position of FBI Director. The CIA's "Republican faction" and the CIA's "Democratic faction" work together to establish CIA control of the government.

Intrinsic to the KGB's assassination of President Kennedy and their plans to kill Presidents Johnson, Nixon, Ford, and Reagan is the fact that the Secret Service is the CIA. As cited in Chapter 1, the CIA has records stating that it has provided "manpower support" to the Secret Service "since 1955," and when the "legal status" of such CIA officers came into question, the Deputy Director of the CIA wrote a memorandum stating, "Such officers detailed by the CIA will be designated officers of the Secret Service."[361]

Once the CIA began taking over Secret Service duties in the 1950s, it was just a matter of time before the entire "Secret Service" would be comprised of CIA officers "detailed by the CIA" to the Secret Service.

CIA officers functioning as Secret Service agents have "police" and "law enforcement powers." They are clearly exercising "internal security functions" and "internal security powers" and performing "internal security duties." But the legislation that created the CIA, the National Security Act of 1947, emphatically states that the CIA cannot legally have "police" or "law enforcement powers," and the CIA is prohibited from having "internal security functions," and "internal security powers," and "internal security duties."[362]

As far as the CIA is concerned, an "agreement" written into a CIA memorandum in 1965 overruled the Act of Congress that created the CIA. As noted in Chapter 1, the Deputy Director of the CIA cannot make laws, and in reality, the "legal status" of "such officers detailed by the CIA" is that the CIA officers are illegally functioning as Secret Service agents. They are literally breaking the law, just like CIA officers with "official covers" as Attorney General and FBI Director.

I first found out that "the Secret Service is the CIA" in 1980 when a CIA officer and I were heading into the CIA field office in the Dirksen Federal Building in Chicago. Instead of driving into the underground parking garage and taking a key-activated elevator up to the CIA offices, which we had done on several occasions, he violated procedure and we went in the front door of the building. We then took a public elevator up to the floor where the Secret Service offices are located. After we walked into a small

---

[361] National Archives Record Number 104-10419-10046
[362] National Security Act, section 104d and section 308a
https://www.dni.gov/index.php/ic-legal-reference-book/national-security-act-of-1947

room with a display case in it, he flashed his badge and a woman behind a window buzzed us in.

We took a few steps through a small office with a desk in it, and as he opened another door, I said, "That's a good idea, having the CIA offices behind the Secret Service offices."

He turned to me, and regardless of the fact that he was disclosing extremely sensitive information, he said, "The Secret Service is the CIA."

After we walked through the second door that he opened, I found myself inside the CIA's Chicago field office, the same CIA field office to which I had been on previous occasions.

The 98th Congress was made aware that the Secret Service is the CIA during the 1984 closed-door Congressional hearings. Soon afterward, CIA officers testified at the hearings and tried to dissuade Congress from believing that the Secret Service is the CIA, but they only ended up confirming it.

One particular CIA officer was at first adamant in his testimony that he was a member of the Secret Service and not a CIA employee, but upon further questioning he admitted to joining the CIA before becoming a member of the Secret Service, although he still maintained he was not in the CIA.

Eventually, he admitted there was no "transfer" when he went from identifying himself as a CIA officer to identifying himself as a Secret Service agent, and he admitted that he would still have to take orders from ranking CIA officials, such as the CIA's head of domestic operations or the Deputy Director of the CIA.

After a prolonged show of resistance in which he tried to justify taking orders from ranking CIA officials while being a member of the Secret Service, he finally admitted, under oath, that he is in the CIA and that the Secret Service is the CIA.

The Deputy Director of the CIA made it clear in his 1965 memorandum that the so-called "designated officers of the Secret

Service" are, in fact, CIA officers who have been "detailed by the CIA" to function as Secret Service agents.[363]

After the KGB was exposed in 1984, Congressman and renegade CIA officer Leon Panetta, along with other renegade CIA officers in Congress and in the CIA hierarchy, knew that it was in their best interest to keep their former CIA Director, Vice President George H. W. Bush, in power. They also knew that President Reagan had no intention of exposing massive bipartisan corruption or upsetting his re-election chances in any way, which meant they could count on him to keep Bush as his Vice President. But George H. W. Bush had been a KGB asset for more than twenty years and had come up through the political ranks because of KGB efforts.

In 1984, Leon Panetta and his CIA colleagues wanted assets of their own that they could put into the Presidency, and Panetta enlisted George W. Bush, the son of Vice President George H. W. Bush, as one of his assets targeted for the Presidency.

Panetta had Bush Jr. commit a felony as part of a secret agreement in which he would use his CIA position to facilitate Bush's political career, details of which are in the next chapter.

James Madison, the "Father of the Constitution" and fourth President of the United States, stated, "The essence of Government is power; and power, lodged as it must be in human hands, will ever be liable to abuse."

---

[363] National Archives Record Number 104-10419-10046

Chapter 7: Learning from the KGB, Killing More Members of Congress, & Taking Control of the United States Government

As noted earlier, every Member of the 98th Congress was present at the 1984 closed-door Congressional hearings that took place after the KGB infiltration was exposed. By that time, after more than thirty years of the KGB's insidious machinations, deep-rooted corruption existed in the CIA hierarchy and at many levels of the CIA.

The KGB's efforts to subvert the U.S. Constitution and take control of the government also caused bipartisan corruption to reach into the upper echelons of the 98th Congress and the Reagan Administration.

I intended to publicly expose what I know about the KGB infiltration and the vast corruption, but a corrupt CIA hierarchy easily used the CIA's massive domestic operations as a Praetorian Guard to prevent me from exposing what I know. Besides a corrupt CIA hierarchy, having a CIA officer as Vice President and having CIA officers in Congress were key to sustaining the corruption. As noted in Chapter 6, Congressman Leon Panetta used his high-ranking position in the CIA and his position in Congress to take the lead in being a vanguard for sustaining the corruption.

The KGB and renegade CIA officers initiated operations targeting me during the years that I was trying to expose the KGB infiltration, and every Member of the 98th Congress, some of whom are still in Congress, can attest to the CIA operations targeting me in 1984.

By the same token, every Member of the 98th Congress was acutely aware that renegade CIA officers were entrenched in the CIA hierarchy and that the CIA had become very corrupted, but Democrats and Republicans knew the ramifications of exposing Members of Congress as CIA officers, especially if those CIA officers were members of their own party.

As Senator and renegade CIA officer Chuck Schumer said, "You take on the intelligence community, they have six ways from Sunday at getting back at you,"[364] not to mention the threatening CIA document stating that the CIA will "generate, alter, or halt human behavior by implying, citing, or using physical or psychological means to ensure compliance."[365]

Congressman Lawrence McDonald, one of the CIA officers in Congress, was a Member of the 98th Congress when he became the thirteenth and final Member of Congress that the KGB killed. He and other CIA officers were put aboard Korean Air Lines Flight "Double-O-Seven," and it was then sent into Soviet airspace, where it was shot down on September 1, 1983.

In 1984, I learned the officially classified reason for Congressman McDonald's plane flying near a Soviet island was to light up Russia's radar defense system. The island had "air bases, radar stations, and other tracking installations,"[366] and the United States was supposed to use electronic intelligence gathering systems to gather data on Russia's radar defense system.

The official cover story for Korean Air Lines Flight 007 was that the pilot "accidentally" flipped the wrong switch, which took the plane off course and eventually through Soviet airspace. This is nothing short of an admission that "accidents" are used as "cover stories" when killing Members of Congress.

The KGB infiltration was exposed just a few months after the Soviet Union shot down Flight "Double-O-Seven," and separate

---

[364] TheHill.com, 1-3-17 http://thehill.com/homenews/administration/312605-schumer-trump-being-really-dumb-by-going-after-intelligence-community
[365] National Archives Record Number 104-10408-10241
[366] New York Times, 9-2-83, p. 4

CIA factions picked up where the KGB officers left off in vying for control of the United States government.

Congressman Leon Panetta led a faction of renegade CIA officers that chose George W. Bush as one of the assets they would put into the Oval Office.

I knew the Bush family as a result of my exposing the KGB infiltration, and I met twice with George W. Bush, his brothers, and his sister in 1984. They told me that he had supplied cocaine to his father, Vice President Bush, on behalf of renegade CIA officers as part of a secret agreement in which the CIA would facilitate his political career.

At our first meeting, George W. Bush angrily shouted, "I want to be Governor of Texas!"

It was during our second meeting that I was informed he had supplied cocaine to his father, Vice President George H. W. Bush. Bush Jr. did not deny entering into the secret agreement with renegade CIA officers, nor did he deny that he supplied cocaine to his father, but he was clearly upset that I was being told about it.

Cocaine use was rampant in the CIA, and Vice President George Bush was addicted to cocaine. I personally saw Vice President Bush using cocaine when I was in Washington in 1984. I also saw President Carter using cocaine at the CIA's Chicago field office in 1980.

The KGB used cocaine to control many of the CIA officers they were handling, especially those who were elected to office, and CIA officers in Congress introduced cocaine to other Members of Congress. There were a number of Congressmen and Senators from both parties who were addicted to cocaine in 1984, especially on the Intelligence Oversight Committees, and everyone in Congress knew about it.

Congressman and CIA officer Leon Panetta was a key player in supplying cocaine to Members of Congress and to CIA personnel, both before and after the KGB was exposed.

In early July 1989, I sent letters to every Democratic member of the House of Representatives to begin impeachment proceedings against President George H. W. Bush, stating that I had seen him in possession of cocaine in 1984 when he was Vice President.

Most Members of the 101st Congress, which began its first session in January 1989, were also Members of the 98th Congress back in 1984. Every Member of the 98th Congress knew of the prevalent cocaine use in the CIA and that elected officials from both parties were using cocaine.

Members who had been in the 98th Congress knew that I had exposed KGB infiltration of the CIA in 1984, and they knew about my futile efforts to do something about the massive corruption, which included the widespread use of cocaine. Since most Members of 98th Congress were also in the 101st Congress, and most of them could vouch for my credibility, I had no doubts that replies to my letters would be sent.

I called several Congressional offices and verified that replies had been sent, but I never received those replies and Congress went into recess in August. The only logical conclusion is that renegade CIA officers intercepted the replies.

President George H. W. Bush, for some reason, felt the need to address the nation from the Oval Office concerning his Administration's anti-drug program on September 5, 1989, two months after I sent my impeachment letters and less than eight months after Bush became President.

Someone came up with "the idea of the President holding up crack" while addressing the nation, which resulted in Bush having a bag of crack cocaine sitting next to him on his desk during his address. The stated purpose was to dramatize the ready availability of drugs. Bush said that Federal agents had recently purchased the cocaine at a park across the street from the White House.

According to the *Washington Post*, Bush had been "preparing for the speech" while on vacation in August, the month after I sent my impeachment letters, and "the idea of the President holding up crack was included in some drafts and Bush quickly approved."[367]

"'He liked the prop,' said one White House aide."

Any Member of Congress looking to explain away Bush being in possession of cocaine in 1984 would then have one; President Bush had cocaine in his possession during his Vice Presidency because it had something to do with U.S. "anti-drug" efforts.

I doubt things would have turned out different if my letter stated that I had seen Bush "using" cocaine in 1984. Bush's cocaine use was just part of the much broader bipartisan corruption that was entrenched in the government, which included Members of Congress from both parties using cocaine. Trying to have Bush impeached was just a shot in the dark at exposing the corruption. I am not surprised that it failed.

Renegade CIA officers also responded to my impeachment effort by killing two Members of Congress. They killed Democratic Congressman Mickey Leland in Ethiopia on August 7, and they killed Republican Congressman Larkin Smith on August 13.

Congressman Leland had the pilots who caused the fatal crash by "pushing too far and flying into an area of bad weather at a very low altitude,"[368] after which the plane crashed into a mountain, and Congressman Smith had the pilot who "appeared nervous and even ran the aircraft off the taxiway shortly before takeoff." The plane then veered from "its planned flight path" and "flew about nine miles to the east" before crashing into a "70-foot pine tree in the Desoto National Forest."[369]

Congressman Smith, a freshman Republican in Congress when they killed him, had spent his entire life in law enforcement dating back to 1966, including six years as Chief of Police in Gulfport, Mississippi, and then five years as Harrison County Sheriff just prior

---

[367] Washington Post, 9-22-89, p. 1
[368] Sarasota Herald-Tribune, 8-25-90, p. 5A
https://news.google.com/newspapers?nid=1755&dat=19900825&id=t-obAAAAIBAJ&sjid=u3oEAAAAIBAJ&pg=2361,5313857&hl=en
[369] New York Times, 8-17-89, section 2, p. 10

to being elected to Congress in 1988.[370] Congressman Smith was on the House Judiciary Committee and the Government Operations Committee. The House Judiciary Committee is responsible for initiating impeachment proceedings against the President.

Renegade CIA officers certainly did not want this new Member of Congress jeopardizing their plans to control the government when he found out about Bush's cocaine use during his Vice Presidency.

As noted in chapter 5, the FBI now has the deaths of Congressmen Leland and Smith categorized as homicides.

Killing Members of Congress, sabotaging the democratic process, and controlling the government are not the only things that renegade CIA officers learned from their KGB progenitors. They also learned that the KGB officers had an easy time of exploiting and manipulating Arab nationalists and Islamic extremists.

The KGB officers admitted that they used a Jordanian-born Arab nationalist named Sirhan Sirhan to assassinate Senator Robert F. Kennedy on June 5, 1968. Senator Kennedy had spoken out in favor of Israel, and Sirhan was vehemently anti-Israeli. Sirhan had at one time lived in Jerusalem while it was partly under Jordanian control, and June 5 was the anniversary of the 1967 six-day war in which Israel defeated Jordan and took over the rest of Jerusalem and the West Bank.

A book about this assassination, *RFK Must Die,* has as its cover a photocopy of Sirhan's diary writings in which Sirhan rambles on and repeatedly writes over and over again, "RFK must die. RFK must be killed. Robert F. Kennedy must be assassinated . . . . Robert F. Kennedy must be assassinated before 5 June 68."

Sirhan used the word "assassinated" seventeen times on the diary page and wrote the initials RFK and the name Robert F.

---

[370] Biographical Directory of the United States Congress; http://bioguide.congress.gov/biosearch/biosearch.asp

Kennedy sixteen times as he rambled on about nothing but his belief that RFK "must" be assassinated. Sirhan also drew a line around a notation at the top of the diary page, dated May 18, 1968, which reads, "My determination to eliminate R.F.K. is becoming more the more of an unshakable obsession."[371]

The book, *RFK Must Die*, details Sirhan's jailhouse interviews in which he professed an intense hatred of Jews and a belief that he would be an "Arab hero" if he assassinated Senator Kennedy.

Thirteen years after manipulating Sirhan Sirhan to assassinate Senator Kennedy, the KGB officers, by their own admission, used a group of Islamic extremists in a foreign assassination.

Tony Chavez, a KGB officer who had been the CIA's head of domestic operations until going to prison in 1984, told me that the KGB officers used the "Egyptian Islamic Jihad" to assassinate Egyptian President Anwar Sadat in 1981. Sadat's bodyguards had been "trained" by the CIA.[372]

Another KGB officer told me that CIA officers were torturing him to get information they needed in order to take over handling the Egyptian Islamic Jihad.

According to the FBI's website, the "founder of the Egyptian Islamic Jihad" was Ayman al-Zawahiri,[373] Osama bin Laden's second-in-command during the September 11 terrorist attacks. The *New York Times* reported that Zawahiri "assumed the helm of the Jihad group by the late 1970s."[374] He was imprisoned in Egypt after the assassination of Sadat in 1981 and coincidentally released from prison in 1984, allegedly because of a "lack of evidence."[375]

---

[371] "RFK Must Die!" (E. P. Dutton & Co., Inc., New York, 1970)
[372] https://www.brookings.edu/blog/order-from-chaos/2021/10/01/what-anwar-sadats-murder-40-years-ago-meant-for-the-middle-east/
[373] https://www.fbi.gov/wanted/wanted_terrorists/ayman-al-zawahiri
[374] New York Times, 9-24-01 https://www.nytimes.com/2001/09/24/world/nation-challenged-heir-apparent-egyptian-seen-top-aide-successor-bin-laden.html
[375] https://www.brookings.edu/blog/order-from-chaos/2021/10/01/what-anwar-sadats-murder-40-years-ago-meant-for-the-middle-east/

The FBI website states that the Egyptian Islamic Jihad, "led by Al-Zawahiri, merged with Al Qaeda" in 1998,[376] two years after the Taliban took control of Afghanistan.

The *New York Times* reported that Mohammed Atef, another one of Osama bin Laden's top lieutenants, led the "Egyptian Islamic Jihad" along with Zawahiri, and they brought their "loyal followers" to Al Qaeda.[377]

In 2003, the NBC website stated that Thirwat Saleh Shihata was "Zawahiri's number 2 man" in the "Egyptian Islamic Jihad," and it stated that Shihata was an "Al-Qaida leader."[378]

Reuters reported that Said al-Masri was "a founding member of al Qaeda." He was also a founding member of the "Egyptian Islamic Jihad," and "following the assassination of Egyptian President Anwar Sadat in 1981, Masri was implicated in the killing along with Zawahiri, and they spent time in jail together."[379]

The FBI stated that Masri "provided funds to three of the Sept. 11 hijackers."[380]

In October 2001, just a few short weeks after the September 11 terrorist attacks, the *New York Times* reported that "the leadership of the Egyptian Islamic Jihad" forms the "backbone for Osama bin Laden in Afghanistan,"[381] and the Egyptian Islamic Jihad is "the terror group whose members became foot soldiers for Osama bin Laden."[382]

Renegade CIA officers, led by Leon Panetta, took over handling the Egyptian Islamic Jihad in 1984 and ultimately used them to

---

[376] https://www.fbi.gov/wanted/wanted_terrorists/ayman-al-zawahiri
[377] New York Times, 10-4-01, https://www.nytimes.com/2001/10/04/international/islamic-jihad-forged-in-egypt-is-seen-as-bin-ladens-backbone.html
[378] https://www.nbcnews.com/id/wbna4686491
[379] https://www.reuters.com/article/us-pakistan-usa-qaeda-qa/qa-who-was-al-qaedas-operations-chief-said-al-masri-idUSTRE65017Q20100601
[380] https://www.wsj.com/articles/SB10001424052748703406604575279392274902642
[381] https://www.nytimes.com/2001/10/04/international/islamic-jihad-forged-in-egypt-is-seen-as-bin-ladens-backbone.html
[382] https://www.nytimes.com/2001/11/21/world/nation-challenged-bin-laden-s-allies-investigation-egypt-illustrates-al-qaeda-s.html

build the Al Qaeda hierarchy during the Clinton Administration. In due time, they linked up Zawahiri, Atef, Masri, and all their "loyal followers" with Osama bin Laden and then used the newly formed terrorist alliance to bring about the September 11 terrorist attacks.

The five 9/11 hijackers who crashed a plane into the Pentagon worked out at a Gold's Gym in Beltway Plaza in Greenbelt, MD, not far from where I lived.[383] I spent considerable time at Beltway Plaza in the years before and after the 9/11 attacks and did most of my shopping there.

The 9/11 hijackers also stayed at a motel in Laurel, MD.[384] I worked in Laurel, MD from 1999 through 2002.

Panetta and his corrupt CIA colleagues took the 9/11 hijackers and hid them right in the middle of the CIA operations targeting me.

In September 2011, Fox News reported, "Declassified documents, exclusive interviews and phone and banking records present an overwhelming case that the 9/11 hijackers relied heavily on a domestic support network."[385]

Zawahiri and his "Jihad group" were not identified in news reports as the Egyptian Islamic Jihad in the 1980s, but the exact phrase that Tony Chavez used in 1984 when he told me who killed Egyptian President Anwar Sadat on behalf of the KGB officers was "the Egyptian Islamic Jihad."

As I noted earlier, it was soon afterwards that another KGB officer told me that CIA officers were torturing him to get information on handling the Egyptian Islamic Jihad. Ayman al-Zawahiri was then released from prison because of an alleged "lack of evidence."

In June 2011, Ayman al-Zawahiri, the "founder of the Egyptian Islamic Jihad," became the new Al Qaeda leader.

Sometime after the 9/11 attacks, high-ranking CIA officer Leon Panetta went to President George W. Bush and, in an effort to get the

---

[383] https://www.baltimoresun.com/news/bs-xpm-2001-09-18-0109180193-story.html
[384] https://www.cbsnews.com/news/the-fbis-hijacker-list/
[385] http://www.foxnews.com/politics/2011/09/02/11-hijackers-relied-on-domestic-support-network-records-show/

top spot at the CIA, Panetta told Bush that he could get Osama bin Laden but that he had to be CIA Director to do it. Panetta knew where bin Laden was located, and after failing to persuade Bush to put him in charge of the CIA, Panetta set his sights on renegade CIA officer John Kerry being elected President in 2004.

Panetta had no doubts that Kerry, his fellow CIA officer and fellow Democrat, would appoint him to be Director of the CIA, but Kerry lost the 2004 election. Panetta knew at that point that he would have to wait at least another four years before becoming CIA Director, and Osama bin Laden was moved to a newly built compound in Abbottabad, Pakistan in 2005.

After the 2008 Presidential election, Panetta went to President-elect Barack Obama and told him the same thing that he told President Bush, that he could get Osama bin Laden but that he had to be CIA Director to do it. Obama chose Panetta for the position of CIA Director two weeks before assuming the Presidency in January 2009, and the Senate unanimously confirmed him.

The United States government was not behind the 9/11 attacks, nor did President Bush have anything do to with them. They were strictly a product of Leon Panetta's renegade CIA officers and Islamic extremists. Panetta saw President Bush as nothing more than a CIA asset.

After U.S. forces raided Osama bin Laden's compound and killed him on May 2, 2011, President Obama appointed CIA Director Leon Panetta to the position of Secretary of Defense.

When Panetta became Secretary of Defense, he replaced another CIA officer, Robert Gates, who had been Secretary of Defense during the last two years of the Bush Presidency and the first two years of the Obama Presidency. Gates had risen to the position of CIA Director when Bush's father, CIA officer George H. W. Bush, was President.

Gates left that position in January 1993 with an eye toward the future as he continued to climb the covert ladder of success, while

Bush Sr. finished off his lengthy CIA career with a four-year stint as President of the United States. CIA officer Leon Panetta then moved up the covert ladder with an "official cover" as President Clinton's OMB Director in 1993. There is nothing like renegade CIA officers jockeying for position in the highest offices of the United States Government.

As noted in Chapter 5, I was able to get information on the CIA killing Members of Congress to FBI Director Louis Freeh during the Administration of Bill Clinton in the 1990s. I included the fact that I exposed KGB infiltration of the CIA in 1984, something the FBI could easily confirm, and I noted that the KGB officers admitted to killing thirteen Members of Congress.

I also noted that my attempt to have President Bush impeached in 1989 resulted in the CIA killing Congressmen Mickey Leland and Larkin Smith. I included all the details that are laid out in Chapter 5 concerning the sixteen Members of Congress that died in "accidents" and "suicides."

FBI Director Louis Freeh told me in person at FBI Headquarters that the FBI investigated and that the FBI now has all sixteen deaths categorized as homicides, which means the FBI confirmed that the CIA killed sixteen Members of Congress in addition to assassinating Senator Robert F. Kennedy.

He also told me that after officially confirming the deaths as homicides, the FBI was prevented from further pursuing the case or saying anything about it, undoubtedly due to Presidential interference.

I later learned that Leon Panetta used his influence with President Clinton to interfere in the FBI investigation.

In May 2001, FBI Director Louis Freeh "unexpectedly announced" that he would be resigning "two years ahead of schedule."[386] His resignation took place on June 25, 2001.

Ten days later, Leon Panetta had his asset, President George W. Bush, nominate CIA officer Robert Mueller to be Director of the FBI.

---

[386] https://www.cbsnews.com/news/another-blow-to-the-bureau/

As noted in Chapter 6, Mueller, while functioning as FBI Director, told me in person that he is in the CIA.

CIA officer Robert Mueller was sworn in as FBI Director on September 4, 2001, one week before the 9/11 terrorist attacks. CIA officer Robert Mueller would be using his "official cover" as FBI Director to investigate the CIA-orchestrated attacks while working directly under CIA officer John Ashcroft, who had an "official cover" as Attorney General.

CIA officer John Ashcroft was serving as a U.S. Senator in violation of the Constitution when President and CIA asset George W. Bush appointed him to be Attorney General in December 2000.

Renegade CIA officers originally wanted Ashcroft re-elected to the Senate in November 2000, and pursuant to those plans, they used the KGB's prescribed method of "sabotage" in "political murders" to get rid of his Democratic opponent, Missouri Governor Mel Carnahan.

On October 16, 2000, twenty-two days before the election, Governor Carnahan died in an airplane "accident" when, according to the NTSB, the pilot experienced "disorientation" due to failure of "the airplane's primary attitude indicator."

The NTSB investigation "could not determine the cause of the failure,"[387] but prior to Governor Carnahan's flight, the plane clearly had a functioning "primary attitude indicator."

Renegade CIA officer John Ashcroft ended up losing his re-election bid to the late Mel Carnahan, and CIA asset George W. Bush appointed him to be Attorney General of the United States forty-five days later. Carnahan's widow, Jean, was appointed to fill the U.S. Senate seat of her posthumously elected husband.

Renegade CIA officers resumed killing Members of Congress two years later during the next election cycle.

---

[387] National Transportation Safety Board; NTSB Report Number: AAB-02-02; Aircraft Accident Brief; Accident Number: CHI01MA011

On October 25, 2002, eleven days before the 2002 midterm elections, they killed Democratic Senator Paul Wellstone of Minnesota in an airplane "accident."

The *Minneapolis Star Tribune* reported that, according to the NTSB, pilots who had flown with Senator Wellstone's pilot, Richard Conry, "expressed concerns about his flying skills. For example, a King Air pilot told investigators that during an instrument approach to the airport in Fort Dodge, Iowa, he had to 'take the controls away' from Conry because Conry was unable to hold altitude.

"Another King Air copilot said that he also took the airplane controls from Conry while they were cruising in poor weather. The copilot told investigators that he turned around to answer a question from passengers and when he swung back around to face the controls, he realized the plane was in a 45-degree bank and descending at 1,000 feet a minute."[388]

The *Star Tribune* also stated that just three days before the flight that killed Senator Wellstone, Conry "endangered Wellstone by flipping the wrong switch on a takeoff from St. Paul. That mistake by Capt. Richard Conry was corrected by his copilot after the plane pitched downward while trying to gain altitude just 300 feet off the ground . . . . 'Oh, that could have been pretty bad,' Conry reportedly told the copilot . . . . When the plane landed safely in Rochester, Wellstone jokingly told Conry to 'get some sleep' . . . . Conry's copilot on that flight later suggested to Conry that he should consider retiring."

The *Star Tribune* reported that, according to the NTSB, Conry was "so concerned about the weather that he briefly canceled the trip before deciding to go ahead with it." It also reported that an air traffic controller who had handled one of Conry's weather briefings "told investigators he was concerned that someone was putting pressure on the pilot of Wellstone's plane to make the flight."[389]

---

[388] Minneapolis Star Tribune Online http://www.startribune.com/politics/11758266.html
[389] Minneapolis Star Tribune Online http://www.startribune.com/politics/11758266.html

Regarding Michael Guess, Conry's copilot on the flight that killed Senator Wellstone, the NTSB stated, "Several pilots who had flown with Guess at Aviation Charter expressed concerns about Guess's flying skills, especially his ability to land the airplane without assistance."

The NTSB "could not determine" which of the two pilots was in control of Senator Wellstone's plane when it crashed as a result of "the flight crew's failure to maintain adequate airspeed."[390]

Recall that when the KGB killed Congressman George Collins, his pilot similarly "failed to maintain flying speed" on his "final approach" to Chicago's Midway Airport in 1972.[391] The FBI now has Congressman Collins's death categorized as a homicide.

As for someone putting pressure on Conry to "make the flight," Congressman Mickey Leland's pilots were "pressured" to make a flight that would end when they crashed into a mountain. Six days later, Congressman Larkin Smith's pilot "appeared nervous and even ran the aircraft off the taxiway shortly before takeoff," after which the plane "veered east from its planned flight path before hitting a 70-foot pine tree in the Desoto National Forest."

Renegade CIA officers can clearly "pressure" a pilot to "make the flight."

Six days after they killed Senator Wellstone, renegade CIA officer and former Senator Walter Mondale, who was Vice President of the United States from 1977 to 1981 and the Democratic nominee for President in 1984, replaced Wellstone as the Democrat's nominee for U.S. Senator from Minnesota. After just four days of campaigning, CIA officer Walter Mondale lost the election by less than 50,000 votes out of more than 2.2 million votes that were cast.

Governor Carnahan and Senator Wellstone were killed just prior to the U.S. Senate elections in 2000 and 2002. Killing a

---

[390] https://www.ntsb.gov/investigations/AccidentReports/Reports/AAR0303.pdf
[391] NTSB Identification: DCA73A0003
https://www.ntsb.gov/_layouts/ntsb.aviation/brief.aspx?ev_id=66703&key=0

candidate immediately before an election is something that renegade CIA officers learned from their KGB progenitors. The KGB officers were planning to kill President Johnson immediately before the 1964 election so that their asset, renegade CIA officer Barry Goldwater, would be elected to the Presidency.

But the murders of Governor Carnahan and Senator Wellstone over a two-year period pale in comparison to the true intent of the CIA-orchestrated 9/11 terrorist attacks.

Killing Members of Congress with vehicles that they are not on board was a tried and proven method on September 11, 2001.

Ten years before the 9/11 attacks, renegade CIA officers killed Senator John Heinz by having a helicopter crash into his plane. Eight years before that, the KGB killed Congressman Larry McDonald by sending his plane into Soviet airspace, where it was destroyed by a missile fired from a Soviet fighter jet, and there had been two other occasions in which Members of Congress were similarly killed with vehicles they were not on board.

It took a train engine, a tractor-trailer, a missile fired from a Soviet jet, and a helicopter crashing into a plane to kill just four Members of Congress in 1957, 1965, 1983, and 1991, but those four deaths would pale in comparison to a jumbo jet loaded with fuel crashing into a Senate Office Building on September 11, 2001, not to mention that renegade CIA officers had a clearly established track record for killing Members of Congress with airplanes.

Renegade CIA officers are obsessed with controlling the government, particularly the Senate. Flight 93, the hijacked plane that crashed in Pennsylvania on September 11 while heading toward Washington, was meant to kill a multitude of U.S. Senators. President Bush was in Florida at the time and was obviously not the target.

The hijacked planes that crashed into the two towers of the World Trade Center and the Pentagon would have easily provided cover for the main purpose of the terrorist attacks, killing United States Senators by crashing a plane into a Senate Office Building.

It certainly cannot be proven that killing Members of Congress was the main intent of the attacks, but what is known and is absolutely indisputable is that Members of Congress were killed by vehicles they were not on board in 1957, 1965, 1983, and 1991, and prior to the September 11 attacks, "airplanes" were used kill eleven Members of Congress and a Governor who was running for the Senate.

Leon Panetta and his band of renegade CIA officers knew that while the CIA performed its legitimate function of identifying and pursuing terrorists, no one would suspect that renegade CIA officers built the Al Qaeda hierarchy and then facilitated the September 11 attacks.

Renegade CIA officers are acutely aware that KGB officers functioned for decades inside the CIA and were completely trusted by their peers. They know that, like their KGB predecessors, they are viewed as loyal Americans and completely trusted within the CIA.

Renegade CIA officers have every intention of strengthening their grip on power, and that was the whole point of the September 11 attacks.

If Flight 93 had reached its destination and crashed into a Senate Office Building instead of going down in Pennsylvania when passengers overpowered the hijackers, Panetta and his corrupt CIA colleagues would have consolidated power in a President they had been handling since 1984. The Constitutional balance of power would have been voided, and if everything had gone according to plan, Panetta and his corrupt CIA colleagues would have reigned supreme alongside their asset, President George W. Bush, as the nation began rebuilding from the tragedy.

CIA officers in government are at the forefront of the CIA's quest to control the government. President Jimmy Carter and Congressman Leon Panetta were the main obstacles to exposing the KGB infiltration during the first three and a half years of my seven-year effort.

Panetta openly stated that it was his intention to protect the KGB infiltration because the KGB officers helped him get into the CIA after the CIA first rejected him.

According to Panetta, the CIA told him that he was rejected because he "got stuck in a rebellion as a teenager," which is something the CIA would determine during the psychological evaluation. Panetta will openly admit that the CIA initially rejected him and he will admit why they rejected him, although he will insist that he did not fail the psychological evaluation. He will also admit that the people who helped him get into the CIA were eventually identified as KGB officers who went to prison in 1984.

After the 1980 election, the main obstacles to exposing the KGB infiltration were Vice President Bush and a virulently corrupt CIA hierarchy, which, of course, included Leon Panetta.

The corrupt hierarchy also included CIA Director William J. Casey, who was addicted to cocaine and was most definitely a renegade CIA officer.

I first met Casey at the CIA's Chicago field office in early 1980. He stated that he was the "Acting Director" of the CIA and later informed me that he was also Ronald Reagan's campaign manager. Later that year, he told me that Reagan would be appointing him to be Director of the CIA after the election.

As I had been looking forward to a new Presidential Administration that was not under KGB control, I tried to clarify with Casey that the KGB infiltration would finally be exposed and come to an end. When I directly asked him if he was going to expose the KGB infiltration after becoming CIA Director, his emphatic reply was, "No."

Shocked by his answer, I asked, "Why not?"

And his exact words were, "Because they supply me with my cocaine."

As noted in chapter 4, Casey manipulated Ronald Reagan into choosing his cocaine-addicted CIA colleague, George H. W. Bush, as a Vice Presidential running mate in 1980.

In 1984, I witnessed President Reagan angrily confront Casey about being manipulated into choosing Bush as a running mate, which happened only after the big push to supposedly "draft" former President Gerald Ford "fizzled."

Reagan made it clear during the confrontation that Casey had given him every impression that he, Casey, was convinced Ford would accept the number two spot on the ticket. Casey finally admitted that he knew Ford had no intention of being Reagan's running mate and that everything had been orchestrated to get Reagan to accept CIA officer George Bush as a running mate at the last minute.

Senator Daniel Patrick Moynihan's CIA pseudonym was John McMahon. Moynihan was Deputy Director of the CIA in 1984 while simultaneously holding the position of Vice Chairman of the Senate Intelligence Oversight Committee. The Senate officially confirmed Moynihan as Deputy Director and then used his CIA pseudonym, John McMahon, for public records so that the American people would not know about the Constitutional violation (CIA Deputy Directors needed Senate confirmation in the 1980s). The CIA also used a photo of a CIA officer they claimed was "John McMahon" for public consumption.

When President Reagan nominated "John McMahon" to be Deputy Director of the CIA in April 1982, the *New York Times* quoted Moynihan as saying, "Mr. McMahon was the only, and I repeat, only, appointment I would have found acceptable."[392]

Adhering to the warped logic that is used to justify having CIA officers in Congress in violation of the Constitution, Senator Moynihan once said to me, "I'm not in the CIA. John McMahon is in the CIA."

CIA officer Daniel Patrick Moynihan was elected as a Democrat to the U.S. Senate in 1976, the same year CIA officers Jimmy Carter and Walter Mondale were elected President and Vice

---

[392] New York Times, 4-26-82, http://www.nytimes.com/1982/04/26/us/no-3-cia-official-called-as-likely-sucessor-to-inman.html

President on the Democratic ticket. It was also the same year high-ranking CIA officer Leon Panetta was elected to Congress, all while CIA officer George H. W. Bush reigned supreme as CIA Director.

With Casey and renegade CIA officer Daniel Patrick Moynihan holding the two top positions in the CIA, and with renegade CIA officer Barry Goldwater being the Republican Chairman of the Senate Intelligence Committee while Moynihan was the Democratic Vice Chairman, and with a number of CIA officers in Congress holding office as Democrats and Republicans, bipartisan corruption existed in a symbiotic relationship in both the executive branch and the legislative branch, just as it did in previous Administrations and previous Congresses.

Regardless of the corruption, everything fell into place in early 1984 and the KGB was exposed, but corrupt CIA official Leon Panetta led the initiative to build upon what the KGB officers had accomplished during thirty-seven years of operating inside the CIA.

The Soviet KGB's subversion of the U.S. Constitution served as a foundation for renegade CIA officers to begin their own quest to control the United States government.

At one point, Panetta boasted that he remembered everything the KGB taught him, which included supplying cocaine to Members of Congress and to CIA employees.

Prior to the KGB infiltration being exposed, CIA officers who were not corrupted naturally wanted to expose the KGB. When I was identifying KGB officers from 1977 to 1984, some of the CIA field officers with whom I interacted filed intelligence reports on the KGB infiltration. It was at my behest that a CIA officer at the Chicago field office contacted former CIA Deputy Director Bobby Ray Inman, former CIA Director William Colby, and former Deputy Director Frank Carlucci, who, as related in Chapter 6, all cooperated with me in exposing the KGB.

But it is something entirely different for CIA officers to expose their corrupt CIA colleagues, who have continued to wield substantial control in the CIA, the United States Congress, and the

Executive Branch, just as their KGB progenitors did. Exposing renegade CIA officers and their plans to control the United States government is definitely more formidable than exposing the KGB infiltration.

As noted in Chapter 6, former Senator John Kerry, the Democratic nominee for President in 2004, is a renegade CIA officer whom the KGB officers had targeted for political office, although he was not elected to Congress until after the KGB infiltration was exposed.

Kerry is among a "Democratic" faction of the CIA that is ostensibly opposed to the "Republican" faction, but the two factions exist in a symbiotic relationship. They have been vying for control of the United States government since the 1950s as they work together to build up CIA control of the United States government.

The KGB officers were never able to have two CIA officers run against each other as Presidential nominees, but renegade CIA officers accomplished the next best thing in 2004. They had Senator John Kerry, a renegade CIA officer, running against President and CIA "asset" George W. Bush. No matter who won the 2004 Presidential election, the renegade CIA officers' warped view of the democratic process would prevail. As noted in Chapter 6, Leon Panetta was hoping that Kerry would defeat his asset, President George W. Bush, so that Kerry would appoint Panetta to be CIA Director.

In a continuing show of renegade CIA officers influencing Presidential appointments, President Barack Obama not only appointed Leon Panetta to be Director of the CIA, but also appointed CIA officer Eric Holder to be Attorney General. Obama's predecessor, CIA asset George W. Bush, had similarly appointed CIA officer John Ashcroft to be Attorney General. Obama also appointed renegade CIA officer John Kerry to succeed Hillary Clinton as Secretary of State in December 2012.

In the six years before Kerry's appointment to be Secretary of State, CIA officers Leon Panetta and Robert Gates waited for their next move up the covert ladder of success. Recall that President George Bush appointed Gates to the position of Secretary of Defense in November 2006, and President Obama retained Gates as Defense Secretary while appointing Panetta to the position of CIA Director.

After two and a half years of having Gates and Panetta in those positions, Obama appointed CIA officer Leon Panetta to replace CIA officer Robert Gates as Secretary of Defense, and, a year and a half later, he appointed CIA officer John Kerry to be Secretary of State. To repeat, there is nothing like renegade CIA officers jockeying for position in the highest offices of the United States Government during any given Presidential Administration.

And while Bush Jr. was appointing Gates to be his Defense Secretary back in November 2006, one of Gates's corrupt CIA colleagues, Michele Bachmann, was celebrating her victory in the 2006 Congressional elections. Bachmann then violated the Constitution for almost four and a half years as a CIA officer in Congress before announcing that she would run for President in 2012. She even touted herself as a "Constitutional Conservative."

CIA officers currently in Congress in violation of the Constitution include Congresswomen Maxine Waters and Frederica Wilson.

Liz Cheney is a CIA officer who was a Member of Congress in violation of the Constitution from 2017 to 2023. She previously had "diplomatic covers" at the U.S. embassies in Budapest and Warsaw and an "official cover" as a Deputy Assistant Secretary of State under President and CIA-controlled "asset" George W. Bush.

Tulsi Gabbard, a Member of Congress from 2013 to 2021, is a CIA officer. Nancy Pelosi chose Gabbard to speak at the Democratic National Convention in September 2012 when she was still a candidate for Congress. She described Gabbard as "an emerging star."[393]

---

[393] https://www.vogue.com/article/making-a-splash-is-tulsi-gabbard-the-next-democratic-party-star

Gabbard joined the Congressional Progressive Caucus after becoming a Member of Congress in 2013, and she was elected to be Vice Chair of the Democratic National Committee.

She further established her leftist "bona fides" when she resigned as DNC Vice Chair in 2016 so that she could endorse socialist Bernie Sanders for President, and Gabbard endorsed CIA "asset" Joe Biden for President after she dropped out of the 2020 Democratic Presidential primary.

CIA officer Tulsi Gabbard left the Democratic Party in 2022 and began espousing conservative views and endorsing Republicans, regardless of an eight year record of aligning herself with the far left. Social media shows that some conservatives are suspicious of her and some think it is great that she "switched sides." She is, in reality, a renegade CIA officer and an integral part of the CIA takeover of the United States government.

In November 2022, CIA officer Tulsi Gabbard began using a "nonofficial cover" as a "paid contributor" with Fox News.[394] As will be seen later in this book, high-profile CIA officials are similarly using "nonofficial covers" as liberals with NBC News and CBS News.

As noted in Chapter 1, CIA Director William Colby testified that there are "full-time employees" of the CIA who are also "full-time employees of major domestic media outlets."[395]

Renegade CIA officers continued to influence Presidential appointments after the Obama Administration.

President-elect Trump chose CIA officer Mike Pompeo for the position of CIA Director ten short days after being elected. Pompeo was a Member of Congress in violation of the Constitution for six years before becoming CIA Director.

Besides my first-hand knowledge that Pompeo is a CIA officer, the Rockefeller Report states that there are no "outsiders" in the CIA's

---

[394] https://www.latimes.com/entertainment-arts/business/story/2022-11-14/tulsi-gabbard-signs-as-a-contributor-for-fox-news
[395] Hearings Before The Select Committee On Intelligence, Part 5, p. 1589
https://www.maryferrell.org/showDoc.html?docId=146901#relPageId=27&tab=page

"top-level management." In any other United States "executive agency," the "chief officer" and "top-level assistants" are "appointed from the outside," but "no such infusion occurs in the CIA."

Pompeo was a clearly high-ranking CIA official while he was a Member of Congress for six years, and he was clearly violating the Constitution.

Mike Pompeo never informed Trump that there was a "Democratic faction" of the CIA vying for control of the government, nor did he inform him about CIA operations targeting the White House. The "Democratic faction" of the CIA most definitely has a symbiotic relationship with the "Republican faction" of the CIA.

President Trump nominated CIA Director Mike Pompeo to be U.S. Secretary of State in March 2018 and he was confirmed in April, thus giving him an "official cover" as Secretary of State.

The CIA's "Republican faction" got Trump to nominate CIA officer Bill Barr to be Attorney General in December 2018.

Barr was "officially" a CIA employee from 1971 to 1978, during which time the CIA paid him to go to law school. He then used a "nonofficial cover" as an attorney in the private sector until he was given an "official cover" at the Reagan White House from 1982 to 1983.[396] I know Barr is a CIA officer because I met him in 1984 while I was trying to expose the corruption in the CIA.

Barr went back to using a "nonofficial cover" in the private sector until landing "official covers" with the Justice Department under President and CIA officer George H. W. Bush from 1989 to 1993, eventually rising to the position of Attorney General during the last two years of the Bush Administration.

Barr then used "nonofficial covers" in the private sector for the next twenty-five years until the CIA's "Republican faction" got Trump to nominate him to be Attorney General.

As noted in Chapter 6, the CIA's "Republican faction" got Trump to appoint CIA officer Christopher Wray to be FBI Director after Trump fired FBI Director and CIA "asset" James Comey in 2017.

In December 2019, with CIA officers Bill Barr and Chris Wray using their "official covers" as Attorney General and FBI Director,

---

[396]https://www.judiciary.senate.gov/imo/media/doc/William%20Barr%20Senate%20Questionnaire%20(PUBLIC).pdf

and with CIA officer Mike Pompeo using his "official cover" as Secretary of State, Trump appointed a CIA officer named Anthony Ornato to be the White House "Deputy Chief of Staff for Operations." Ornato had previously been "detailed by the CIA" to be a "designated officer of the Secret Service," and he was the Deputy Assistant Director of the Secret Service when Trump appointed him to the high-ranking White House position.[397]

As for the KGB officers who started the ball rolling on corrupting and controlling the United States government, "John McCone," Director of the CIA when President Kennedy was assassinated, was one of the KGB officers who was exposed in 1984. The real John McCone died at a relatively young age, and a KGB officer named "Ligachev" assumed his identity.

Ligachev attended the University of California using McCone's identity, and in due time, he worked his way up into several high-ranking positions in government until becoming CIA Director in 1961. Having a KGB officer in the position of CIA Director was essential to orchestrating the assassination of President Kennedy.

In 1987 and 1988, the CIA had the elderly Ligachev once again impersonate McCone and sit for three interviews at the University of California. The idea was to dissuade any effort to publicize that KGB infiltration of the CIA had been exposed and that McCone was one of the KGB officers. There would ostensibly be no explanation for how McCone could be doing interviews in 1987 and 1988 if McCone was a KGB officer named Ligachev who went to prison in 1984.

Before 1984, the closest any of the KGB officers had ever come to being exposed was during the 1950s when Senator Joseph McCarthy said he had a list of a few dozen people who were secretly Communists, but McCarthy then began accusing thousands of people of being Communists. Many were simply vouching for the credibility of what they thought were loyal

---

[397] https://www.foxnews.com/politics/donald-trump-anthony-ornato-deputy-chief-staff-operations

Americans, and others were just antithetical to McCarthy's heavy-handed tactics. McCarthy's effort itself would have been easy to infiltrate and sabotage by anyone who masked their intentions with a zeal to expose Communists.

"McCarthyism" was born, and McCarthy's effort failed miserably. KGB officers continued to enter the United States, assume the identities of deceased Americans, and then join the CIA during the 1950s. McCarthy was ultimately beneficial to them because they were much better off when he and his effort lost all credibility.

After solidifying their positions as ostensibly loyal Americans, the KGB officers began killing Members of Congress in 1957. Six years later, the Soviet KGB took aim at the President of the United States.

All Members of the 98th Congress were acutely aware of how corrupted the CIA was in 1984. They were all aware that there were CIA officers in Congress and that Members of Congress from both parties used cocaine. They were made aware that KGB officers inside the CIA had killed Members of Congress, and an abundance of testimony at the closed-door Congressional hearings in 1984 proved that the KGB-dominated CIA killed President Kennedy in 1963.

But the preponderant attitude amongst the powers-that-be and the power brokers in Congress was that the American people should not find out about this pernicious corruption, and the Reagan Administration took the same position.

Republicans would not point the finger of guilt at other Republicans, and Democrats would not point the finger of guilt at other Democrats. There was an unspoken secret agreement that everyone would continue with business as usual while the American people were kept in the dark regarding the massive bipartisan corruption. Republicans and Democrats were focused on the upcoming primaries and elections in 1984 and on the political battles between the Reagan Administration and the Democratic-controlled House of Representatives.

Neither the Reagan Administration nor the United States Congress had any intention of exposing massive bipartisan corruption in 1984, and they had no intention of doing anything about the egregious corruption in the Central Intelligence Agency.

President Reagan, with his re-election looming, had no intention of sacrificing Vice President Bush on the altar of Constitutionality.

President Reagan's chief of staff, James A. Baker, rebuffed my attempt to get his perspective in 1984 when, in a brash display of opportunism, he exclaimed, "I have my own future to think about."

CIA officer George Bush appointed Baker to be Secretary of State after being elected to the Presidency in 1988.

Four Members of the 98th Congress, Dan Quayle, Al Gore, Dick Cheney, and Joe Biden, all of whom had intricate knowledge of the vast bipartisan corruption, went on to become Vice President of the United States, and Biden went on to become President of the United States.

I know first-hand that the infamous Leon Panetta enlisted Joe Biden as an "asset" and targeted him for the Presidency back in 1984.

As noted in chapter 4, none of this is about politics. This is about virulently corrupt elements of the CIA destroying our Constitution and corrupting our government far beyond what anyone could imagine. It is about corruption, murder, intrigue, and assassinating our elected officials.

Chapter 8: Orchestrating the Assassination of a President

While the information in this book is not about politics, Senator Barry Goldwater's KGB handlers did use "politics" to lure President Kennedy to his death on November 22, 1963, and KGB asset Barry Goldwater was more than happy to cooperate.

In what appeared to be nothing more than political posturing, the KGB had Goldwater using inflammatory and oftentimes nonsensical rhetoric while visiting key electoral states in the months leading up to the assassination. Goldwater clearly showed that he planned to run for President in 1964 while adamantly denying that he had any intention of running for President, all for the purpose of luring President Kennedy to his death.

Elements of the KGB's grand production sprouted at a Political Action Conference on July 12, 1963, when Senator Barry Goldwater, "the leading candidate for the Republican Presidential nomination in 1964, arrived at the Statler-Hilton Hotel, just three blocks from the White House, to have breakfast with 500 of his admirers."[398]

With exactly nineteen weeks remaining before his KGB handlers would assassinate President Kennedy, KGB asset Barry Goldwater "charged that President Kennedy was trying to 'coexist with international communism wherever it thrives, even in the Western Hemisphere.'" Goldwater made several statements attacking the way Kennedy dealt with communist expansionism, adding that "today's

---

[398] Washington Post, 7-13-63, p. 2

liberal is so frightened of the future that he is incapable of acting in the present."

His attacks on the President "were greeted with applause, shouts, cheers, whistles and the stomping of feet and the Senator's harsh words set the tone for a long day of speeches by other Members of Congress," some of whom were evidently opposed to civil rights and integration.

Congressman Bruce Alger of Texas "declared that 'Bobby is behind every bush,' and the audience howled at this thrust at Attorney General Robert F. Kennedy," the President's brother and a leading proponent of President Kennedy's civil rights program.

The only Democrat to address the conference was Senator Strom Thurmond of South Carolina, a Southern Democrat who was "one of the principal opponents of Mr. Kennedy's civil rights program."

Nineteen days later, on July 31, 1963, Goldwater bolstered what was apparently a newly found segregationist stance. While addressing the U.S. Senate, Goldwater "accused Attorney General Robert F. Kennedy of using 'police state' powers in an effort to desegregate communities around military bases . . . . He and several Southern Democrats denounced a Pentagon directive authorizing military commanders to designate as off limits for servicemen communities which practice 'relentless discrimination' against Negroes."[399]

"What he fears, Goldwater said, is 'the threat of a military takeover should things change in this country and we find that the military commanders have become used to running politics and the social life of the community.'"

Goldwater, in aligning himself with segregationist "Southern Democrats," clearly stated that the Pentagon was creating a "police state" and threatening a possible "military takeover" of the United States government by doing nothing more than forbidding military personnel from going into segregationist communities.

---

[399] Washington Post, 8-1-63, p. 9

The *Washington Post* touted CIA officer Barry Goldwater as the "front-runner for the Republican Presidential nomination" on August 14, 1963, when it reported on Senate hearings to ratify a partial nuclear test ban treaty. The treaty, which banned testing nuclear weapons in the air to stop the spread of radioactive fallout around the globe, was ratified by the Senate in September by a margin of eighty to nineteen. During the August hearings, Goldwater claimed that the treaty would "open 'a possibly fatal gap' in this nation's defenses against an enemy missile attack."[400]

Goldwater's clear position is that Russia would be able to destroy the United States in a nuclear onslaught unless the United States tested nuclear weapons in the air.

Exactly nine weeks before the KGB would lure President Kennedy to his death, Goldwater's KGB handlers had him directly threaten President Kennedy's 1964 re-election bid while Goldwater continued to backpedal on the idea that he would run for President.

On September 20, 1963, CIA officer and KGB asset Barry Goldwater announced that he had formed a California advisory committee "'for consultation' about the California primary," but he firmly maintained it was "not an announcement that I intend to seek the Presidential nomination."[401]

It is no surprise that they chose the electoral prize of California to directly threaten Kennedy's re-election. As noted in Chapter 2, California had one Republican Senator going into the 1964 election, and a second Republican Senator was elected in 1964. San Francisco, which hosted the Republican National Convention in 1964, had a Republican Mayor and had nothing but Republican Mayors from 1912 to 1964, and California was conservative enough to elect staunch Goldwater supporter Ronald Reagan as its Governor in 1966.

California went to the Republican Presidential candidate in 1952, 1956, and 1960, and back in 1948, incumbent President Harry Truman barely edged out Republican candidate Thomas Dewey in

---

[400] Washington Post, 8-14-63, p. 1
[401] Washington Post, 9-21-63, p. 2

California by less than one half of a percentage point. The electoral prize of California was most definitely a GOP target in 1964.

Six days after KGB asset Barry Goldwater issued his threat, President Kennedy spoke in Salt Lake City, Utah, where he "sharply attacked the foreign policies advocated by Senator Barry Goldwater" and "took issue point by point with proposals put forth by the Senator . . . . The speech marked the first time that the President has tried to refute in a detailed way the foreign policies that Goldwater has stressed . . . . Utah, like the other mountain states the President is visiting on his five-day, ten state Western tour, is a center of Goldwater strength."[402]

Kennedy deleted a reference to the fact that Goldwater often spoke about "total victory," but in what seems to be a naively ironic parody of the fate that awaited him, Kennedy did say, "We have history going for us today."

Four days later, a September 30th front page headline in the *Dallas Times Herald* was forebodingly symbolic of the fate that awaited President Kennedy in Dallas, stating, "First Shots Fired: JFK Tour Trains Democrat Guns on Goldwater."

With fifty-three days remaining before JFK's scheduled assassination in Dallas, the *Dallas Times Herald* made it clear that "in the wake of a Presidential tour of the West that will be followed by forays into the South," Senator Barry Goldwater was "the Democratic Party's No. 1 political target," adding that the President's upcoming trip to Texas had been "expanded into a two-day visit in which the President will seek to shore up Democratic leaders sorely beset by a Dallas-based Goldwater boom."[403]

It also stated President Kennedy was planning "a major appearance" in the electoral prize of California to "counteract a recent massive rally in Goldwater's behalf that all but filled Dodger's stadium in Los Angeles."

---

[402] Washington Post, 9-27-63, p. 1
[403] Dallas Times Herald, 9-30-63, p. 1

"Kennedy's Salt Lake City speech on foreign policy was a clear attack against the principles advocated by Senator Goldwater. It is already a certainty that a similar speech will be included in those to be made in Texas . . . . For all practical purposes, the Kennedy-Goldwater clash that many expect in 1964 is already under way."

On October 3, three days after the *Dallas Times Herald* reported that "Democrat Guns" were trained on Goldwater, KGB asset Barry Goldwater returned to the electoral prize of California, and while "deep in the heartland of Western conservatism," he told the California Federation of Republican Women that the Kennedy Administration was "establishing 'a Soviet-American mutual aid society.'"[404]

The KGB asset attacked President Kennedy's New Frontier proposals and said: "In less than a month the New Frontier has offered to pick up the check for half the cost of a joint shot to the moon, stop testing nuclear weapons in the air and, finally, bail out the highly vaunted Soviet farm collective with what I'm willing to bet will be tons of free American wheat."

Goldwater sharpened his attack, stating, "There is an old line somewhere that goes: If you can't lick 'em, join 'em. But I for one am not quite ready to lie down and play Rover to Kremlin tunes . . . . Along the New Frontier the idea is to conform or keep quiet.

"Nothing must be done to ruffle Mr. Khrushchev's feelings or lead him to think that we are superior to the Soviets in any category. We don't hear a tough note out of this Administration unless it is directed at one of our tried and proven allies."

CIA officer Barry Goldwater's "tried and proven allies" were the repressive dictatorships that the KGB-controlled CIA propped up in Latin America to foster Communist insurgencies, and contrary to Goldwater's claim that President Kennedy was lying down and "playing Rover to Kremlin tunes," it was less than a year earlier that President Kennedy's naval blockade of Cuba forced Soviet Premier Nikita Khrushchev to withdraw nuclear missiles from Cuba.

---

[404] New York Times, 10-4-63, p. 20

Six days after Goldwater's crack about President Kennedy being "tough" only with "our tried and proven allies," President Kennedy held a news conference and stated that "the United States is wholly opposed to military coups in Latin America, no matter what justification is made for them . . . . In addition to their threat to the whole process of democratic government and progress, he said, military 'dictatorships are the seed-beds from which communism ultimately springs up.'"[405]

When asked if he expected Goldwater to end up being the Republican nominee who would challenge his 1964 re-election bid, President Kennedy, who was scheduled to be assassinated in forty-four days, warned that Goldwater will have "a trying seven or eight months which will test his endurance and his perseverance and his agility."

On the following day, October 10, 1963, CIA officer and KGB asset Barry Goldwater spoke in the electoral prize of Pennsylvania and "lashed out at the 'corruption-ridden machines' which he said are the key to national Democratic victories . . . . Goldwater delivered a slashing attack on the New Frontier's connections with the big city machines in the North and East.

"Mr. Goldwater, rated a leading prospect for next year's Republican Presidential nomination, said the Kennedy Administration's choice was clear: 'Government of the Kennedys, by the Kennedys and for the Kennedys.'

"His appearance in this key state was widely viewed as another sign that he is seriously considering becoming a candidate for the GOP nomination next year."[406]

Goldwater also proclaimed, "The vitality of American leadership in the cold war has waned to the vanishing point."

And while in Pennsylvania, Goldwater held a news conference, telling reporters that he "would be willing to debate President Kennedy on television if he is the Republican Presidential

---
[405] Washington Post, 10-10-63, pp. 1 & 14
[406] Dallas Morning News, 10-11-63, p. 1 and New York Times, 10-11-63, p. 26

nominee in 1964, but he stressed that he had not made up his mind about seeking the nomination. When asked when he would make a decision, he said, 'I don't know when it will be.'"[407]

In the plan to lure President Kennedy to his death, Goldwater now had the electoral prizes of California and Pennsylvania under his belt as points of interest in a "possible" Presidential bid, and the day after his Pennsylvania visit, where he claimed he was still undecided about running for President, his KGB handlers had him make a most noteworthy visit.

On Friday, October 11, 1963, exactly six weeks before Goldwater's KGB handlers would assassinate President Kennedy, CIA officer Barry Goldwater flew to San Antonio, Texas, where he received "a red carpet welcome" and "rode from the airport in an open convertible" while "a crowd of fans chanted 'We want Barry' and waved 'Goldwater for President' signs."[408]

"Goldwater, rated by pollsters as a leader among potential candidates for the 1964 Republican Presidential nomination, waved and leaned over to shake hands."

The *Dallas Morning News*, reporting on Goldwater's speech in San Antonio, stated: "Senator Barry Goldwater charged here Friday night that the Kennedy Administration is following the most disastrous foreign policy in the nation's history . . . . 'The policy stands wall-eyed in Berlin and cross-eyed in Paris and blind in Cuba' . . . . Senator Goldwater waded into the Administration after receiving an award for his contribution to national defense from the Military Order of World Wars, made up of active and retired commissioned officers."[409]

"The front-runner for the Republican Presidential nomination told the officer veterans that he was going to give them some plain, hard talk about the world situation . . . . His speech was interrupted eighteen times by applause from an obviously conservative and anti-

---

[407] Dallas Morning News, 10-11-63, p. 8
[408] Washington Post, 10-12-63, p. 2
[409] Dallas Morning News, 10-12-63, p. 6

Kennedy military audience . . . . He rounded the world in his indictment and was particularly critical about the handling of Latin American affairs."

Goldwater also held a news conference in San Antonio in which he addressed civil rights and further aligned himself with segregationists, stating, "I'd like to see us calm down in the whole field . . . . The whites, in many instances, have beefs."[410] (Goldwater's statement that "whites" have "beefs" in the drive to end segregation was clearly a milestone in the nonsensical statements that he incorporated into his escalating rhetorical conflict with President Kennedy.)

And while speaking to reporters back in Pennsylvania before his Texas visit, Goldwater spiced up the flavor of his upcoming grand reception by "from time to time" responding to questions with the words "If I were a candidate,"[411] which made the front page of the *Dallas Morning News* on October 11, as it was the first time that Goldwater did not issue a straightforward denial that he might eventually become a candidate.

Goldwater literally prefaced his "red carpet welcome" in the electoral prize of Texas with the words "If I were a candidate," and Goldwater, who had told reporters in Pennsylvania several times that he was "not a candidate," exuded the aura of being the Republican nominee for President as he "rode from the airport in an open convertible" while his fans chanted "We want Barry" and waved "Goldwater for President" signs.

Besides his news conference in Pennsylvania and his news conference in San Antonio, renegade CIA officer Barry Goldwater "stopped over at Dallas Love Field" while on his way to his grandiose reception and held a "brief five-minute press conference."[412]

---

[410] Dallas Morning News, 10-12-63, p. 7
[411] Dallas Morning News, 10-11-63, p. 1
[412] Dallas Morning News, 10-12-63, section 4, p. 1

Dallas Love Field is the airport from which President Kennedy would be riding when he was assassinated.

And during his Love Field news conference, Goldwater found it necessary to refute a copyrighted story in the *Dallas Morning News* stating that Goldwater would announce his Presidential bid in early January. When asked about plans to announce his candidacy, Goldwater replied, "There is no truth in it. It is absolutely not true."

Eight days later, Goldwater visited the electoral prize of California for the third time in less than a month and fired off another "foreign policy" volley in a speech sponsored by the *San Bernardino Sun-Telegram* on October 19. Goldwater accused the Kennedy Administration of "endangering the nation through 'flagrant news management'" and "attacked the Administration's handling of the announcements of four recent international developments."[413]

Eleven days after his third California visit, Goldwater spoke in the electoral prize of New York, and in a speech "sponsored by the publication Financial World," Goldwater proclaimed that "President Kennedy has touched off a 'crisis of confidence' that is harming the nation's economy. The Arizona conservative said the Kennedy administration's economic performance 'adds up to nearly a thousand days of wasted spending, wishful thinking, unwarranted intervention, wistful theories and waning confidence.'"[414]

Goldwater was again speculative about becoming a candidate, stating that "if he becomes a candidate for the White House, he will seek delegate backing in New York State."

In an interview on November 10, thirty days after riding from a Texas airport "in an open convertible," the front-runner for the GOP nomination stated, "Any interference in this Administration's bungling of foreign policy would work for the better."[415]

With twelve days remaining before President Kennedy's scheduled assassination, KGB asset Barry Goldwater, who constantly brought

---

[413] Washington Post, 10-21-63, p. 8
[414] Arizona Republic, 10-31-63, p. 18
[415] Washington Post, 11-11-63, p. 7

up "foreign policy" in his attacks on the President, was even more speculative about running for President in 1964, using the phrases "not yet decided . . . until I am convinced . . . . If and when . . . unless I decide . . . whether or not I decide."

When President Kennedy was assassinated on November 22, 1963, he was "on his way to the Trade Mart to make a speech. It was to be a bold speech. Here in the stronghold of political conservatism and before an audience made up largely of critics of New Frontier policies at home and abroad, he was going to accuse right-wing extremists of talking 'just plain nonsense.'"[416]

"Mr. Kennedy and Mrs. Kennedy were riding in the rear seat of a top-down Lincoln Continental . . . . Thousands had cheered the First Family as the motorcade drove in from Love Field."

"The assassination occurred just as the President's motorcade was leaving downtown Dallas at the end of a triumphal tour through the city's streets . . . . The original plans called only for a fast ride from the airport to a lunch at the Trade Mart . . . . Mr. Kennedy himself had made the decision to ride in the slow-moving motorcade."[417]

Back in January 1963, the *Washington Post* reported: "President Kennedy himself, it can be said with knowledge, does not think his re-election will be easy or can be taken for granted."[418]

On October 5, 1963, forty-eight days before the scheduled assassination, the *Washington Post* reported: "President Kennedy is now much preoccupied with his chances of winning a second term. Governor Connally, on his way out of the White House, had this to say to reporters: 'I told the President that he would have a hard race in Texas. It would be unrealistic to think we are not going to have a tough fight there next year.'"[419]

---

[416] Washington Post, 11-23-63, pp. 1 & 9
[417] New York Times, 11-24-63, p. 1
[418] Washington Post, 1-8-63, p. 11
[419] Washington Post, 10-5-63, p. 1

"Connally acknowledged that Goldwater had 'considerable strength' in Texas but suggested that after the Democrats do a job on the Senator, some of his strength might vanish. Goldwater will certainly be on Mr. Kennedy's mind when he visits Texas on November 21-22."

Six days after the *Washington Post* stated that Goldwater would "certainly" be on Kennedy's mind when he visits Texas, Goldwater was riding from a Texas airport in "an open convertible" while his enthusiastic fans lined the streets chanting "We want Barry" and waving "Goldwater for President" signs.[420]

FBI Director J. Edgar Hoover testified to the Warren Commission, "One of President Kennedy's staff made the statement that the whole fault in this matter was that, in the choice between politics and security, politics was chosen. That is exactly what happened."[421]

---

[420] Washington Post, 10-12-63, p. 2
[421] Warren Commission Hearings, Volume V, p. 107

Chapter 9: Preparing for President Johnson's Assassination and a Goldwater Presidency

Pursuant to the KGB's two-pronged assassination plan, the Soviet Union used a wide array of Communist propaganda organs to put forth that "racists" were behind President Kennedy's assassination while blatantly accusing Barry Goldwater and his supporters of being complicit in the assassination.

The prolonged and intense propaganda campaign also warned that right-wing "madmen" were plotting to take over the United States government. As noted earlier, the KGB was planning to assassinate President Johnson three days before the 1964 election to catapult segregationist Barry Goldwater into the Presidency.

Goldwater's support for segregation was well established by 1964. Recall that the *New York Times* reported on a Goldwater rally at Madison Square Garden in May 1964, stating, "The Negro choir that had been hired to sing The Battle Hymn of the Republic had to overcome a rebellion in its ranks." One singer stated, "I can't help feeling strange here tonight because I know how Senator Goldwater stands on civil rights."[422]

Another singer, who "had to sing baritone" because of "desertions," complained, "It's like singing for the Ku Klux Klan."

The KGB officers envisioned that after President Johnson's assassination and Goldwater's subsequent election to the

---

[422] NYT Article, May 13, 1964 titled, "Goldwater Fills Rally At Garden" http://www.nytimes.com/1964/05/13/goldwater-fills-rally-at-garden.html?_r=0

Presidency, they would use the long tentacles of the CIA to push the idea that "President-elect Goldwater" was a racist "madman" who conspired with his supporters to kill two U.S. Presidents in less than a year. They envisioned that the entire nation would soon be launched into violent partisan and racial turmoil with people revolting against the pro-segregation "President Barry Goldwater" and the conspiracy to seize power.

David Murphy, Chief of the CIA's Soviet Russia Division, was immediately suspicious of the Soviet propaganda.

On November 23, 1963, one day after President Kennedy's assassination, Murphy sent a cable "via closed channel" to CIA Counterintelligence Chief James Angleton on the subject of "Possible KGB Role in Kennedy Slaying."

Murphy's cable states: "Within minutes of the first news, Moscow radio statements as heard in London attributed the assassination to 'right-wing elements.' Only as the true identity of the believed assassin became known did Moscow begin to complain that U.S. reactionaries were using Oswald as a pawn.[423]

"Was Oswald, unwittingly or wittingly, part of a plot to murder President Kennedy in Dallas as an attempt to further exacerbate sectional strife and render the U.S. Government less capable of dealing with Soviet initiatives over the next year?"

Murphy also stated, "We can expect major Soviet pressures over the next several months, for which the Soviets have made careful, long-range preparations."

Official documents confirm Murphy's suspicions and his expectation of "major Soviet pressures over the next several months."

"Twelve minutes" after it was announced that President Kennedy was dead, Moscow radio carried "the first TASS bulletin on his death," stating that Kennedy "had fallen victim to rightwing extremists,"[424] and on the following day, as a veritable deluge of

---

[423] National Archives Record Number 104-10431-10078
[424] National Archives Record Number 104-10404-10067, p. 3

propaganda got under way, Moscow radio reported, "Kennedy was a victim of racist fanatics."[425]

In another Moscow radio broadcast on November 23, Soviet propagandist Valentin Zorin stated "it is quite obvious" that the assassination is "a political crime, carefully prepared and planned."[426]

Zorin noted that the assassination "took place in the southern state of Texas, which is commonly known as the stronghold of American racists . . . . It is here that Senator Goldwater, an aspirant to the Presidency and the idol of the American rightists, enjoys support."

Goldwater's name came up again the next day when *Izvestiya*, the Soviet Union's official state-run newspaper, described the "political atmosphere" when President Kennedy was assassinated "as one in which 'wild men,' such as Senator Goldwater, come out violently against coexistence with the Soviet Union," and a Communist radio broadcast stated that "the American racists" were responsible for "eliminating Kennedy."[427]

On November 25, Soviet propagandist Valentin Zorin stated that President Kennedy's policies "aroused violent criticism and fierce resistance from an influential group of die-hard politicians known as the 'madmen.'" Zorin noted Goldwater's "unbridled attacks on the policy of the late President," adding, "For many months, Goldwater maliciously attacked Kennedy and his policy, demanding its radical revision."[428]

And while Valentin Zorin was implicating Goldwater in the assassination, an article in the Soviet newspaper *Pravda* was titled, "How the 'Wild Men' Prepared the Crime in Dallas." The

---

[425] Warren Commission Document 322, p. 159
[426] Warren Commission Document 1135, p. 168
[427] National Archives Record Number 104-10302-10012, p. 9 and Warren Commission Document 322, p. 162
[428] Warren Commission Document 1135, p. 177

CIA stated that *Pravda* was adamant about "blaming the Kennedy assassination on 'right extremists.'"[429]

A United States Information Agency report revealed that Soviet "propagandists" specifically accused the "Goldwater group" of being "reactionaries" who "abetted" President Kennedy's assassination. The report also stated that "the main thrust of Soviet and East European comment and analysis" was a claim that "President John F. Kennedy was a victim of right-wing terrorists who hope to establish an 'ultra-conservative dictatorship' in America."[430]

The CIA's Daily Summary of November 25 stated that Che Guevara, who came to power with Fidel Castro in the 1959 Cuban Revolution, gave a speech in which he proclaimed, "Everything indicates that in the next months and years, world peace will be threatened by the most unscrupulous, ferocious, and warlike monopolistic oligarchy, with the most murderous potential that the history of humanity has ever known."[431]

The next day, four short days after the assassination, Soviet propaganda correlated President Kennedy's assassination to the 1964 Presidential election. The official government newspaper *Izvestiya* boldly proclaimed that an "intensified struggle" would determine "the course of the election campaign which is now developing," and it warned, "Madmen ready to play a hazardous game with the destinies of the American people, 'wild men,' Fascist racists – these are the ones who were up in arms against Kennedy. Is it not they who directed the killer's bullet into the head of the President?"[432]

A CIA report of November 26 states that Moscow warned of "rightwing 'wild men'" who would "test President Johnson's resolve to pursue present policy lines . . . . 'Rightwing ultras' are consistently blamed for the assassination . . . . Soviet media see Oswald's murder as an effort to silence him -- proof that rightwing fanatics were

---

[429] National Archives Record Number 104-10434-10335, p. 5
[430] Warren Commission Document 322, p. 109
[431] National Archives Record Number 104-10302-10021, p. 8
[432] National Archives Record Number 104-10434-10335, p. 6

behind the assassination," and the Soviet Bloc countries of Eastern Europe maintained that President Kennedy was killed because of his "championing of Negro rights."[433]

On the same day, Moscow's International Service reported, "Without a doubt, direct responsibility for the Dallas tragedy should be borne by the Ku Klux Klan and the ultra reactionary forces in the United States."[434]

Communist propaganda brought up "the unhealthy climate of right-wing extremism," and the CIA stated that "Soviet propagandists portray a sick American society beset by the cancerous growth of right-wing political extremism."[435]

As noted earlier, David Murphy, the CIA's Soviet Russia Chief, wrote that the Soviets had made "careful, long-range preparations" for the "pressures" they would exert after the assassination.

A CIA memorandum of December 13, 1963, corroborates Murphy's view, stating that "for over a year," the intention of Soviet propaganda was to portray the United States as being "in the grips of a deep social and moral crisis, with a massive rightist plot moving toward power."[436]

The Communist Party in the United States blamed the assassination on "pro-Fascists, ultra-right forces, Dixiecrats, and racists" who will "stop at nothing to undermine the democratic institutions of the country and to threaten international peace."[437]

The official Soviet news agency TASS forebodingly warned, "Kennedy's death raises a number of other questions, not the least of which is who will be elected President in 1964. Until yesterday, most felt that Kennedy was ensured re-election. Will Johnson be the Democratic candidate in 1964? Are the chances of the

---

[433] National Archives Record Number 104-10434-10064, p. 5
[434] Warren Commission Document 322, p. 156
[435] Ibid., pp. 96 & 109
[436] National Archives Record Number 104-10434-10203, p. 3
[437] National Archives Record Number 104-10434-10335, p. 3

Republicans enhanced? There is no answer yet to these questions, although the pre-election balance is apparently changing."[438]

President Johnson's assassination three days before the election would clearly change the "pre-election balance" and significantly enhance the "chances" of KGB asset Barry Goldwater. Soviet KGB officers had every intention of making sure Johnson would not be "the Democratic candidate" on election day.

Radio Moscow brought up Goldwater again on November 28, stating, "A bloody crime has been committed in the United States . . . . Who is responsible for this crime? The press throughout the world has been paying much attention to ultra rightwing groups in the United States . . . . The influential Senator Barry Goldwater is known as one of the leaders of the ultra rightwing in the United States."[439]

A CIA memorandum states that TASS filed a dispatch for Radio Moscow's "international program" on December 4, 1963, stating, "Racists and extremists killed the President." The CIA described the TASS dispatch as part of "a standard propaganda attack on 'Southern racists'" and "the Republican Party."[440]

A United States Information Agency report on December 6, 1963, states that Cuban leaders were "fearful" that President Johnson "would become the victim of 'dark and sinister' ultra-rightist forces." The report also stated that "Goldwater" is one of the names that "crop up" when Soviet media "repeatedly recall extremist opposition" to President Kennedy's "civil rights stand."[441]

"Communist propaganda organs in Eastern Europe" maintained that "the rightists, in their impotence to reverse President Kennedy's liberal policies, have now resorted to 'political terror' to gain their ends."[442]

Cuban Premier Fidel Castro gave a two-hour speech on November 23, the day after the assassination, "devoted entirely to the

---

[438] National Archives Record Number 104-10434-10335, p. 4
[439] Warren Commission Document 1135, p. 208
[440] National Archives Record Number 104-10412-10316, p. 4
[441] Warren Commission Document 322, pp. 90 & 176
[442] National Archives Record Number 104-10434-10203, p. 5

assassination . . . . Castro pictures the United States as beset by a struggle between 'moderates and ultra-reactionaries' and forecasts a stronger hand for the latter. The ultra-reactionaries, as defined by Castro, are those demanding a stronger policy against Cuba and those who opposed the test ban treaty and civil rights legislation."[443]

It was Goldwater who demanded "a stronger policy against Cuba." Goldwater "opposed the test ban treaty," and he was clearly opposed to President Kennedy's "civil rights legislation." Fidel Castro, with knowledge of the KGB's plan to assassinate President Johnson and catapult Goldwater into the Presidency, was forecasting a "stronger hand" for Goldwater.

Castro "devoted considerable time to an attempt to throw doubt on the guilt of the accused assassin and to insinuate that Oswald, whether guilty or innocent, was actually a tool of the extreme rightists," and he "declared that the assassination can only benefit 'those ultra-rightist and ultra-reactionary sectors, among which President Kennedy could not be counted.' These 'most reactionary forces are now breaking loose within the United States.'"[444]

Castro gave another speech on November 27 stating he is "determined to 'prove' the late President died at the instigation, if not by the hand of, ultra-reactionaries in the United States."[445]

With hopes that Goldwater's election to the Presidency would result in a Civil War in the United States, Radio Moscow's first "commentary" on the assassination noted President Kennedy's handling of "racial discrimination" and stated, "100 years ago rabid reactionaries killed another great American President, Abraham Lincoln."[446]

The "commentary," reminding everyone of the Civil War, was broadcast "sixty times to audiences worldwide."

---

[443] National Archives Record Number 104-10434-10064, p. 15
[444] National Archives Record Number 104-10404-10022
[445] National Archives Record Number 104-10404-10023
[446] National Archives Record Number 104-10434-10064, p. 8

On November 26, the CIA's Daily Report stated, "Soviet Commentators uniformly place the responsibility for President Kennedy's assassination on 'ultra rightwing' circles."[447]

The CIA also reported, "President Kennedy's attempts, within the limits imposed by internal opposition, to meet the demands of the Negroes and to secure legislation giving them equal rights are also recalled by the East European radios." Commentaries in Yugoslavia "hail the late President . . . . and his anti-racist domestic policies."[448]

"Havana has also broadcast to North America a speech by the extremist American Negro expatriate Robert Williams referring, in typically vituperative language, to the dangers ahead 'with racist Lyndon B. Johnson in the White House.'"[449]

Robert Williams' exact words in his speech to North America were: "With racist Lyndon B. Johnson in the White House, it becomes more expedient than ever that Afro-Americans mount an all-out drive for freedom now."[450]

The Mexican Communist Party, as quoted on Cuban Radio, stated, "The responsibility for the murder of President Kennedy falls on the shoulders of those who attacked his policies from ultra-rightist positions."[451]

On November 30, 1963, Poland's "Director General in the Ministry of Foreign Affairs," Jerzy Michalowski, wrote an article in which he brought up the last U.S. President to die in office, President Franklin Roosevelt, whose 1945 death catapulted Vice President Harry Truman into the Presidency to fill the remainder of Truman's term, after which Truman was elected to a four-year term in 1948.

Michalowski pointed out that a Presidential election would take place "in eleven months," and he stated that President Johnson will

---

[447] Ibid., p. 10
[448] Ibid., pp. 12 & 13
[449] Ibid., p. 16
[450] National Archives Record Number 104-10434-10241, p. 9
[451] National Archives Record Number 104-10441-10087, p. 22

"play the role adopted by Truman" in filling the remainder of President Kennedy's term.[452]

Michalowski then stated, "But perhaps his successor will be somebody else," meaning "somebody else" would be elected to a four-year term in 1964.

Michalowski asked if the "hot line between the White House and the Kremlin" would "remain the center of a peaceful dialogue," and he brought up "the bill on civil rights" and "three years of activity concerning laws about Negroes." Michalowski noted that Kennedy "fought boldly the racist elements in the Southern States."

Michalowski continued, "The Democrats of the South supported backwardness, racism, and violence . . . . The bullet which pierced the President's head was intended to maintain the States in medieval racial barbarism. Will it be successful?"

The "Democrats of the South" to whom Michalowski was referring were vehemently opposed to civil rights. They mounted a lengthy but unsuccessful filibuster to block the 1964 civil rights legislation, and the entirety of Michalowski's December 5, 1963, article was a clear warning that a segregationist-oriented rightwing faction would seize power in the 1964 election.

In addition to Michalowski's article, "Numerous articles are appearing in the press on the 'unanswered questions' regarding the assassination and on the activities and organization of extreme right wing elements in the United States."[453]

A United States Information Agency report on December 6, 1963, stated, "The alleged plots now are seen everywhere as racist and rightist,"[454] and on the same day, "The Soviet Union charged today that President Kennedy was 'eliminated' by rightwing

---

[452] National Archives Record Number 104-10404-10018, pp. 4-6
[453] National Archives Record Number 104-10404-10019, p. 6
[454] National Archives Record Number 104-10404-10242

extremists to change the balance of political forces in the United States."455

On December 9, "Moscow TASS International Services in English" stated that there is an "atmosphere of hatred, violence, and lawlessness reigning in the Southern States of America."456

The TASS broadcast pointedly stated, "The circumstances of the murder show that the late President fell victim to racists and rightwing extremists," and "many Republicans" are "sympathetic toward the Southern racists . . . . These Republicans are striving to relieve the racists and rightwing extremists of responsibility for the death of President Kennedy." (Five Southern Democratic States that supported segregation went to Republican Barry Goldwater in the 1964 election, the only five states that Goldwater won besides his home state of Arizona.)

A CIA report on December 11, 1963, stated that a Soviet official voiced "widely held views" that "the only ones who could profit by this act are the extreme reactionary forces," and the official added, "We are prepared for a status quo in the international situation, at least until after the Presidential election in the US."457

With the objective of assassinating President Johnson three days before the election to get ultra conservative, pro-segregation Barry Goldwater elected to the Presidency, the Soviet Union and its allies could not help but bring up the 1964 Presidential election and correlate it to "racists and rightwing extremists" killing President Kennedy.

Soviet news organizations proclaimed that "racists" were "accomplices in Kennedy's murder" and that they hoped to "do away with the Constitution and democracy and replace them with a 'dictatorship of strongmen.'"458

---

[455] Warren Commission Document 1135, p. 64
[456] National Archives Record Number 104-10404-10252
[457] National Archives Record Number 104-10404-10240, pp. 3-4
[458] Warren Commission Document 322, p. 111

The Soviet news organizations also stated that President Kennedy's "stand on civil rights" was of "particular concern to the reactionary groups," and it "infuriated the diehards."[459]

A CIA report on February 13, 1964, almost three months after the assassination, stated that the Soviets "maintained firmly" that there was "a large scale right-extremist plot."[460]

The U.S. Embassy in Moscow sent a telegram to Secretary of State Dean Rusk on March 18, 1964, four months after the assassination, stating, "Soviet press has consistently used every means in an attempt to demonstrate that Kennedy assassination perpetrated by rightwing plot . . . . Embassy believes Soviets will continue to play up 'plot' theory."[461]

One week later, on March 25, 1964, CIA Deputy Director for Plans Richard Helms wrote: "The most widely circulated rumor about Oswald holds that he was in some way enmeshed in an assassination plot engineered by right-wing extremists in the United States . . . . It is now clear that the Soviet Union played a major role in fostering the rumor and in deliberately keeping it alive . . . . Communism's propagandists have kept up a drum fire of allegations that the assassination was the work of the extreme right-wing in this country."[462]

The Soviet Union could not have been more blatant in their four-month campaign of accusing Barry Goldwater, racists, and the extreme right-wing of assassinating President Kennedy, and the United States Embassy in Moscow clearly stated that the Soviets "will continue to play up 'plot' theory."

The CIA reported that Soviet Premier Nikita Khrushchev engaged in a "45-minute conversation" with a journalist on May 24, 1964, six months after the assassination. Khrushchev told the journalist that there was "some kind of conspiracy to assassinate

---

[459] Warren Commission Document 1135, p. 117
[460] National Archives Record Number 104-10434-10335, p. 12
[461] National Archives Record Number 104-10404-10015
[462] National Archives Record Number 104-10412-10337, pp. 3-4 & 16

President Kennedy." and Khrushchev put forth "some dark thoughts about the American Right Wing being behind this conspiracy."[463]

On September 23, 1964, one day before the Warren Commission released its report, Moscow's *New Times* stated that the Warren Report "will adhere to the FBI-police version that Kennedy was murdered by a lone operator, Lee Oswald, for no rational reason . . . . Most Europeans and many politically oriented Americans believe otherwise. They suspect Kennedy was the victim of a rightist political plot."[464]

Thirty-eight days after Moscow's *New Times* claimed that President Kennedy had fallen prey to "a rightist political plot," the KGB officers who killed Kennedy were planning to make President Johnson "the victim" of another supposedly "rightist political plot."

Exactly five weeks before the 1964 election, an article in the Soviet Bloc country of Czechoslovakia on September 29 stated that "the lawyer" that the Warren Commission appointed to represent Oswald is "a leader of the Goldwater movement" and had "attended only one hearing of the Commission . . . . Two members of the Commission are Southern racists who support Goldwater."[465]

Senator Richard Russell of Georgia and Congressman Hale Boggs of Louisiana, both of whom were on the Warren Commission, were Southern Democrats from segregationist states that went to Goldwater in 1964.

Senator Russell led the "Southern Bloc" of Senators that filibustered the 1964 Civil Rights Act,[466] stating on March 30, 1964, "We will resist to the bitter end any measure or any movement which would have a tendency to bring about social equality and intermingling and amalgamation of the races in our states."[467]

---

[463] National Archives Record Number 104-10408-10068, p. 3
[464] National Archives Record Number 104-10412-10147, p. 10
[465] Ibid., p. 13
[466] http://www.dirksencenter.org/print_basics_histmats_civilrights64_contents.htm#senate
[467] http://www.latimes.com/nation/la-oe-civil-rights-quotes-20140629-story.html

On October 2, Bulgarian commentators proclaimed, "The madmen in the U.S. are making an open bid for power."[468]

On October 8, as the countdown continued twenty-three days before President Johnson's scheduled assassination, the United States Embassy in Warsaw, Poland sent information to the U.S. State Department about an "anti-U.S. propaganda theme" that was "heard in many countries in Europe and elsewhere" in which the propaganda harped on the question, "Who killed President Kennedy?"[469]

The Embassy also sent articles from several Communist news agencies, one of which stated, "It is known what circles in the U.S. hated Kennedy due to his realistic foreign policy as well as his internal policy, above all with regard to civil rights for the Negroes."[470]

What the article was really saying is: "Everyone knows that Senator Barry Goldwater, the Republican who has strong support among the segregationist Southern Democrats, hated President Kennedy's foreign policy as well as his internal policy, 'above all with regard to civil rights for the Negroes.'"

The KGB capped off their propaganda campaign with another reminder of the Civil War. An October 1964 article stated that when Abraham Lincoln was assassinated in 1865, it was "on the orders of the then reactionaries from the Southern States who were against the liberation of the Negroes."[471]

If the KGB officers had succeeded in killing President Johnson to catapult Goldwater into the Presidency, the KGB's "covert propaganda campaigns" would have shifted into overdrive with a renewed and intensified campaign that would forcefully tell the American public that "President Goldwater" is a die-hard racist

---

[468] National Archives Record Number 104-10322-10079, p. 20
[469] National Archives Record Number 104-10404-10008, p. 2
[470] National Archives Record Number 104-10404-10008, p. 6
[471] National Archives Record Number 104-10404-10008, p. 8

"madman" who conspired with his supporters to assassinate two American Presidents in less than a year.

In Fidel Castro's speech on November 23, 1963, he asked, "What is behind all this? What sinister maneuver are they hatching behind all this? Who can be responsible for the assassination of President Kennedy? And who benefits from the assassination?"[472]

The CIA's Office of Current Intelligence stated, "Castro warned that it is not possible at this point to answer these questions."[473]

But Castro would have "answers" when President Johnson was assassinated and Barry Goldwater was elected to the Presidency. The purported fear of Cuban leaders that Johnson "would become the victim of 'dark and sinister' ultra-rightist forces" would seemingly be realized, and Castro would seemingly have his "proof" that Presidents Kennedy and Johnson "died at the instigation, if not by the hand of, ultra-reactionaries in the United States."

Soviet propagandists would proclaim that Goldwater and his supporters have again "resorted to 'political terror' to gain their ends," and they would remind the American people that President Kennedy "was a victim of right-wing terrorists who hope to establish an 'ultra-conservative dictatorship' in America."

A worldwide propaganda campaign would discredit the United States with the same message, and "the alleged plots" would once again be "seen everywhere as racist and rightist."[474]

In his November 23 cable with the subject line "Possible KGB Role in Kennedy Slaying," David Murphy, Chief of the CIA's Soviet Russia Division, put forth the possibility that President Kennedy's assassination could be "an attempt to further exacerbate sectional strife."[475]

---

[472] National Archives Record Number 104-10302-10021, p. 7
[473] National Archives Record Number 104-10404-10022, p. 3
[474] National Archives Record Number 104-10404-10242
[475] National Archives Record Number 104-10431-10078

The "sectional strife" would have been cataclysmic in the wake of President Johnson's assassination and Barry Goldwater's election to the Presidency.

But the KGB's plan to use a Goldwater Presidency to discredit the United States and incite the masses came to a screeching halt when they failed to assassinate President Johnson.

The Suffolk County Police, as noted in Chapter 2, foiled President Johnson's assassination when they discovered the KGB's intended patsy, Robert Babcock, sitting along President Johnson's motorcade route with a telescopic rifle on the seat beside him and a loaded shotgun in the trunk.

As will be seen in Goldwater's testimony examined later in this chapter, the KGB had total control over him and included him in their plans to kill Members of Congress and plans to assassinate President Johnson.

KGB officers inside the CIA had nothing to fear from their fellow CIA officer and his ostensibly "anti-Communist" views. Goldwater's supposed "conservatism" was, in fact, a fabricated part of his "nonofficial cover" as a U.S. Senator.

On the day President Kennedy was assassinated, the CIA intercepted a phone call to the Cuban Embassy in Mexico City, and in the call, it is evident that an "unidentified man" and a Cuban intelligence officer named Luisa Calderon knew about plans to assassinate President Kennedy. It is also evident that the "unidentified man" knew about the long-term objective of promoting racial conflict in the United States.

In discussing the assassination and the subsequent arrest of Oswald, the unidentified man told Luisa Calderon, "The reason, let's say it may be that they are trying to find out something about that fellow because . . . ."[476]

Whereupon he was interrupted by Calderon, who stated, "Wait a minute. Can you tell me?"

---

[476] National Archives Record Number 104-10404-10426, p. 36

The unidentified man replied, "We thought it had been, or if by chance looked like to the public, that it was a segregationist or in opposition to integration that had assassinated Kennedy, then let's say there might even be a Civil War in the United States. Let's say that given time, and more contradictions, the critical situation that has happened in that country, than we were talking here . . . . They will find a resolution to that fellow, no?"

When Luisa Calderon interrupted the unidentified man and asked, "Can you tell me," she was clearly aware that he knew something that she did not know. And his reply is evidence he knew, "Given time . . . there might even be a Civil War in the United States."

The unidentified man may or may not have known about the plans to assassinate President Johnson right before the 1964 election, but he obviously knew about the hope that if it "looked like to the public" that someone "in opposition to integration" was behind President Kennedy's assassination, it could lead to a "Civil War in the United States."

Oswald being a left-winger was apparently one of the "contradictions" to which the unidentified man was referring, as it would make no sense that Oswald, a supposed Communist sympathizer, would assassinate a liberal President so that Vice President Lyndon Johnson, a Southern conservative from Texas, would become President. On November 22, 1963, the unidentified man was expecting that "given time," there would be "more contradictions."

Even more important, the CIA transcript of the conversation shows that both Luisa Calderon and the unidentified man had definitive foreknowledge of President Kennedy's assassination. The transcript states that when the conversation began, the unidentified man "calls Luisa" and "asks if she knows the latest news."[477]

Calderon responds by saying, "Yes, of course. I knew about it before Kennedy."

---

[477] National Archives Record Number 104-10404-10426, p. 35

The unidentified man then "laughs and comments that that is very bad."

In 1975, the CIA claimed that Luisa Calderon did not say that she "knew about it before Kennedy." The CIA alleged that a correct translation of her words would be, "I heard about the shooting of Kennedy almost at the time the event took place."[478]

But if Luisa Calderon actually said that she "heard about the shooting of Kennedy almost at the time the event took place," it would make no sense that the unidentified man would then "laugh and comment that that is very bad."

What's more, Calderon interrupted the "unidentified man" to ask if he could tell her the reason for President Kennedy's assassination, not to mention that CIA translators most certainly knew how to translate Spanish into English in 1963.

The CIA's 1975 claim that Luisa Calderon's words were mistranslated is obviously a cover story, and as this book makes clear, "cover stories" are standard operating procedure in the CIA.

Most interesting, Cuban Premier Fidel Castro was interviewed at the Brazilian Embassy in Cuba on September 7, 1963, two and a half months before President Kennedy was assassinated, and Castro declared, "United States leaders should think that if they are aiding terrorist plans to eliminate Cuban leaders, they themselves will not be safe."[479] (The CIA supported Cuban exiles in their plans to overthrow the Castro government in 1963.)

The reporter who conducted the interview was Daniel Harker, and his article was headlined, "Goldwater 'Toughness' Challenged By Castro."

Harker wrote that besides threatening the safety of U.S. leaders, Castro said, "We have heard that Goldwater is tough . . . . Well, if he is elected let him try his tough policies on Cuba. We know how to defend ourselves and we will not be afraid to face him."

---

[478] House Select Committee on Assassinations, Volume XI, p. 494
[479] National Archives Record Number 104-10422-10028, pp. 3 & 4

Harker then wrote, "At this point, Mr. Castro ended his discussion of the Presidential election, saying he was not interested in getting involved in United States politics."

Two and a half months before President Kennedy's assassination, Cuban Premier Fidel Castro clearly warned that current U.S. leaders "will not be safe," and in referring to Barry Goldwater, Castro used the words "if he is elected."

The dichotomy in Castro's words is astounding. He never said anything about Goldwater not being safe "if he is elected." Castro warned only that current U.S. leaders "will not be safe," even though Goldwater's anti-Castro rhetoric went well beyond that of President Kennedy.

Castro likewise never said anything about knowing "how to defend ourselves" in the face of current "tough policies on Cuba" or about being "afraid to face" current U.S. leaders. He flat out said that current U.S. leaders "will not be safe" and that Cuba will not be "afraid to face" Goldwater.

As for Castro's statement that he "was not interested in getting involved in United States politics," the CIA documented that Soviet diplomats and "numerous Soviet Bloc diplomats" were definitely interested in getting involved in U.S. politics when Goldwater announced his candidacy in January 1964.

Soviet Bloc diplomats characterized Goldwater as a "fascist," and one of the diplomats stated there was a "secret army of the right in the United States with ramifications into the Pentagon that would seize power someday."[480]

In 1984, Senator Barry Goldwater testified before a closed-door session of the House of Representatives that he was in the CIA and that he was well acquainted with CIA officers who had been exposed as KGB officers. Three specific KGB officers with whom he was well acquainted were John McCone, Director of the CIA from 1961 to 1965; Tony Chavez, the head of domestic operations for a number of

---

[480] National Archives Record Number 104-10308-10008, p. 5

years until the KGB infiltration was exposed in 1984; and Vincent Puritano, head of the CIA's domestic operations in the early 1960s.

At another point in 1984, Goldwater again testified under oath while the only people in the room were his trusted CIA colleagues and me. In an extremely defiant and bellicose tone, Goldwater stated that the CIA officers who were ultimately exposed as KGB officers let him know that plans were in the works to assassinate President Kennedy. He stated that after the assassination, they not only made him aware that they were behind it, but also informed him of their intention to assassinate President Johnson right before the election to bring about a Goldwater victory in 1964.

Goldwater stated that he was expecting President Johnson to be assassinated on Saturday, October 31, 1964 as part of the plan to get him elected to the Presidency on Tuesday, November 3.

Never expecting his statements to see the light of day and obviously thinking no one would ever believe he said these things, Goldwater boldly admitted that the KGB officers let him know they had plans to kill Congressman Henderson Lanham in 1957. Goldwater testified that he knew beforehand of definitive plans to kill each of the other twelve Members of Congress who died at the hands of the KGB, just like he knew beforehand of definitive plans to assassinate President Johnson.

He also testified that he knew beforehand of plans to assassinate Presidents Nixon, Ford, and Reagan.

In analyzing Goldwater's words, it seemed like a pep talk for his corrupt CIA colleagues, who were bent on carrying on with the objective of controlling the government. As cited in Chapter 1, Goldwater said the CIA should be allowed to keep "domestic subversives" in the United States under surveillance.[481] Goldwater's hypocrisy in that statement is unfathomable.

A railroad employee who worked in a tower near the Texas School Book Depository when President Kennedy was assassinated submitted a sworn affidavit to the Dallas Police

---

[481] New York Times, 12-28-74, p. 8

Department stating that, at about 11:55 a.m. on November 22, 1963, he observed a car that "had a Goldwater for '64' sticker in the rear window" coming down a street that dead ends in the railroad yard. The car "just drove around slowly and left the area," after which another car came into the area at about 12:15 p.m. and the man in the car "appeared to have a mike or telephone."[482]

A few minutes after the second car left, another car with a "Goldwater for '64' sticker" pulled into the area and stayed "longer than the others." It left at about 12:25 p.m. and a few minutes later, the railroad employee "heard at least three shots very close together," which was obviously the sound of President Kennedy being assassinated.

---

[482] https://texashistory.unt.edu/ark:/67531/metapth339624/ Dallas Municipal Archives, University of North Texas, President John F. Kennedy / Dallas Police Dept. Collection

Chapter 10: The KGB, the CIA, & Oswald's Feigned Defection to Russia

President Kennedy's accused assassin, Lee Harvey Oswald, was killed while in Dallas Police custody less than forty-eight hours after the assassination.

Oswald was alleged to be a Communist sympathizer who defected to Russia, but a CIA document titled "Excerpts From Unpublished Writings of Lee Harvey Oswald" quotes Oswald as having written, "When I first went to Russia in the winter of 1959 my funds were very limited, so after a certain time, after the Russians had assured themselves that I was really the naive American who believed in Communism, they arranged for me to receive a certain amount of money every month . . . . It was arranged by the MVD [Russian Ministry of Internal Affairs] . . . . It really was payment for my denunciation of the US in Moscow in November 1959."[483]

A CIA memo from March 1964 refers to Oswald's writings and states, "In his writings, Oswald is highly critical of Soviet rigged elections, the massing of crowds for staged demonstrations, travel restrictions, regimentation, and the lack of freedom of press, speech, and religion."[484]

On November 29, 1963, the CIA sent a message to the White House stating that while Oswald was enroute to the Soviet Union, he "passed through Sweden during October 1959" and was

---

[483] National Archives Record Number 104-10408-10104, p. 3
[484] National Archives Record Number 104-10439-10009, p. 15

"unsuccessful in obtaining a visa to the USSR in Helsinki, which resulted in his returning to Stockholm."

The CIA message also stated, "Two days after he arrived in Stockholm, Oswald traveled directly to Moscow . . . . There was no record that there was any request for a USSR visa processed through normal channels for Oswald at any time during 1959 . . . . It was difficult to explain how Oswald might have received his visa in two days without going through normal channels."[485]

The CIA sent out a cable in July 1964, stating that Headquarters "wants to know minimum time required to obtain Soviet tourist visa."[486]

The response in a CIA cable three days later states, "Normal visa processing takes seven days, which can be shortened 'in exceptional cases' to five days. Impossible in two or three days."[487]

A CIA document pertaining to CIA "Operations" dated September 19, 1961, less than two years after Oswald went to the Soviet Union, defines an agent as: "A person who acts in our behalf, at our instigation and in consonance with our direction."[488]

As for Oswald being "a person who acts in our behalf, at our instigation and in consonance with our direction," Oswald's Marine Corps record shows that on February 25, 1959, he was tested on his Russian language "comprehension" skills, including his ability to "understand" Russian, his ability to "read" Russian, and his ability to "write" in Russian.[489]

On August 17, 1959, less than six months after being tested on his Russian language skills, Lee Harvey Oswald "submitted a request for a 'dependency' discharge from the Marine Corps." The alleged reason for the "dependency discharge" was the "hardship of his mother."[490]

---

[485] National Archives Record Number 104-10408-10061, p. 6
[486] National Archives Record Numbers 104-10437-10048
[487] National Archives Record Numbers 104-10437-10049
[488] National Archives Record Number 104-10408-10241, p. 5
[489] Warren Commission Hearings and Exhibits, Volume XIX, p. 746
[490] National Archives Record Number 104-10009-10078, p. 15

After submitting his request, Oswald first "appeared before the Hardship/Dependency discharge board," which "recommended that he be released from active duty for reason of dependency," and his discharge from the Marines was approved on August 31, two weeks after Oswald submitted his request.[491]

Two days after Oswald's discharge was approved, a CIA memorandum addressed the "legal travel operations into the USSR," stating that the CIA's Soviet Russia Division "will conduct all legal travel operations involving the use of U.S. citizens."[492]

On September 4, Oswald applied for a passport. His application states that the countries to which he would be traveling included France, England, Finland, and Russia.[493]

Then, on September 11, 1959, one week after applying for a passport, Oswald was officially released from "active duty" in the Marines, whereupon he was transferred into the Marine Corps Reserve with obligated service until December 8, 1962. He then went to Fort Worth, Texas, where he visited with his mother for "approximately three days" and told her that he would like to "travel abroad," after which he went to New Orleans.[494]

On September 16, five days after his release from active duty in the Marines due to the alleged "hardship of his mother," Oswald paid $215 to travel to France aboard the SS Marion Lykes, a "passenger-carrying freighter." He boarded the ship on September 19 and "wrote his mother that he had booked passage for Europe."[495]

The ship set sail on September 20, 1959, and Oswald arrived in France on October 6. He subsequently departed for England the same day, arriving in England on October 9. The next day, he boarded a flight that would take him to Helsinki where, as previously noted, he was unsuccessful in obtaining a Soviet visa,

---

[491] Warren Commission Hearings and Exhibits, Volume XVII, p. 664
[492] National Archives Record Number 104-10310-10192, pp. 2 & 3
[493] National Archives Record Number 104-10009-10078, pp. 16-18
[494] Warren Commission Document 321, pp. 12 & 14
[495] Warren Commission Document 818, pp. 10-11

after which he went to Stockholm and waited two days for a Soviet visa, even though "there was no record that there was any request for a USSR visa processed through normal channels for Oswald at any time during 1959."[496]

The only explanation for Oswald getting a visa "without going through normal channels" and getting it in "two days" is that the CIA created one for him. A 1961 CIA document states that the CIA Deputy Director of Operations "is authorized to suspend procedures" when "operational and security aspects of an agent's management are so sensitive as to require processing through special channels." The document also states that one of the "basic requirements" in a "secure operation" is "to keep to an operational minimum the number of persons aware of the true aims of the operation."[497]

Oswald's fabricated visa, for which there was "no record" of a request, lists "Helsinki" as the place where it was issued, and the "signature" of the person issuing the visa is "illegible."[498]

On October 16, eight months after the Marine Corps tested Oswald on his Russian language "comprehension" skills and forty-four days after the CIA memorandum about "legal travel operations into the USSR," Oswald arrived in Moscow, where "he was handled" by "a KGB agent."[499]

A CIA paper dealing with the alleged defection states, "All such defectors would be interrogated by the KGB" and "surrounded by KGB informants wherever they re-settled in the USSR."[500]

Fifteen days after arriving in the Union of Soviet Socialist Republics, Oswald went to the U.S. Embassy in Moscow and claimed that he was renouncing his American citizenship, stating afterward, "I will never return to the United States for any reason."[501]

---

[496] National Archives Record Numbers 104-10009-10078, pp. 21-24 & 104-10408-10061, p. 6
[497] National Archives Record Number 104-10408-10241, pp. 3, 4, & 11
[498] Warren Commission Hearings and Exhibits, Volume XVIII, p. 164
[499] National Archives Record Number 104-10310-10121, p. 4
[500] National Archives Record Number 104-10019-10021, p. 7
[501] Warren Commission Document 692, p. 122

The Embassy reported that Oswald "was aggressive, arrogant, and uncooperative," and in response to his alleged desire to renounce his citizenship, the Embassy "advised Oswald by mail of his right to renounce citizenship, such renunciation in manner prescribed by law being valid, and that he might appear on any normal business day and request documents be prepared."[502]

But Oswald never went back to do the paperwork, and a U.S. State Department memo in December 1961 states that Oswald "did not, in fact, renounce United States citizenship . . . . Mr. Oswald did not expatriate himself and remains a citizen of the United States."[503]

Eleven months before the State Department memo, Oswald wrote a letter to the Secretary of the Navy due to receiving an undesirable discharge for traveling to the Soviet Union. A short fifteen months after the alleged attempt to renounce his citizenship, Oswald told the Secretary of the Navy that he is "still a U.S. citizen" and "had gone to the Soviet Union to reside only for a 'short time.'"[504]

Oswald also wrote a letter to a Marine Corps General on March 22, 1962, stating, "I have never taken steps to renounce my U.S. citizenship . . . . I refer you to the United States Embassy, Moscow, or the U.S. Department of State, Washington, D.C., for the verification of this fact."[505]

According to the State Department officer who dealt with Oswald during the phony attempt to renounce his citizenship, Oswald appeared to have been "tutored in connection with his apparent attempts to renounce his American citizenship," and Oswald's trip to the Soviet Union was suspiciously a "competently arranged trip."[506]

---

[502] Warren Commission Document 363, pp. 71-72
[503] Ibid., p. 70
[504] National Archives Record Number 104-10322-10044, p. 4
[505] Ibid., p. 8
[506] Warren Commission Document 843, pp. 1, 4, & 5

The State Department officer also reported, "Oswald evidently knew something of the procedure for renunciation of citizenship when he came into the office. This seemed a bit unusual since it was so soon after his first departure from the United States on his first trip abroad traveling as a private citizen."

The Warren Commission told CIA officials in March 1964, "The letters Lee Oswald wrote to the American Embassy in Moscow while he was trying to get permission for himself and his wife Marina to return to the United States might have been 'coached.'"[507]

A Warren Commission staff member told the CIA officials that "these letters reflected a higher degree of sophistication and knowledge of passport procedures than would be expected of a man of Lee Harvey Oswald's known character."

The FBI documented that an Associated Press reporter spoke with Oswald at his hotel soon after his claim that he wanted to "relinquish his United States citizenship and remain in Russia." The reporter "engaged him in a conversation" and "asked Oswald why he was going to remain in Russia."[508]

The FBI report states, "Oswald replied, 'I've got my reasons,' but did not elucidate."

On June 18, 1962, five days after he returned from Russia, Oswald had Pauline Bates, a stenographer in Fort Worth, Texas, type up notes that he made while in Russia.

Pauline Bates testified to the Warren Commission that the notes, both typed and handwritten, were in Russian and that Oswald spent three days translating them for her. She also stated that she was "anxious to get on it" because Oswald "had just come back from Russia and had notes" and it was a "real interesting job."[509]

She told the Warren Commission, "I started asking him some questions – 'Why did you go to Russia?' - and a few things like that. Some of them he'd answer and some of them he wouldn't . . . . He

---

[507] National Archives Record Number 104-10422-10284, pp. 2 & 8
[508] Warren Commission Hearings and Exhibits, Volume XXVI, p. 99
[509] Warren Commission Hearings and Exhibits, Volume VIII, pp. 341-343

wasn't very talkative. And whenever I did get him to talk, I had to drag it out of him. He didn't talk voluntarily."

The information that Pauline Bates "dragged" out of Oswald included the fact that he would "scribble notes" while in Russia "whenever he could" and then "surreptitiously" type them when "Marina would cover for him . . . muffle the tone of the typewriter and everything . . . . He said she would cover or watch for him so that nobody would know that he was making them . . . try to steer anybody away while he was doing this, because he could have got in trouble."

She testified that the notes were "about the living conditions and the working conditions in Russia. And they were very bitter against Russia . . . . It was the terrible living conditions and the terrible working conditions . . . . The notes were very, very bitter about Russia.

"He smuggled them out of Russia. And he said that the whole time until they got over the border, they were scared to death they would be found, and, of course, they would not be allowed to leave Russia."

Oswald also told Pauline Bates that while he was in the Marine Corps, he "had taken elementary Russian - a course in elementary Russian." As noted earlier, six and a half months before he left on a "passenger-carrying freighter" with Russia as his ultimate destination, the Marines tested Oswald on his ability to understand Russian, read Russian, and write in Russian.

The FBI reported that when they interviewed Oswald on June 26, 1962, thirteen days after he returned to the United States, "Oswald declined to answer the question as to why he made the trip to Russia in the first place" and stated he "would not be willing to take a polygraph test."[510]

Oswald was put on the CIA's Counterintelligence "Watch List" on November 9, 1959, nine days after he told U.S. embassy

---

[510] National Archives Record Number 104-10322-10044, p. 13 and FBI Oswald Mexico City File (105-3702) - 1980 release, File No. 105-3702, section 1, p. 18

officials that he was renouncing his American citizenship and would "never return to the United States for any reason."

The card with Oswald's name on it simply states, "Recent defector to the USSR, Former Marine," but it is also stamped "Secret: Eyes Only,"[511] which means it was of the highest restriction when it comes to who sees it, and anyone who sees it knows they are not supposed to ask any questions about Lee Harvey Oswald.

Very few people were supposed to know that Oswald was acting on behalf of the CIA in his feigned defection to Russia. In an executive session of the Warren Commission on January 27, 1964, Congressman Hale Boggs asked former CIA Director Allen Dulles, "Did you have agents about whom you had no record whatsoever?"[512]

Dulles replied, "The record might not be on paper," adding that if anything were "on paper," it "would have hieroglyphics that only two people knew what they meant, and nobody outside of the Agency would know."

A full two weeks prior to President Kennedy's assassination, the upper echelons of the U.S. intelligence community were focused on Oswald.

On November 8, 1963, FBI Director J. Edgar Hoover sent a letter to the CIA Deputy Director for Plans, Richard Helms, with fourteen pages of information on Oswald, the "Fair Play for Cuba Committee" that Oswald joined in 1963, and on a group of anti-Castro Cubans with whom Oswald had a confrontation while passing out pro-Castro leaflets on August 9, 1963.[513]

Hoover's information said that the FBI had interviewed Oswald "at his request" in the "First District Police Station" in New Orleans on August 10, 1963, the day after he was arrested for scuffling with anti-Castro Cubans. While speaking with the FBI, Oswald expounded on a man named "Hidell," who, according to Oswald, had enlisted him to pass out the pro-Castro leaflets.

---

[511] National Archives Record Number 104-10406-10112, p. 140
[512] Warren Commission Executive Session, Jan. 27, 1964, p. 152
[513] National Archives Record Number 104-10406-10096, pp. 4 & 8-10

Oswald also told the FBI that he received two membership cards from the Fair Play for Cuba Committee. He received the first card, which had been signed by the Executive Secretary Vincent Lee, in late May 1963, and then "a short time later," Oswald received a membership card "signed A. J. Hidell" that "made him a member of the New Orleans chapter."

The FBI report on the interview states, "Oswald had in his possession both cards and exhibited both of them . . . . He said that he had spoken with Hidell on the telephone on several occasions . . . . He said that he has never personally met Hidell."

Oswald stated that he distributed the pro-Castro leaflets, which led to the scuffle and his arrest, because he "received a note through the mail from Hidell" requesting that he do so. The pro-Castro leaflets "bore the name of A. J. Hidell" and a "nonexistent" Post Office Box.

The CIA's "Counterintelligence staff" first handled Hoover's information, after which it went to the CIA's "Special Activities Staff." And on the day of President Kennedy's assassination, Hoover's information on how Oswald openly talked about being handled by someone named Hidell was being "processed" by the CIA's "Special Investigations Office."[514]

An FBI report states that when Oswald was arrested on November 22, 1963, both membership cards from the Fair Play for Cuba Committee were among "the articles contained in the wallet of Lee Harvey Oswald at the time of his arrest." One card was issued to L. H. Oswald and "signed A. J. Hidell, chapter president," and the other card was "signed V. T. Lee, Executive Secretary."[515]

The name Hidell is also associated with the rifle allegedly used to shoot President Kennedy. It was purchased through the mail from Klein's Sporting Goods in Chicago under the name "A.

---

[514] National Archives Record Number 104-10406-10095, p. 7
[515] Warren Commission Hearings and Exhibits, Volume XXIV, p. 17

Hidell" in March 1963 and sent to "A. Hidell" at Post Office Box 2915 in Dallas, where Oswald received his mail.[516]

A CIA report states that when Oswald was arrested after the assassination, he was also in possession of two United States "selective service cards," both of which were "phony." One had the name "Lee Harvey Oswald" and the other had the name "Alek J. Hidell."[517]

The CIA report also states, "As is well known, the Soviets are adept at issuing fake documentation." (The CIA, of course, is equally adept at issuing fake documentation.)

The Secret Service did a detailed examination of the phony "Hidell" selective service card and a Marine Corps "Certificate of Service" that had been "issued to Alek James Hidell."

A Treasury Department report states that they were each made by taking "photographs" of the front and back of an "original card," after which the two photographs were "glued together to simulate an original card."[518]

The report states, "The original card bore a name and other information, which insertions were selectively removed or prevented from showing in the photographs either by retouching or masking." It also states that the "operations" necessary to produce the phony cards had to be performed on either "the photographic negative" or on a "print" from the negative, or on "both negative and print in order to achieve a final print which simulated an original blank form."

Since the assassination of President Kennedy and the subsequent killing of Oswald, the official position has been that the name Hidell is an alias that Oswald was using. But a CIA cable on November 24, 1963, stated that the FBI "had not established as of 12 noon on November 23 whether Hidell exists" or whether Hidell is an "alias

---

[516] National Archives Record Number 104-10408-10007, p. 43
[517] National Archives Record Number 104-10439-10009 p. 5
[518] National Archives Record Number 124-10369-10062, pp. 200-201

used by Oswald."⁵¹⁹ (The FBI obviously did not consider the possibility that Oswald's CIA handler used the name Hidell as an alias.)

If "A. J. Hidell" was an alias that Oswald was using, then why did Oswald "request" an interview with the FBI after his arrest in August and expound to the FBI on who "A. J. Hidell" is?

Further, why did Oswald display to the FBI the two different membership cards from the Fair Play for Cuba Committee?

The FBI agent to whom Oswald spoke during the August interview testified to the Warren Commission that Oswald never disclosed "why he had requested the interview."⁵²⁰

If it was Oswald's idea to print up and distribute pro-Castro leaflets, why did they have a "nonexistent" Post Office Box instead of the Post Office Box where Oswald received his mail?

Where would Oswald obtain "fake documentation" in the form of two official looking, government-issued selective service cards, both of which the FBI determined were "phony?"

Where would Oswald obtain a phony Certificate of Service in the Marine Corps with the name Hidell on it, and where would he get the "original card" needed to create it?

Why did FBI Director J. Edgar Hoover send fourteen pages of information on Oswald, the Fair Play for Cuba Committee, and anti-Castro Cubans to CIA Deputy Director for Plans Richard Helms two weeks before President Kennedy's assassination, and why was it handled by the CIA's "Counterintelligence staff," the CIA's "Special Activities Staff," and the CIA's "Special Investigations Office?"

This communication at the highest levels of the U.S. intelligence community two weeks before the assassination had to have a reason. Oswald most definitely had a connection to the CIA, regardless of the fact that CIA Director and KGB officer John

---

⁵¹⁹ National Archives Record Number 104-10400-10295
⁵²⁰ Warren Commission Hearings and Exhibits, Volume IV, p. 435

McCone would later testify to the Warren Commission that Oswald had absolutely no association whatsoever with the CIA.

When Oswald was being interrogated shortly before he was killed on November 24, 1963, he told Secret Service Inspector Thomas J. Kelley that he had received "a letter signed by Alex Hidell" after he wrote to the Fair Play for Cuba Committee headquarters in New York.[521]

Again, if the name Hidell was an alias that Oswald was using, and Oswald had just shot the President of the United States with a rifle purchased under the name Hidell, why would Oswald expound on the name "Hidell" when talking to a Secret Service agent, which is exactly what he did when he talked to the FBI three months earlier?

As for McCone's denial that Oswald had anything to do with the CIA, McCone was forewarned of exactly what he would be expected to say during his testimony.

On May 12, 1964, two days before his testimony, the Warren Commission's General Counsel, Lee Rankin, called McCone and said in part, "All they want to deal with is the question of your knowledge about Oswald being an agent or informer or anything of that character . . . . This testimony is going to be made public. I thought you might want to keep that in mind."[522]

When McCone testified about Oswald, his exact words to the Warren Commission were, "The Agency never contacted him, interviewed him, talked with him, or received or solicited any reports or information from him, or communicated with him directly or in any other manner."[523]

But on November 6, 1961, Robert Amory, the CIA's Deputy Director of Intelligence, sent a memorandum to the CIA Deputy Director for Plans on the subject of "Positive Intelligence Exploitation of Former Residents of the USSR."[524]

---

[521] Warren Commission Hearings and Exhibits, Volume XX, p. 443
[522] National Archives Record Number 104-10408-10102
[523] Warren Commission Hearings and Exhibits, Volume V, p. 120
[524] National Archives Record Number 104-10310-10194

Amory's purpose in sending the memorandum was to "reaffirm my strong interest in the positive intelligence exploitation of former residents of the USSR."

The Deputy Director wrote that the intelligence exploitation "requires screening the places of residence of as many former Soviet residents as possible," which makes it obvious that it would have been CIA policy to contact both Lee Harvey Oswald and his wife.

Richard Helms, upon taking over as Deputy Director for Plans in February 1962, immediately replied to Amory. Four months before Oswald would return to the United States with his Soviet wife after his two-and-a-half-year sojourn in Russia, Helms acknowledged the "continued interest" in the "intelligence exploitation of repatriates and other former residents of the USSR."[525]

Helms also stated, "All Headquarters components of this office," meaning the CIA's Directorate for Plans, "have been alerted to the importance of the intelligence potential inherent in the repatriate flow," which, again, means it would have been important for the CIA to contact Oswald.

A memorandum dated November 25, 1963, from an obviously ranking CIA officer with "subordinates" states, "I remember that Oswald's unusual behavior in the USSR had struck me from the moment I had read the first dispatch on him, and I told my subordinates something amounting to 'Don't push too hard to get the information we need because this individual looks odd.'

"We were particularly interested in the info Oswald might provide on the Minsk factory in which he had been employed, on certain sections of the city itself, and of course, we sought the usual biographic information that might develop foreign personality dossiers,"[526] which is further proof that the CIA would have a reason to contact Oswald.

---

[525] National Archives Record Number 104-10310-10179
[526] National Archives Record Number 104-10434-10230

It is clear from the evidence that Oswald had been recruited for a "fake defector" program in the CIA. I have personal knowledge of such a program, and there is no doubt that the CIA enlisted Lee Harvey Oswald to feign defection to the Soviet Union. There is no doubt that Soviet KGB officers inside the CIA were handling him upon his return to the United States.

I was involved in an incident with the CIA in the spring of 1977 in which the CIA was attempting to thwart an action initiated by an alleged defector named Philip Agee. CIA Director Richard Helms recruited Agee to infiltrate the KGB by feigning defection in 1969.

Toward that end, Agee wrote a book titled *Inside the Company: CIA Diary*, which was published in 1975. It detailed his twelve-year CIA career, including his alleged disagreements with CIA policy and alleged sympathy for leftist insurgents in Latin America.

In 1980, shortly after William J. Casey told me that he was the "Acting Director" of the CIA, Casey personally told me, "Philip Agee has infiltrated the KGB," and I met Agee shortly afterward. I also met Richard Helms, as Agee was still reporting directly to Helms.

Casey never should have disclosed such extremely sensitive information, but his cocaine addiction obviously impaired his judgment. I was only the fifth person who knew that Agee had infiltrated the KGB. Casey, Helms, and two other CIA Directors knew about it, but none of the CIA Deputy Directors knew about it, and the information on Agee was withheld from two CIA Directors, one of whom was George H. W. Bush.

As I pressed hard to expose the KGB infiltration of the CIA in 1980, I personally learned that Agee had actually defected by feigning infiltration of the KGB. I also became aware that Agee had a close personal relationship with the KGB officers and double agents inside the CIA. In 1981, I heard some double agents happily referring to him as "Jeremy," as Agee's CIA pseudonym was Jeremy S. Hodapp.[527]

---

[527] Inside The Company; CIA Diary, p. 133 (*Bantam Books, 1975*)

When I finally exposed the KGB infiltration and double agents in 1984, it was because one of President Kennedy's three assassins, a woman from the CIA's New York field office, came to see me and made inquiries about Philip Agee, who had not told her or any of his subversive associates that he had originally been recruited to "infiltrate" the KGB.

Being on an intelligence gathering mission and thinking that she and her KGB superiors were in charge of everything, she willingly went with me to the CIA's Chicago field office, where we administered sodium amytal (truth serum) and verified that she was a double agent and one of President Kennedy's three assassins. We also verified there were 497 KGB officers inside the CIA and more than 800 double agents. (As I recall, she actually said there were 498 KGB officers inside the CIA, which would be due to her being unaware that one of the KGB officers had been killed in 1982.)

As I have noted, at my behest a CIA officer contacted two former CIA Deputy Directors and a former CIA Director, and they worked with me to expose the KGB infiltration. When CIA Director Casey got involved, he tried to interfere but we circumvented his interference and succeeded without his help.

Agee's ostensibly "fake" defection, the KGB's use of three assassins inside the CIA to assassinate President Kennedy, and the documented information cited throughout this book leads to the inescapable conclusion that Lee Harvey Oswald, President Kennedy's accused assassin, was recruited to feign defection to the Soviet Union in 1959, not to mention that when Oswald was put on the CIA's "Watch List," the card with his name on it was stamped "Secret: Eyes Only."

When Oswald was arrested on November 22, 1963, a reporter at Dallas Police Headquarters asked, "Did you shoot the President?"

Oswald replied, "No. They've taken me in because of the fact that I lived in the Soviet Union. I'm just a patsy."[528]

In order to set him up as President Kennedy's accused assassin, Soviet KGB officers inside the CIA had to be handling Oswald upon his return to the United States in June 1962. I surmise it was CIA Director John McCone and his fellow the KGB officers who were responsible for bringing Oswald back from the Soviet Union.

In 1984, the KGB officers admitted that their plans to assassinate President Kennedy began to take shape when Kennedy took the oath of office on January 20, 1961.

On February 1, 1961, less than two weeks after Kennedy became President, Oswald wrote to the U.S. embassy in Moscow requesting the return of his U.S. passport, stating, "I desire to return to the United States."[529]

The KGB's desire to bring Oswald back to the United States explains why Soviet authorities granted his wife permission to "leave the Soviet Union and travel to the United States" when, "in practice, permission for a Soviet wife to accompany her foreign national husband abroad is rarely given."[530]

Marina "received her exit document" from Soviet authorities in May 1962,[531] and Oswald returned home with her in June.

The CIA was rife with Soviet KGB officers, including the CIA Director himself, and they wanted an American residing in the Soviet Union to return to the United States as part of a plan to assassinate the President, all of which means Soviet authorities would grant permission for Marina to leave.

The Soviet Union was intricately involved in President Kennedy's assassination, as was Senator and CIA officer Barry Goldwater, which is more than evident in the next chapter.

---

[528] https://www.pbs.org/wgbh/pages/frontline/shows/oswald/etc/script.html
https://web.archive.org/web/20050403000422/http://www.pbs.org/wgbh//pages/frontline/programs/transcripts/1205.html
[529] Warren Commission Hearings and Exhibits, Volume XVIII, p. 262
[530] National Archives Record Number 104-10434-10389, pp. 4-5
[531] Warren Commission Document 107, p. 21

Chapter 11: Goldwater's Prospects for the Presidency, Help from George W. Bush's Father and George W. Bush's Grandfather

As noted in Chapter 8, Senator Barry Goldwater worked with his KGB handlers to lure President Kennedy to his death while consistently denying that he would run for President in 1964.

One of his denials came three and a half months before President Kennedy's assassination.

On August 5, 1963, the *Washington Post* reported: "Senator Barry Goldwater has returned a campaign contribution . . . . saying he has no plans to seek the Presidency."[532]

In returning the contribution, Goldwater wrote: "I have already announced my intention of seeking a third Senate term in 1964 and have established a campaign organization for this purpose. If you care to resubmit your contribution for this effort, I would of course be most grateful."

On September 22, 1963, two days after KGB asset Barry Goldwater announced the formation of an advisory committee "'for consultation' about the California primary,"[533] the president of the University of New Hampshire Republican Club invited Goldwater to visit New Hampshire, site of the first Presidential primary in March 1964.[534]

---

[532] Washington Post, 8-5-63, p. 2
[533] Washington Post, 9-21-63, p. 2
[534] Washington Post, 10-5-63, p. 1

Goldwater declined the invitation, writing, "My plans at present are to run for re-election to the U.S. Senate . . . . The balance of my schedule for this year has been completely filled for some time."

Goldwater's "schedule," which had been "completely filled for some time," included riding from a Texas airport "in an open convertible" while his fans lined the streets chanting "We want Barry" and waving "Goldwater for President" signs.535

Back on June 1, 1963, a *Washington Post* columnist wrote: "I think his reluctance to make the final decision is real . . . . Goldwater cherishes his position in the Senate . . . . It is the forum from which he has won the undisputed leadership of the conservative forces in the United States.

"Since he must run for re-election in Arizona next year, he would not relish losing his Senate seat in a possibly futile campaign for the White House. He does not assume that President Kennedy cannot be defeated, but he considers at this stage the odds are clearly on the side of the President's re-election."536

The "odds" of Kennedy's re-election clearly changed on November 22, 1963.

The *Dallas Morning News* reported that when Goldwater spoke to reporters in Pennsylvania on October 10, the day before his grandiose reception in Texas, Goldwater "said he really preferred to stay in the Senate and thought his services might be more useful there."537

Eight days after his grandiose reception in Texas, Goldwater stated, "Actually, I'm trying to think of reasons why I should become a candidate and I'm coming up with some negative answers."538

Then, on November 10, twelve days before President Kennedy was scheduled to be assassinated, Goldwater responded to a reporter's questions by stating, "I don't intend to announce something I am not

---

[535] Washington Post, 10-12-63, p. 2
[536] Washington Post, 6-1-63, p. 11
[537] Dallas Morning News, 10-11-63, p. 8
[538] Washington Post, 10-21-63, p. 8

yet decided upon doing . . . . There are others who are equally insistent that I wait until I am convinced it is something I should do . . . . If and when I become a candidate . . . I have not decided to become a candidate . . . . I haven't done any campaigning for myself and won't unless I decide in January to seek the Republican nomination."[539]

A Harris Poll published just four days before President Kennedy's assassination analyzed the balance between liberals and conservatives, stating: "The key, however, rests with middle-of-the-road voters . . . . It is immediately evident that the balance of power rests with the politically more numerous moderate group . . . . President Kennedy, however, already has a substantial edge among moderates. It remains to be seen just how well Goldwater can cut down this advantage."[540]

President Kennedy's popularity was a clear deterrent to a Goldwater candidacy, and after the assassination, it was immediately clear that Vice President Johnson's ascendance to the Presidency was a far greater deterrent.

It is a simple fact that if ultra conservative Barry Goldwater were to become the Republican nominee for President, everyone who intended to vote for President Kennedy would simply vote for President Johnson. They certainly would not be switching their allegiance to Goldwater.

What's more, Texan Lyndon Johnson, being a Southern Democrat, was a popular figure with segregationist Southern Democrats who despised President Kennedy and would have never voted for him. Moderate Republicans, too, would see Johnson as an acceptable alternative to extremist Barry Goldwater. As such, Johnson would clearly take votes away from Goldwater in addition to getting all the votes that would have gone to President Kennedy.

---

[539] Washington Post, 11-11-63, p. 7
[540] Washington Post, 11-18-63, p. 10

On November 24, 1963, the *New York Times* stated: "The prospect of Mr. Johnson's nomination appeared likely to produce a liberal Republican opponent."[541]

The article said this was to "capitalize" on President Johnson's "greatest potential weakness" which was "his lack of appeal to independent and liberal voters." Liberals and independents were not at all fond of Southern Democrats like Lyndon Johnson, whereas a liberal Republican trying to unseat Johnson would definitely appeal to them.

Syndicated columnists Evans and Novak wrote in the *Washington Post* on December 5, 1963, about the "sharp falloff, sharper than was first apparent, in Senator Barry Goldwater's strength after President Kennedy's death . . . . Now, even some of his own supporters admit that a totally different kind of candidate is required against President Johnson."[542]

On December 11, the *Washington Post* reported: "Politicians in both parties have felt that the Senator's chances for the nomination were hurt by the accession of President Johnson, a Southerner."[543]

On December 27, the *Washington Post* reported that the National Committee for an Effective Congress, "a nonpartisan political committee," received a staff report stating that Lyndon Johnson's ascendance to the Presidency "damaged Goldwater's chances of landing the nomination." The report said that Republicans "are now looking for a middle-of-the-road candidate."[544]

The December 27 article also gave the views of the Republican Mayor of San Francisco, where the Republican National Convention was to be held in 1964: "Republican Mayor George Christopher of San Francisco said yesterday that Arizona Senator Barry Goldwater has lost ground in the race for the Republican Presidential nomination."

---

[541] New York Times, 11-24-63, p. 4
[542] Washington Post, 12-5-63, p. 23
[543] Washington Post, 12-11-63, p. 4
[544] Washington Post, 12-27-63, p. 2

Christopher stated there was "a remarkable change in sentiment" due to "the death of President Kennedy and the probability that President Johnson will be the Democratic nominee in 1964. Before Mr. Kennedy was assassinated, Christopher said, he had believed Goldwater was the leading contender for California's 86 GOP national convention votes."

To repeat, if ultra conservative Barry Goldwater were to become the Republican nominee for President, President Johnson would get virtually every vote that had been intended for President Kennedy, who already had a "substantial edge among moderates" and a clear "advantage" over Goldwater, and Texan Lyndon Johnson, being a Southern Democrat, would also get votes from Southern Democrats who despised President Kennedy and would have never voted for him. Johnson would also get votes from moderate Republicans who saw Goldwater as an extremist.

On Friday, January 3, 1964, exactly six weeks after his KGB handlers assassinated President Kennedy, Goldwater announced his candidacy for the Republican nomination for President, even though back on August 4, 1963, he pointedly said he had "no plans to seek the Presidency," and even though on September 22 his definitive plans were to "run for re-election to the U.S. Senate." He announced his Presidential bid even though on October 10 he "said he really preferred to stay in the Senate and thought his services might be more useful there."

Goldwater announced his candidacy regardless of the fact that on October 19 he was "trying to think of reasons" why he should become a candidate and "coming up with some negative answers," and he announced his candidacy regardless of the fact that Kennedy's death apparently sounded the death knell for the impetus that was supposed to push Barry Goldwater into the 1964 Presidential race.

KGB officer and CIA Director John McCone enlisted former President Eisenhower in preparation for the political situation that Goldwater would face after President Kennedy's assassination. McCone met with Eisenhower on September 19, 1963, and one of the topics they discussed was South Vietnam, where Henry Cabot Lodge was serving as U.S. Ambassador.[545]

McCone also had a "brief conversation" with Eisenhower at the White House on November 23, the day after President Kennedy's assassination.[546]

On December 10, 1963, eighteen days after President Kennedy's assassination, former President Eisenhower publicly declared that Henry Cabot Lodge should run for the GOP nomination for President.

The *Washington Post* reported, "To a great many of the Goldwater followers, none of the Eastern, internationalist liberal Republicans is more unacceptable than Lodge. His entry into the race for the nomination would stiffen their determination to nominate Goldwater.

"Whatever General Eisenhower's intentions, it is apparent that a Lodge candidacy could hurt the chances of aspirants of Lodge's stripe, like Rockefeller, Nixon and Scranton."[547]

In an interview back on June 18, 1963, Goldwater stated, "I'm the only conservative being mentioned. If a fight develops, it will be among the liberals."[548]

Another liberal Republican was used to help Goldwater six months before Eisenhower (whatever his intentions) stoked the fire of an all-but-extinguished Goldwater candidacy. This other Republican was one of the Eastern liberals and had been a Senator throughout the Eisenhower Administration, namely, Prescott Bush of Connecticut, the father of CIA officer George H. W. Bush and grandfather of CIA asset George W. Bush.

---

[545] National Archives Record Number 104-10306-10012, p. 5
[546] National Archives Record Number 104-10408-10099, p. 3
[547] Washington Post, 12-11-63, p. 4
[548] Washington Post, 6-18-63, p. 2

On June 7, 1963, Prescott Bush made a scathing attack on Goldwater's chief rival for the Republican nomination, New York Governor Nelson Rockefeller.

The attack was detailed in an Associated Press article carried by the *Washington Post*, which read: "Former United States Senator Prescott Bush has denounced the recent marriage of New York Governor Nelson A. Rockefeller and said he does not think Rockefeller is fit to be President.

"'Have we come to the point in our life as a nation,' Bush asked, 'where the Governor of a great state, one who perhaps aspires to the nomination for President of the United States, can desert a good wife, mother of his grown children, divorce her, then persuade a young mother of four youngsters to abandon her husband and their four children and marry the Governor?'

"Have we come to the point where one of the two great political parties will confer upon such a one its highest honor and greatest responsibility? I venture to hope not."[549]

This vitriolic denunciation of a "Governor" who was "not fit to be President" sounded like a campaign speech, and it was remarkably out of place because Bush made his statements at the "commencement exercises" of Rosemary Hall, an exclusive girls' school in Connecticut, where "Bush spoke yesterday on 'shifting standards of behavior.'"

After telling the high school graduating class about his "hope" that Rockefeller would not be the Republican nominee for President, Bush told the students that "our people" would be destroying "the sanctity of the American family" if the Republicans nominated Rockefeller, and Bush solicited public support for his position.

"Bush said that whether Rockefeller's actions are approved will depend on educators, opinion makers, churches and others, and on 'whether our people are ready to say phooey to the sanctity of the American family.'"

---

[549] Washington Post, 6-8-63, p. 2

As if that were not enough, one week later Prescott Bush touted what he called "overwhelming approval" of the anti-Rockefeller position that he espoused in front of a high school graduating class.

A UPI article carried by the *Washington Post* on June 15, 1963, read: "Former Senator Prescott Bush says he has received telegrams and letters showing 'overwhelming approval' of his criticism . . . . The former lawmaker said yesterday that out of about 10 letters and telegrams 'only two expressed opposition to my views and all the rest were favorable.' He added that he received mail from New York, Minnesota, Indiana and other Midwestern states."[550]

Prescott Bush obviously contacted the press to tell them that eight letters and telegrams were evidence of "overwhelming approval" of what he had told a high school graduating class; that the Republican Party must nominate someone other than Nelson Rockefeller for President.

On October 24, 1963, four months after Prescott Bush did his part in tamping down Rockefeller's prospects, syndicated columnists Evans and Novak devoted their column to a "Goldwater surge" in Bush's home state of Connecticut, writing, "The odds soared against Rockefeller after his remarriage and after former Republican Senator Prescott Bush castigated him as unfit to carry the banner."[551] (To use Evans and Novak's wording, Bush "castigated" the Governor of New York in front of a high school graduating class as "unfit" to be the Republican nominee for President.)

Noting that Connecticut is "the center of the Party's eastern liberal heartland," Evans and Novak quoted a liberal Connecticut Republican as saying, "The Goldwater crowd has a horse off and running with lots of money riding on the nose. We don't even have a horse."

They went on to state that with Prescott Bush attacking the Governor of New York in front of a high school graduating class, "The odds are now at least even that Senator Barry Goldwater,

---

[550] Washington Post, 6-15-63, p. 2
[551] Washington Post, 10-24-63, p. 21

conservative idol from far-off Arizona, may wrap up Connecticut's sixteen votes at the San Francisco convention next summer."

What makes Prescott Bush's criticism even more interesting is that the *New York Times Index* for 1963 lists more than thirty references under the subheading "marriage" of Nelson A. Rockefeller, and it shows that Prescott Bush was the only U.S. politician who criticized it.

Members of the clergy also criticized it, and most interesting, a reference on November 7, 1963, reads, "Premier Khrushchev, in apparent reference to the Governor, scores 'parasitic capitalists' who 'live life of luxury, drinking, carousing or changing wives.'"[552] This was fifteen days before his KGB officers inside the CIA assassinated President Kennedy in an effort to get Barry Goldwater elected President of the United States.

On November 21, 1963, the eve of President Kennedy's assassination, a *Washington Post* article mentioned "Mrs. Rockefeller" and said her "marriage to the Governor on the heels of divorces by both brought some protests within Republican ranks."[553] ("Some protests within Republican ranks" is a clear reflection of how unique Prescott Bush's vituperative attack was.)

Another *Washington Post* article on November 21 reported, "Senator Thruston Morton, chairman of the Republican Senate Campaign Committee, said Senator Barry Goldwater is far ahead in the running for the Republican Presidential nomination," and Senator Morton "doesn't know where Nelson A. Rockefeller can count on delegate votes outside of New York."[554]

With one day remaining before President Kennedy's assassination, it is clear that Prescott Bush's widely reported vitriol had reverberated nationally.

It is hard to imagine that anyone but stalwart Rockefeller supporters would continue to think the New York Governor

---

[552] 1963 New York Times Index p. 679
[553] Washington Post, 11-21-63, p. 5
[554] Washington Post, 11-21-63, p. 5

should be President after Prescott Bush portrayed him in such a despicable light. Soviet Premier Nikita Khrushchev referring to the wealthy Rockefeller as a parasitic capitalist, who lives a life of luxury, drinking, carousing, and changing wives, certainly reinforced Bush's bitter denunciation of a man who was "not fit to be President."

A Gallup poll back in January 1963 had Rockefeller well ahead of Goldwater. 46% of Republicans planned on voting for Nelson Rockefeller in the Republican primaries, and only 26% planned on voting for Barry Goldwater.[555]

But the KGB had to change that, and KGB officer John McCone had direct input with both Nelson Rockefeller and Prescott Bush, just like he had direct input with former President Eisenhower prior to Eisenhower energizing Goldwater supporters with his suggestion that Henry Cabot Lodge run for the GOP nomination.

McCone's calendar shows he attended a black-tie dinner "in honor of Senator and Mrs. Bush" on January 9, 1963, hosted by none other than former CIA Director Allen Dulles,[556] and McCone attended another black-tie dinner "in honor of Senator Bush" on January 25.[557]

His input with Rockefeller came twenty-seven days after attending the second black-tie dinner honoring Prescott Bush. McCone's daily calendar shows that on February 21, 1963, he left Virginia on a Gulfstream jet headed for a noon meeting with Rockefeller in New York. McCone then flew back to Virginia at 1:55 p.m.[558]

Thirty-nine days later, on April 1, 1963, Nelson Rockefeller's mistress, socialite Margaretta Murphy, divorced her husband to marry Nelson Rockefeller, a marriage that took place on May 4, seventy-two days after the McCone-Rockefeller meeting.

On June 18, 1963, just four days after Prescott Bush wreaked havoc on Rockefeller's chances of winning the Republican

---

[555] Washington Post, 1-13-63, p. 6
[556] National Archives Record Number 104-10306-10000, p. 5
[557] Ibid., p. 10
[558] National Archives Record Number 104-10306-10000, p. 18

nomination, two UPI reporters who interviewed Goldwater wrote: "He used to tell reporters bluntly that he did not have a chance to be nominated, and he would privately acknowledge that no Republican had much hope of derailing President Kennedy's bid for a second term . . . . Now he radiates optimism on and off the record."[559]

His KGB handlers had been killing Members of Congress with Goldwater's knowledge and apparent consent for six years. They exercised definitive control in the government, and they were bent on putting him into the Presidency, while Nelson Rockefeller, Goldwater's chief rival for the GOP nomination, had been completely discredited by divorcing his wife and marrying his mistress. Why wouldn't Goldwater radiate optimism?

The UPI reporters quoted Goldwater as saying, "I don't want this nomination, but it may be forced on me."

Goldwater also said, "With the right candidate, 1964 could be a Republican year after all."

After President Kennedy was assassinated, KGB asset Barry Goldwater knew perfectly well that he would be the GOP nominee, and he knew perfectly well that the only thing that would make 1964 "a Republican year after all" is President Johnson's assassination right before the election.

The Warren Commission Report states that "President Kennedy's visit to Texas" had been "under consideration for almost a year before it occurred."[560] It also states that President Kennedy made the decision to visit Texas on June 5, 1963, less than two weeks before the interview in which Goldwater was reported to be "radiating optimism on and off the record."

Goldwater's KGB handlers knew that President Kennedy would go toe-to-toe with their candidate in Texas, hoping to score a knockout punch before Goldwater ever decided to run.

---

[559] Washington Post, 6-18-63, p. 2
[560] Warren Commission Report, p. 28

Luring President Kennedy into his "open convertible" Dallas visit, where he hoped for the knockout punch, was made easier by having Goldwater state on October 10 that he "really preferred to stay in the Senate and thought his services might be more useful there,"[561] and eight days after riding from a Texas airport in an open convertible, Goldwater stated, "Actually, I'm trying to think of reasons why I should become a candidate and I'm coming up with some negative answers."[562]

President Kennedy clearly wanted to reinforce those "negative answers." He needed to send Goldwater a message that he should "stay in the Senate" and not risk "losing his Senate seat" in a "futile campaign for the White House." As such, President Kennedy's reception in Texas had to upstage Barry Goldwater's reception in Texas.

In previous statements in August and September, Goldwater completely ruled out running for President, claiming he would run for re-election to the Senate, but his escalating rhetorical conflict made it abundantly clear that he was spoiling for a fight.

His sporadic backpedaling was crafted to have President Kennedy look forward to "a triumphal tour through the city's streets" when "Mr. Kennedy himself made the decision to ride in the slow-moving motorcade."

President Kennedy was just minutes away from making a speech in which he was "going to accuse right-wing extremists of talking 'just plain nonsense.'"[563] Goldwater's handlers, in turn, had three assassins that said, "Welcome to Dallas, Mr. President."

It's no wonder that Goldwater was radiating optimism by June 18, 1963. He and his KGB handlers were the powers-that-be with whom President Kennedy would have to contend, and CIA officer Barry Goldwater apparently thought things were going his way in his quest

---

[561] Dallas Morning News, 10-11-63, p. 8
[562] Washington Post, 10-21-63, p. 8
[563] Washington Post, 11-23-63, pp. 1 & 9

for the Presidency, especially with President Kennedy having recently made the decision to visit Texas.

When Goldwater returned a campaign contribution on August 4, 1963, claiming he had "no plans to seek the Presidency," he also wrote: "Circumstances might develop which could compel me to alter my present course."[564]

The only "circumstances" that "compelled" Goldwater to seek the Presidency were President Kennedy's assassination and Goldwater's expectation that his KGB handlers would assassinate President Lyndon Johnson immediately before the election.

When Goldwater announced his candidacy, he was "asked whether he would concede Texas" to President Johnson in the election.

With the expectation that President Johnson would be assassinated before the election, Goldwater replied, "I don't concede anybody anything."[565]

---

[564] Washington Post, 8-5-63, p. 2
[565] Washington Post, 1-4-64, p. 6

Chapter 12: Getting the United States Government to Cover Up an Obvious Conspiracy in a Presidential Assassination

On November 29, 1963, seven days after KGB officers inside the CIA assassinated the President of the United States, President Johnson established "The President's Commission on the Assassination of President Kennedy," commonly known as the Warren Commission.

Nicholas Katzenbach, a CIA officer operating with an "official cover" as Deputy Attorney General, was the CIA's initial point man in pushing President Johnson to establish a Presidential Commission. (Katzenbach testified at the closed-door Congressional hearings in 1984 that he is in the CIA.)

Katzenbach initiated the push for a Presidential Commission on Saturday, November 23, one day after President Kennedy's assassination.

He continued to push for a Commission on Sunday, and his three-day effort culminated in a memo to the White House on Monday, November 25, stating, "The public must be satisfied that Oswald was the assassin; that he did not have confederates who are still at large; and that the evidence was such that he would have been convicted at trial,"[566] which means Katzenbach's proposed Commission would have a "no conspiracy" mandate and be tasked with making a case for the deceased Oswald being the lone assassin.

---

[566] House Select Committee on Assassinations, Volume XI, pp. 411-412

On Tuesday, November 26, KGB officer and CIA Director John McCone observed President Johnson's "considerable contempt" for Katzenbach's efforts, after which McCone became the CIA's point man in pushing Johnson to establish a Presidential Commission.

Chief Justice Earl Warren admitted that Johnson established the Warren Commission seven days after the assassination because Johnson came to have a profound fear that Soviet Premier Nikita Khrushchev and Cuban Premier Fidel Castro were behind the assassination. President Johnson feared that their involvement could get the United States into, in Earl Warren's words, "a nuclear war."

The retired Chief Justice was interviewed in December 1972 and stated that when he went to the White House on November 29, 1963, President Johnson "told me he felt conditions around the world were so bad at the moment that he thought it might even get us into a war; a nuclear war."[567]

Two hours before going to the White House, Earl Warren met with Attorney General Robert F. Kennedy, telling him that he "did not believe a Chief Justice should undertake non-judicial duties while sitting on the Supreme Court."

But when he went to the White House, Johnson told Warren that he had "asked for a report from Defense Secretary Robert S. McNamara for an estimate on how many Americans would be killed in a Soviet nuclear attack."

Johnson was given a figure of 40 million, and the fear of a possible nuclear war caused Warren to "agree to head the inquiry."

The simple fact is that no matter what the Warren Commission found out, they would abide by their instructions to tell the American public that there was no conspiracy to assassinate President Kennedy.

When President Johnson called Senator Richard Russell on November 29 to enlist him for the Warren Commission, he told

---

[567] New York Times, 12-9-72, p. 25

Russell about Chief Justice Warren refusing Bobby Kennedy's request to serve on a Presidential Commission, stating, "Bobby and them went up to see him today and he turned them down cold and said, 'No' . . . . Two hours later I called him and ordered him down here, and he didn't want to come. I insisted he come."[568]

Johnson told Senator Russell that Chief Justice Warren "came down here and told me no twice," and President Johnson pointedly told Russell, "We've got to take this out of the arena where they're testifying that Khrushchev and Castro did this and did that and chuck us into a war that can kill 40 million Americans in an hour."[569]

Warren met with the Commission staff on January 20, 1964, and a staff memorandum from the meeting states that Warren "discussed the circumstances under which he had accepted the chairmanship of the Commission." Warren told the staff that "rumors" that were "circulating in this country and overseas" had to be "quenched," or the rumors "could conceivably lead the country into a war which could cost 40 million lives. No one could refuse to do something which might help to prevent such a possibility."[570]

The CIA initially supplied President Johnson and the Warren Commission with information that implicated Castro in the assassination, and they later told the Warren Commission that anti-Castro Cubans were responsible for assassinating President Kennedy. The anti-Castro Cubans' alleged motive was to blame Castro for the assassination and thus provoke a U.S. invasion of Cuba.

But if it were true that anti-Castro Cubans assassinated President Kennedy, it would mean Soviet Premier Nikita Khrushchev and Cuban Premier Fidel Castro instantaneously knew that the assassination was a rightwing conspiracy perpetrated by "those demanding a stronger policy against Cuba." As noted in Chapter 9, "twelve minutes" after it was officially announced on November 22

---

[568] LBJ Library, LBJ Phone Calls; Telephone Conversation between the President and Senator Russell, 29 Nov 1963, 8:55PM, p. 7
[569] Ibid., p. 2
[570] Warren Commission staff meetings; Warren Commission Memo of Staff Meeting of 20 Jan 1964 https://www.maryferrell.org/showDoc.html?docId=10391

that "President Kennedy was dead," Moscow radio carried "the first TASS bulletin on his death" stating he "had fallen victim to rightwing extremists," and Castro stated with absolute certainty that "those demanding a stronger policy against Cuba" were behind the assassination.

Chapter 9 contains voluminous reports from the CIA and the United States Information Agency stating that nations all around the world thought Kennedy was killed as a result of a right-wing conspiracy. The Soviets and their allies went as far as to repeatedly accuse Barry Goldwater and his supporters of being behind the assassination. There was no one "testifying that Khrushchev and Castro did this and did that," and the only rumors "circulating in this country and overseas" were rumors that President Kennedy was killed as a result of a right-wing conspiracy.

When CIA officer Nicholas Katzenbach wrote his memo to the White House on November 25, 1963, stating "the public must be satisfied that Oswald was the assassin," he also wrote that a perspective should be proffered "which will satisfy people in the United States and abroad that all the facts have been told, and that a statement to this affect be made now . . . . We should have some basis for rebutting the thought that this was a Communist conspiracy."[571]

As has been made clear in this book, it most certainly was a "Communist conspiracy," and Cuban Premier Fidel Castro was party to it all along.

Two and half months before the assassination, as noted in Chapter 9, Fidel Castro held a three-hour interview at the Brazilian Embassy in Cuba and warned that "United States leaders" (meaning President Kennedy) "will not be safe" if they give aid to anyone with "plans to eliminate Cuban leaders."

Castro said he was prepared to "fight them and answer in kind." In other words, Castro would eliminate President Kennedy if the

---

[571] House Select Committee on Assassinations, Volume XI, pp. 411-412

United States continued to support anti-Castro Cubans and their plans to eliminate Castro.[572]

On September 7, 1963, the day that Castro threatened "United States leaders," one of his underlings went into action to make it seem like President Kennedy's assassination would mean Castro had made good on his threat.

Lieutenant General Brent Scowcroft, President Ford's National Security Advisor, wrote a memo stating that on September 7, 1963, Cuban official Rolando Cubela, who was "highly placed in the Castro government," initiated a meeting with the CIA during which Cubela claimed that he had a "specific plan" to "foment a coup against Castro."[573]

CIA documents state that Cubela told the CIA that the only possible way to "effect a coup" against Castro was through an "inside job," and Cubela was "waiting for a plan of action from the United States Government."[574]

Cubela wanted "high-level assurances of support for a successful coup." The high-level assurances, of course, could only come from "U.S. leaders" who "support" a coup against the Castro regime.

Scowcroft wrote that "at Cubela's instigation," the CIA "began to support" the coup plan, which included, "as a first step, the assassination of Fidel Castro."[575]

And while Cubela was instigating CIA support for a coup that would kill Castro, the U.S. Coordinating Committee for Cuban Affairs met on September 12, 1963, and "agreed unanimously that there was a strong likelihood Castro would retaliate in some way against the rash of covert activity in Cuba."[576]

"Within weeks" of the September 12 meeting, the CIA, under the leadership of KGB officer John McCone, "escalated the level of its

---

[572] National Archives Record Number 104-10422-10028, pp. 3 & 4
[573] National Archives Record Number 178-10004-10101
[574] National Archives Record Number 178-10004-10103
[575] National Archives Record Number 178-10004-10101
[576] National Archives Record Number 104-10431-10124, p. 12

covert operations" against Cuba and informed Cubela that the United States "supported" his plans for a coup.577

On October 11, 1963, Rolando Cubela, described as "a high level Cuban government official,"578 told the CIA that he wanted "a meeting with a senior U.S. official, preferably Robert F. Kennedy, for assurance of 'moral support'" for his coup plans, which included Castro's assassination.579

On October 29, 1963, fifty-two days after Castro threatened the safety of "United States leaders," Desmond Fitzgerald, Chief of the CIA's Special Affairs Staff, met with Cubela and told him that he was the "personal representative" of Attorney General Robert F. Kennedy.

Fitzgerald also gave Cubela the task of assassinating Fidel Castro, telling him that "the United States is prepared to render all necessary assistance to any anti-communist Cuban group which succeeds in neutralizing the present Cuban leadership."580 (Neutralize is a CIA code word for kill.)

The meeting took place "despite warnings from certain CIA staffers that the operation was poorly conceived and insecure."581

Two days later, a CIA document stated that if the coup against Castro were going to be "supportable" by the United States, those involved must "neutralize the top echelon of Cuban leadership."

The document emphasized that "the situation in Cuba at the time of U.S. intervention" must be one in which "Fidel Castro, and possibly Raul Castro, President Dorticos, and Che Guevara" have been "neutralized by the insurgents."582

A CIA document on "Highly Sensitive Activities" states, "At the very moment President Kennedy was shot in Dallas, a CIA officer was meeting with a Cuban agent in Paris and giving him an

---

577 Ibid.
578 National Archives Record Number 104-10431-10124, p. 8
579 National Archives Record Number 104-10065-10094, pp. 12-13
580 National Archives Record Number 104-10065-10094, pp. 13-14
581 National Archives Record Number 104-10431-10124, p. 18
582 National Archives Record Number 104-10307-10007, pp. 3 & 9

assassination device for use against Castro."[583] The "Cuban agent" was Rolando Cubela, and prior to November 22, Cubela "spoke repeatedly of the need for an assassination weapon."[584]

CIA documents state that the Cubela episode began in March 1961 when he and another Cuban allegedly "wanted to defect" and "needed help" in escaping from Cuba, but no such defection took place because "Cuban police were aware" of Cubela's "intention and plans."[585]

In August 1962, the CIA decided to use Cubela, the alleged defector, as an asset inside Cuba, but in a meeting with the CIA on August 20, 1962, Cubela "refused to be polygraphed."[586]

Nine days after refusing to take a lie detector test, Cubela flew back to Havana and "did not leave Cuba" again until September 1963, which resulted in the CIA having "no contact" with him from August 1962 until he initiated a meeting with the CIA on September 7, 1963,[587] the very day that Fidel Castro threatened to retaliate against U.S. leaders if they gave aid to anyone trying to "eliminate Cuban leaders."

The CIA finally terminated contact with Cubela in June 1965.[588]

To summarize, then, Cubela claimed that he wanted to defect but never left Cuba, allegedly because the Cuban police knew he was a defector. And even though he was allegedly pegged as a traitor by Cuba, he was still "highly placed in the Castro government."

A year and a half after his claim about wanting to defect, the CIA wanted to use him as an asset inside Cuba, but Cubela refused to take a lie detector test. He then had "no contact" with the CIA until the day that Castro threatened the safety of "United States leaders" if they gave aid to anyone with plans to "eliminate Cuban leaders," at which time Cubela coincidentally initiated a meeting with the CIA

---

[583] National Archives Record Number 104-10310-10259, p. 8
[584] National Archives Record Number 104-10065-10094, p. 15
[585] Ibid., p. 5
[586] National Archives Record Number 104-10065-10094, p. 7
[587] National Archives Record Number 104-10143-10001, p. 8
[588] National Archives Record Number 104-10310-10259, p. 8

and told them that he had a "specific plan" to "foment a coup against Castro." He said he wanted "high-level assurances of support" as he waited for a "plan of action from the United States Government" that would result in Castro's death.

Then, Cubela said he wanted to meet with Attorney General Robert F. Kennedy, another "United States leader," so that Cubela could get "moral support" for his plan to assassinate Castro. A CIA official met with Cubela and told him that he was the "personal representative" of Robert F. Kennedy and that the United States would provide "all necessary assistance" to "any anti-communist Cuban group" that would kill Castro.

Cubela then spoke repeatedly of needing "an assassination weapon," and, coincidentally, at the very moment that President Kennedy was killed, a CIA officer was in Paris giving Cubela "an assassination device for use against Castro."

Cubela, whose CIA code name was AMLASH, was nothing but a provocateur who, from the day Castro threatened the safety of "United States leaders," enticed the CIA to actively plan Castro's assassination. When President Kennedy was assassinated, the assumption was supposed to be that Fidel Castro had made good on his threat to retaliate.

President Johnson would then fear Soviet and Cuban involvement in the assassination and the possibility of "a nuclear war," and he would establish a Presidential Commission with a "no conspiracy" mandate.

CIA Director and KGB officer John McCone did his part to foster the idea that Castro had retaliated and to foster President Johnson's fear of a nuclear war.

On November 24, 1963, McCone informed Johnson about the CIA's "plans against Cuba,"[589] and more important, after his official "morning meeting" with the President, McCone met with President Johnson "in his private residence" and "suggested" that

---

[589] National Archives Record Number 180-10142-10036, p. 60

he get "an early briefing on the Soviet long-range striking capability" and Soviet "air defense posture."[590]

The CIA continued to foster concerns about Castro and Khrushchev in the week following the assassination, and then, after the Warren Commission was established, the CIA solidified those concerns without putting forth an absolute certainty that Castro killed Kennedy. The CIA eventually transitioned into claiming "anti-Castro Cubans" assassinated President Kennedy.

To generate an immediate fear of a Soviet-Cuban connection to the assassination, a KGB officer inside the CIA impersonated Lee Harvey Oswald at the Soviet and Cuban Embassies in Mexico City in late September 1963. The KGB officer claiming to be Oswald told embassy personnel that he was trying to obtain a visa to travel to Cuba and the Soviet Union. It was, however, more than obvious that it was not Oswald.

On October 8, 1963, the CIA's Mexico City station sent a cable to CIA Headquarters stating that "an American male" who identified himself as "Lee Oswald" phoned the Soviet Embassy on October 1. The cable also stated that someone who "appears to be American" had been photographed entering the Soviet Embassy at 12:16 p.m. and leaving six minutes later. The American was "six feet" tall with an "athletic build," a "receding hairline," and a "balding top."[591]

Two days later, CIA Headquarters sent cables to the State Department, the FBI, and the Department of the Navy stating that on October 1, "An American male, who identified himself as Lee Oswald, contacted the Soviet Embassy in Mexico City . . . . The American is described as approximately 35 years old with an athletic build, about six feet tall, with a receding hairline."[592]

CIA Headquarters also sent a cable to the CIA's Mexico City station on the same day to inform them that there is a 23-year-old defector named Oswald, who has "light brown wavy hair," is "five feet

---

[590] National Archives Record Number 104-10301-10000, p. 25
[591] National Archives Record Number 104-10413-10001
[592] National Archives Record Number 104-10404-10314

ten inches" tall, and weighs "one hundred sixty five pounds."[593] The cable put forth that the "Lee Oswald" who contacted the Soviet Embassy is "probably identical" with a Lee Oswald who defected in 1959.

On October 15, the CIA's Mexico City station sent a cable to Headquarters asking them to "please pouch photo Oswald," meaning send someone to Mexico with a photograph of Oswald in a diplomatic pouch.[594]

The CIA waited nine days before sending a cable to the Department of the Navy requesting "two copies of the most recent photograph" of Oswald. The cable also stated, "We will forward them to our representative in Mexico, who will attempt to determine if the Lee Oswald in Mexico City and subject are the same individual," which means the CIA had no knowledge of Oswald actually being in Mexico. The cable also stated that an earlier CIA cable had been in regard to the "possible presence of subject in Mexico City."[595]

On November 22, 1963, thirty-eight days after the CIA's Mexico City station requested a photograph of Oswald, one had still not been received, and thus when President Kennedy was assassinated, the CIA's Mexico City station had no way to factually determine if Lee Harvey Oswald, President Kennedy's accused assassin, had been to the Soviet and Cuban Embassies.[596]

Upon hearing a Voice of America broadcast that "Lee H. Oswald" had been arrested in Dallas on November 22, the CIA's Mexico City station cabled Headquarters that they were sending photos of the "only visitor" to the Soviet Embassy on October 1 "who could be identical with Oswald."[597]

On the following day, November 23, the Mexico City station sent a cable stating they had seen photographs of Oswald on

---

[593] National Archives Record Number 104-10015-10048, p. 3
[594] National Archives Record Number 104-10413-10004
[595] National Archives Record Number 104-10413-10006
[596] National Archives Record Number 104-10428-10166, p. 17
[597] National Archives Record Number 104-10413-10007

television the night before, and it was "obvious" that the photographs they sent were not photographs of Oswald.⁵⁹⁸

The KGB officer impersonating Oswald had been photographed "coming out of both the Soviet and Cuban Embassies" in 1963, and the Warren Commission published one of the photographs as Commission Exhibit 237.⁵⁹⁹

CIA documents state that on November 26, "The Mexico station received through the open mail, directly from the Department of the Navy, a photograph of Oswald."⁶⁰⁰ By that time, no one doubted that the deceased Oswald was the assassin and that he had gone to Mexico.

In due time, the CIA explained that "Oswald" did not actually go to the Soviet Embassy on October 1. They maintained that after six alleged visits to the Soviet and Cuban embassies on September 27 and September 28, Oswald simply called the Soviet Embassy on October 1, whereupon he stated, "This is Lee Oswald."⁶⁰¹

But prior to October 1, the CIA had no information to indicate Oswald had been to either embassy because the KGB officer impersonating Oswald did not use the name "Lee Oswald" in any of his phone conversations.⁶⁰²

More important, the CIA had several photographic observation points covering the Soviet and Cuban embassies, but they had absolutely no photographs of Oswald visiting either embassy.

CIA Headquarters sent a cable to the Mexico City station on November 23 instructing them to send a CIA officer "with all photos" of Oswald at the Soviet and Cuban Embassies "to HQ on next available flight."

For some reason, President Kennedy's assassination meant that Oswald's "possible presence" in Mexico City was now a definite

---

⁵⁹⁸ National Archives Record Number 104-10413-10008, p. 10
⁵⁹⁹ National Archives Record Numbers 104-10400-10270 and Warren Commission Hearings and Exhibits, Volume XVI, p. 662
⁶⁰⁰ National Archives Record Number 104-10428-10166, p. 17
⁶⁰¹ National Archives Record Number 104-10413-10049, p. 4
⁶⁰² National Archives Record Number 104-10019-10023, pp. 9 & 11

presence. For some reason, it meant that "the Lee Oswald in Mexico City" was indeed a defector named Lee Oswald, and as such, CIA Headquarters wanted all the photos of "Oswald" at the Cuban and Soviet Embassies.[603]

But the CIA's Mexico City station sent back a cable on November 23 stating they had done a "complete recheck" of the photographs of "all visitors" to the Soviet and Cuban Embassies from September 1 through the "first half November," and it "shows no evidence Oswald visit,"[604] and a CIA memorandum on December 13, 1963 states, "None of our several photo observation points in Mexico City had ever taken an identifiable picture of Lee Oswald."[605]

A 1967 CIA memorandum confirms, "No photograph was taken, acquired, or received of Oswald alone or with any individual in front of the Cuban Embassy, the Soviet Embassy, or anywhere else in Mexico."[606]

The CIA documented that their "criteria for selecting subjects for photographing" is as follows: "If the target is unknown, and/or a previous photograph has not been taken, the observer takes one."[607] (Oswald was unknown and the CIA did not have a "previous photograph" of him.)

A CIA memorandum on November 27, 1963, states, "We have photographic coverage during daylight hours," and "their consulates are located in the embassies and therefore the coverage of the embassies would include coverage of the consulates. The photographic coverage of the mentioned installations is of a continuous nature during daylight hours."[608]

Another CIA memo states that during September 1963, Soviet Embassy hours were from 9 a.m. to 6 p.m., and "offices in the

---

[603] National Archives Record Number 104-10413-10155
[604] National Archives Record Numbers 104-10413-10008, p. 11
[605] National Archives Record Number 104-10413-10000, p. 5
[606] National Archives Record Number 104-10412-10170, p. 4
[607] National Archives Record Number 104-10414-10093
[608] National Archives Record Number 104-10438-10234

Soviet compound may be visited by appointment only." It also states, "Visitors may enter the Cuban Consulate" from 10 a.m. to 2 p.m., Monday through Friday.[609]

The CIA documented that Sylvia Duran, the Cuban Consulate employee who spoke with the KGB officer impersonating Oswald, "works at the Cuban Consulate from 10:00 a.m. to 2:00 p.m. daily."[610]

Oswald's alleged visits would have clearly occurred "during daylight hours" when the "photographic coverage" of the embassies "is of a continuous nature." If Oswald had made six visits to the Soviet and Cuban Embassies, CIA observers at each embassy would have had ample opportunity to take several pictures of him coming and going.

In 1975, the CIA claimed they had no photograph of Oswald visiting the Cuban Embassy on Friday, September 27, 1963, because "The camera, based upon the recollection of officers still in service at headquarters, was down on the 27 because of mechanical malfunction."[611]

But on November 23, when the CIA's Mexico City station did a "complete recheck" of the photographs of all visitors to the Soviet and Cuban Embassies from September 1 through the first half November, the complete recheck that "shows no evidence Oswald visit,"[612] they made no mention of a malfunctioning camera at the Cuban Embassy on September 27.

The allegedly malfunctioning camera explained only why Oswald was not photographed visiting the Cuban Embassy on Friday, September 27, but as for the alleged visit to the Soviet Embassy on that day, the CIA stated, "Why Oswald was missed in his probable entry to the Soviet installation on the 27th is not yet explained,"[613] which means they have no explanation.

---

[609] National Archives Record Number 104-10414-10368
[610] National Archives Record Number 104-10413-10070
[611] National Archives Record Number 104-10147-10110, p. 15
[612] National Archives Record Number 104-10413-10008, p. 11
[613] National Archives Record Number 104-10147-10110, p. 15

And as for no photographs of Oswald during his alleged visits to the two embassies on Saturday, September 28, the CIA claimed, "Both the Cuban and Soviet Embassies were closed to the public on Saturdays," and "photographic coverage was normally suspended" on Saturdays.

How could Oswald have visited either embassy on Saturday, September 28, if both embassies were closed to the public that day?

Three years later, in 1978, the CIA came up with a new story in a memorandum to the House Select Committee on Assassinations about the "camera bases" at the Soviet Embassy, stating, "There were two separate bases which covered the Soviet gate," and one camera base "was not working on September 28, 1963, a Saturday, although it did work four out of the eight Saturdays in September and October 1963 . . . . Coverage for the Soviet gate on Saturdays was standard operating procedure."[614]

So, the new story is that photographic coverage was not suspended on Saturdays, but they had no photograph of Oswald coming and going from the Soviet Embassy due to one of the two cameras not working on some Saturdays, whereas their previous story was that the camera covering the Cuban Embassy was not working on Friday, September 27.

Again, there had been no mention of a malfunctioning camera when the CIA's Mexico station did the "complete recheck" of all visitors to the Soviet and Cuban Embassies from September 1 through the first half of November. And since they were specifically looking for photographs of Oswald on September 27 and 28, it certainly would have been important to say something about cameras not functioning on those two particular days.

The CIA's 1978 story continues by stating the other camera base covering the Soviet Embassy "would have been working on the afternoon of the 27th and on Saturday the 28th," but it is "the base whose production is unaccountably missing. The Agency has not

---

[614] National Archives Record Number 104-10428-10029, pp. 6-7

as yet offered any explanation as to why the production is 'missing.'"615

The CIA "acknowledged" to the Assassination Records Review Board that back in 1963, the Mexico City station had "three photographic surveillance operations targeting the Soviet compound; and one photographic surveillance operation, which employed at least two cameras, targeting the Cuban compound."616

CIA photo of the KGB officer who impersonated Oswald taken outside the Soviet Embassy.

On March 12, 1964, the Warren Commission told the CIA that no government agency could "fill in the very large gaps still existing in Lee Harvey Oswald's visit to Mexico."

The Commission also stated "there were many days during which we knew nothing about his whereabouts" and "the evenings of his entire trip were unaccounted for."617

Further, the Warren Commission stated the "registry" at the hotel where Oswald allegedly stayed "showed the name of Oswald," but the hotel clerk "completely denies any other memory of Oswald's being

---

615 National Archives Record Number 104-10428-10029, p. 7
616 Final Report of the Assassinations Records Review Board, p. 85
617 National Archives Record Number 104-10422-10284, p. 5

at the hotel . . . . All the subordinate hotel personnel, such as cleaning ladies, etc., likewise deny any memory of Oswald."

A CIA document from December 1963 addresses Oswald's alleged time in Mexico, stating, "No source then at our disposal had ever actually seen Lee Oswald while he was in Mexico."[618]

Two Church Committee staffers examined the CIA's records on Oswald and the alleged Mexico visit, and in correspondence to another staffer, they wrote, "The unidentified individual visited the Soviet Embassy on October 1 and October 4, 1963 and impersonated Lee Harvey Oswald."[619]

The staffers also wrote that according to "a dispatch from Mexico City to Headquarters," the CIA's Western Hemisphere Division Chief "knew the identity of the individual."

The evidence is overwhelming that it was not Oswald at either the Soviet Embassy or the Cuban Embassy, but the entire cover-up hinged on Oswald's alleged visits to the Soviet and Cuban Embassies, which would cause President Johnson to fear that Soviet Premier Nikita Khrushchev and Cuban Premier Fidel Castro were behind President Kennedy's assassination.

The CIA kept Oswald in Houston while a KGB officer was impersonating him in Mexico.

An FBI report on the "day by day location of Lee Harvey Oswald" states that on September 23, Oswald told Ruth Paine that "he would go to Houston, where he had a friend and would look for work."[620]

A CIA report states that on September 23, 1963, when Oswald's wife and daughter left New Orleans for Irving, Texas, "Oswald did not go with them," stating that he "wanted to visit a friend in Houston, Texas."[621]

The FBI report on the "day by day location" of Oswald also states that on October 4, "Oswald arrived at the Paine residence" and told

---

[618] National Archives Record Number 104-10019-10021, p. 10
[619] National Archives Record Number 157-10014-10120, p. 78
[620] Warren Commission Hearings and Exhibits, Volume XXIV, p. 693
[621] National Archives Record Number 104-10434-10177, p. 12

Mrs. Paine that "he had been in Houston but had not found work" and he was "in Dallas for a few days before coming out to the house."

A Secret Service report states that Mrs. Paine "recalls Oswald being at her home for several days and stating that he had been in Houston, Texas, seeking employment, and that he had returned to Dallas several days prior to his arrival at the Paine home."[622]

The *Washington Post* reported that Ruth Paine said Oswald phoned his wife on October 4, 1963, "and related that upon leaving New Orleans, he had scouted around Houston for a job without success and had been looking around in Dallas the last few days."[623]

After the KGB infiltration of the CIA was exposed in 1984, one of the KGB officers admitted to impersonating Oswald at the Soviet and Cuban Embassies. His face perfectly matched the photograph taken at the Soviet Embassy on October 1, 1963, but he was completely bald by 1984. He also admitted to being one of the two KGB officers who assassinated President Kennedy.

The previously cited Warren Commission Exhibit 237, the Mexico City "unidentified mystery man," is a photograph of one of President Kennedy's three assassins.

During a visit to the Soviet Embassy, the KGB officer impersonating Oswald spoke with a KGB officer named Kostikov, who "specialized in handling Soviet agents operating under deep cover in the United States,"[624] which, of course, included KGB officers inside the CIA.

Kostikov was "believed to work for Department Thirteen of the First Chief Directorate of the KGB. It is the Department responsible for executive action, including sabotage and assassination."[625]

Oswald's alleged embassy visits and the alleged meeting with Kostikov immediately became the central focus of the assassination following Oswald's arrest.

---

[622] Warren Commission Hearings and Exhibits, Volume XXIV, p. 870
[623] Washington Post, 12-2-63, p. 3
[624] National Archives Record Number 124-10371-10117, p. 94
[625] National Archives Record Number 104-10422-10191, p. 11

Upon hearing that Oswald had been arrested for the assassination, the CIA's Mexico City station checked its telephone taps and discovered that the person who used Oswald's name on October 1 was unmistakably the same person who called and then visited the Soviet and the Cuban Embassies several times in late September.[626]

The Church Committee Report states, "For the first twenty-four hours after the assassination, the CIA's attention focused primarily on Oswald's September 27, 1963, visit to Mexico City."

It also states that "on the morning of November 23," CIA Director John McCone met with President Johnson and his National Security Advisor, McGeorge Bundy, to "brief them on the information CIA Headquarters had received from its Mexico City station,"[627] which means KGB officer John McCone immediately initiated the effort to implicate Khrushchev and Castro.

And there was no letting up in McCone's efforts to have the President worry about Soviet and Cuban involvement and the possibility of a nuclear war. As noted earlier, it was the on following day, November 24, that McCone informed Johnson of the CIA's "plans against Cuba,"[628] which included plans to assassinate Castro.

Then, after his official morning meeting with the President, McCone met with President Johnson "in his private residence" and suggested that he get "an early briefing on the Soviet long-range striking capability" and Soviet "air defense posture."[629]

A fabricated letter sent to the Soviet Embassy in Washington D.C. was meant to give credence to Oswald's alleged Mexico City visit. The Soviet Ambassador to the United States, Anatoly Dobrynin, sent a telegram to Moscow on November 26, 1963, declaring that someone had forged the letter as a "provocation."

---

[626] National Archives Record Number 104-10019-10023, pp. 9 & 11
[627] Church Committee: Book V, p. 24
[628] National Archives Record Number 180-10142-10036, p. 60
[629] National Archives Record Number 104-10301-10000, p. 25

The letter, allegedly written by Oswald, is on file as a Warren Commission Exhibit. In it, "Oswald" allegedly wrote, "I had not planned to contact the Soviet Embassy in Mexico, so they were unprepared. Had I been able to reach the Soviet Embassy in Havana as planned, the embassy there would have had time to complete our business . . . . Please inform us of the arrival of our Soviet entrance visas as soon as they come."[630]

Dobrynin's telegram to Moscow states, "This letter is clearly a provocation. It gives the impression we had close ties with Oswald and were using him for some purposes of our own. It was totally unlike any other letters the embassy had previously received from Oswald. Nor had he ever visited our embassy himself. The suspicion that the letter is a forgery is heightened by the fact that it was typed, whereas the other letters the embassy had received from Oswald before were handwritten."[631]

Oswald had written letters to the Soviet Embassy in Washington to inform them of the current address of his wife, Marina, pursuant to her Soviet-issued visa requirements. He also wrote to the Embassy on July 1, 1963, requesting that they "rush" an "entrance visa" for his wife and make "transportation arrangements" for her to go back to the Soviet Union. And as Anatoly Dobrynin noted in his telegram to Moscow, all of Oswald's letters were handwritten, not typed like the letter implying Oswald had been to the Soviet Embassy in Mexico and had plans to go to Cuba and the Soviet Union.[632]

Dobrynin goes on to say in his telegram to Moscow, "One gets the definite impression that the letter was concocted by those who, judging from everything, are involved in the President's assassination. The competent U.S. authorities are undoubtedly aware of this letter since the embassy's correspondence is under constant surveillance."

---

[630] Warren Commission Hearings and Exhibits, Volume XVI, p. 33
[631] Documents Handed to President Clinton by Russian President Boris Yeltsin, p. 95, on file at the National Archives
[632] National Archives Record Number 104-10322-10044, p. 14 and Warren Commission Hearings and Exhibits, Volume XVI, p. 30

As for Oswald's desire that the Soviet Embassy "rush" an entrance visa for his wife and make "transportation arrangements" for her to go back to the Soviet Union, Oswald "was beating his wife Marina" three months after he returned to the United States with her in June 1962.[633]

And Oswald continued to beat his wife. An FBI agent interviewed the apartment manager where the Oswalds lived from November 1962 to March 1963, and his report states, "They had considerable difficulty with Mr. Oswald who apparently drank to excess and beat his wife on numerous occasions. They had numerous complaints from the other tenants due to Oswald's drinking and beating his wife."[634]

The FBI interviewed the owner of the building where the Oswalds were living in April 1963 and again found that Oswald's neighbors had complained that he was "beating his wife."[635]

On February 17, 1963, two weeks before the Oswalds moved out of their apartment, Oswald's wife, Marina, wrote to the Soviet Embassy stating, "I beg your assistance to help me return to the Homeland in the USSR . . . . I am requesting you to extend to me a possible material aid for the trip . . . . My husband remains here since he is an American by nationality. I beg you once more not to refuse my request."[636]

One month later, on March 17, 1963, Marina made an official "Declaration" in writing to the Soviet Ambassador, stating, "I am applying for a visa for entry into the USSR and beg you not to deny my request. My husband remains in the U.S.A."[637]

The Soviet Embassy replied to Marina on April 18, 1963, stating she would have to "come to Washington in order to visit the Consulate Section of our Embassy," and if it was "difficult" for her to do that, she would have to write a letter stating why she

---

[633] Warren Commission Hearings and Exhibits, Volume IX, pp. 231 & 310
[634] Warren Commission Hearings and Exhibits, Volume XVII, p. 773
[635] Warren Commission Document 7, p. 106
[636] Warren Commission Hearings and Exhibits, Volume XVI, p. 10
[637] Warren Commission Hearings and Exhibits, Volume XVI, p. 20

requested "this permission for entering the USSR for permanent residence."[638]

The Soviet Embassy sent another letter to Marina on June 4, 1963, telling her once again, "If it is difficult for you to visit us, we request you to advise us by letter concerning reasons which made you request this permission for entering the USSR for permanent residence."[639]

Oswald and his wife were clearly unhappy with each other, which explains why, on July 1, 1963, he requested in his hand-written letter that they "rush" an "entrance visa" for his wife and make "transportation arrangements" for her to go back to the Soviet Union.

In addition to the typed letter that someone sent to the Soviet Embassy on November 9 alleging that Oswald had visited the Soviet Embassy in Mexico and that he, too, was anxiously awaiting a Soviet visa, information was sent from inside the Soviet Union to implicate Lee Harvey Oswald.

The FBI reported that three letters were sent to Oswald from inside the Soviet Union in the months of September and October 1963. The letters alleged that Oswald had "plans to return to the Soviet Union," which ties in with the alleged Mexico trip in September and an alleged desire to obtain visas to Cuba and the Soviet Union.[640]

In the months of September, October, and November, action had clearly been taken to make it seem like Oswald had definite plans to return to the Soviet Union, but as stated in Chapter 10, Oswald was originally recruited to feign defection to the Soviet Union, and a CIA document quotes Oswald as having written, "When I first went to Russia in the winter of 1959 my funds were very limited, so after a certain time, after the Russians had assured themselves that I was really the naive American who believed in Communism, they arranged for me to receive a certain amount of money every month,"

---

[638] Warren Commission Hearings and Exhibits, Volume XVI, p. 22
[639] Warren Commission Hearings and Exhibits, Volume XVI, p. 24
[640] Warren Commission Document 107, p. 63

not to mention that Oswald was "highly critical of Soviet rigged elections, the massing of crowds for staged demonstrations, travel restrictions, regimentation, and the lack of freedom of press, speech, and religion."[641]

The idea that Oswald was in Mexico City in September and desperately trying to get a visa to return to the Soviet Union is absurd and was completely manufactured to create the fear that Castro and Khrushchev were involved in the assassination. As noted earlier, the Church Committee Report states, "For the first twenty-four hours after the assassination, the CIA's attention focused primarily on Oswald's September 27, 1963, visit to Mexico City."[642]

On November 23, Sylvia Duran, the woman who spoke to the KGB officer at the Cuban Embassy, was "arrested and interrogated about Oswald" at the behest of the CIA's Mexico City station,[643] and the arrest was being discussed at the highest levels of the Cuban government.

The CIA intercepted a conversation between Cuban President Osvaldo Dorticos and the Cuban Ambassador to Mexico, Joaquin Hernandez, on November 26. The CIA's Mexico City Station immediately sent a transcript to Headquarters in a "Flash" cable, meaning it had the highest priority and was more than an emergency. The first page of the cable states, "Please note Dorticos preoccupation over question of money."[644]

The Cuban President asked Ambassador Hernandez, "The Federal Police of that country attempted to force Sylvia Duran to say, with promises of leniency, that we had offered money to the American?"[645]

"No, no, nothing about money," replied the Cuban Ambassador.

---

[641] National Archives Record Numbers 104-10408-10104, p. 3 & 104-10439-10009, p. 15
[642] Church Committee: Book V, p. 24
[643] National Archives Record Number 104-10004-10202, p. 16
[644] National Archives Record Number 104-10404-10175, p. 2
[645] National Archives Record Number 104-10404-10114, p. 16

President Dorticos then asked, "And they tried to detain her, to oblige her to make a statement," and the Cuban Ambassador replied, "She was detained and questioned with respect to this visit and the request for a visa," and after the Cuban Ambassador explained more of what took place during the interrogation, President Dorticos again inquired, "Did they ask her some other question about money?"[646]

"No. No absolutely," replied Ambassador Hernandez, who told President Dorticos that the Mexican authorities had asked Sylvia Duran about her relationship with her husband and any relations with Oswald, and President Dorticos again, for the third time, asked about money.

"And they spoke of money?" he said.

"No. No. She has not told me anything about money . . . . That is, she has not told me that they spoke to her about that," replied Ambassador Hernandez.

Upon hearing the Cuban Ambassador deny for the third time that the Mexican Federal Police tried to get Sylvia Duran to say that Cuba "had offered money to the American," President Dorticos made reference to the Cuban Consul in Mexico, Alfredo Mirabal, stating, "Mirabal said to a friend something about that."

President Dorticos concluded by telling the Cuban Ambassador to "question her some more. Investigate more and call me here," which resulted in the Cuban Ambassador calling President Dorticos again in the evening, at which time the Cuban President again wanted to know "whether she had been threatened so that she would declare that the people at the Consulate had given money to this person, the American."[647]

The Cuban Ambassador once again replied, "No, no. Nothing of the sort."

Cuban President Osvaldo Dorticos clearly thought that a story would be generated in which "Oswald" received "money" from someone at the Cuban Consulate, and he clearly thought that the

---

[646] National Archives Record Number 104-10404-10175, pp. 7-8
[647] National Archives Record Number 104-10404-10114, p. 22

Mexican Federal Police would generate the story after arresting Sylvia Duran at the behest of the CIA.

Alfredo Mirabal, whom Dorticos identified as his source for thinking that a story would be generated about Cuba paying Oswald to kill President Kennedy, was Cuba's "chief of intelligence" in Mexico and was "directly in touch" with Cuba's top intelligence chief in Cuba.[648]

On Wednesday, November 27, the Mexican Federal Police picked up Cuban Embassy employee Sylvia Duran again, and a CIA cable to their Mexico City station stated, "We want to ensure that neither Sylvia Duran nor Cubans get impression that Americans behind her re-arrest. In other words, we want Mexican authorities to take responsibility for whole affair."[649]

The idea that Oswald took a payoff at the Cuban Embassy to kill President Kennedy was clearly supposed to be an integral part of the story, which would obviously result in President Johnson thinking Castro was behind the assassination.

On November 25, 1963, the CIA used a Nicaraguan informant to generate such a story, and on the following day, November 26, the CIA's Mexico City station sent a cable to Headquarters stating, "At this moment, station officer and local security officer are interviewing Nicaraguan who claims that on 18 September he saw Lee Oswald receive six thousand five hundred dollars in meeting inside Cuban Embassy."[650]

The Nicaraguan was eventually identified as Gilberto Alvarado Ugarte, "an informant" for a Nicaraguan Security Service officer who is "a CIA source."[651]

Alvarado first "called the American Embassy" on Monday, November 25, and later met with two Embassy security officers. He told them directly that he saw the Cubans pay Oswald $6,500,

---

[648] National Archives Record Number 104-10408-10148, p. 4
[649] National Archives Record Number 104-10404-10160
[650] National Archives Record Number 104-10406-10112, p. 94
[651] National Archives Record Number 104-10400-10055, pp. 12-13

which would be more than $65,000 in the year 2023. Alvarado then repeated his story to a CIA "station officer" on November 26, after which two CIA officers "interrogated" him.[652]

Four days later, on November 30, 1963, one day after President Johnson established the Warren Commission to prevent a nuclear war due to Castro's alleged involvement in killing President Kennedy, Alvarado "admitted to Mexican security officials in writing that his whole story of having seen Lee Oswald receive money in the Cuban embassy in Mexico City was false."[653]

The CIA stated, "Alvarado clearly was a trained intelligence agent."[654]

FBI Director J. Edgar Hoover called President Johnson on November 29 and told him that the Cuban payoff story is "giving us a great deal of trouble."[655] But when Hoover called Johnson, the President was apparently unaware of an internal CIA cable two days earlier in which the CIA stated there is "mounting evidence that Alvarado is fabricating his story of seeing Oswald take money in the Cuban Embassy . . . . We find it incredible that the Cubans would brief and pay an assassin in front of a stranger."[656]

Another internal CIA cable on November 27 said Oswald "applied for unemployment insurance in New Orleans on 17 September," one day before he was allegedly taking a payoff at the Cuban Embassy in Mexico City, and the cable states that Oswald's "New Orleans landlady believes he was there continuously between 17 and 25 September." This cable, too, said the information "gives further reason to believe Alvarado is fabricating,"[657] but as with the other cable on November 27, Johnson was obviously not informed of it.

---

[652] National Archives Record Number 104-10422-10009
[653] National Archives Record Number 104-10400-10055, pp. 12-13
[654] National Archives Record Number 104-10408-10056, p. 13
[655] Lyndon Baines Johnson Library, LBJ Phone Calls; Telephone Conversation between the President and J. Edgar Hoover, 29 Nov 1963, 1:40PM, p. 2
[656] National Archives Record Number 104-10434-10080
[657] National Archives Record Number 104-10434-10089

A CIA Memo for the Record on November 27 also addresses Oswald's whereabouts when he was supposedly at the Cuban Consulate in Mexico. It states, "A check of airlines indicates that he did not leave New Orleans that day or the following one, and every indication, including the statements by his landlady, would lead to the conclusion that he remained in New Orleans until 25 September 1963."[658]

As noted earlier, on November 23 the CIA's Mexico City station did a "complete recheck" of "all visitors" to the Soviet and Cuban Embassies from September 1 through the "first half November," and it "shows no evidence Oswald visit,"[659] which by itself would prove that Alvarado was lying about seeing Oswald at the Cuban Embassy on September 18.

Besides keeping President Johnson in the dark about Alvarado's story being a fabrication, CIA Director and KGB officer John McCone sent a cable to President Johnson's National Security Advisor, McGeorge Bundy, on November 27 vouching for Alvarado and his credibility.

McCone stated that Alvarado had been questioned "until 2 a.m. this morning," and "the wealth of detail Alvarado gives about events and personalities involved with Oswald in Cuban Embassy is striking." McCone also stated that the CIA officer who questioned Alvarado "was impressed by Alvarado," who "is now hiding" in a CIA safe house.[660]

And to add weight to the idea that there was now solid information linking Castro to the assassination, McCone ominously warned, "We cannot guarantee Alvarado's safety."

An internal CIA cable from the following day, November 28, states that an "investigation of Oswald's activities" had determined that Oswald "was in New Orleans on September 19, 1963," one day after he was allegedly in Mexico taking a payoff. It also states that

---

[658] National Archives Record Number 104-10434-10104
[659] National Archives Record Number 104-10413-10008, p. 11
[660] National Archives Record Number 124-10371-10115, pp. 20-21

the CIA "can confidently regard Alvarado as fabricator" and that Alvarado "might respond to the suggestion that he has been having delusions and needs psychiatric treatment,"[661] but as with the two cables and the memo from the previous day, Johnson was not informed of it.

CIA Director John McCone had a meeting with President Johnson early on November 28, but McCone did not inform the President of Alvarado's deception. McCone did, however, send a letter to National Security Advisor McGeorge Bundy, and he included a "Memorandum for the President through Mr. McGeorge Bundy" in which McCone once again vouched for Alvarado.

McCone informed Johnson in his wordy "Memorandum for the President through Mr. McGeorge Bundy" that in his meeting with President Johnson that day, "Time prevented me from mentioning this morning's developments in Mexico City."[662]

The memorandum started out with McCone's "developments," which recapped in precise detail everything about Oswald's alleged visit to Mexico at the end of September and who Alvarado was and his story about an alleged payoff to Oswald on September 18. It also recapped how the CIA was "holding Alvarado voluntarily in a safe house" and "checking every detail of his story." (Johnson was already aware of all these alleged "developments.")

As with his cable to Bundy the day before, McCone harped on Alvarado's credibility, telling Johnson that Alvarado "has advised our station in great detail of his alleged knowledge that he actually saw Oswald given $6,500 in the Cuban Embassy in Mexico City on September 18th." McCone's November 28 memorandum sounds like a repeat of his November 27 cable, and McCone is obviously trying to communicate that he just cannot get over how Alvarado is giving details of a conspiracy involving Castro, even if he did write that Alvarado's "knowledge" of a Cuban payoff to Oswald was now seen as "alleged knowledge."

---

[661] National Archives Record Number 104-10434-10121
[662] National Archives Record Number 104-10438-10227, pp. 3-4

The only thing that would cast a negative light on Alvarado's story was relatively hidden in the fifth paragraph of McCone's eight-paragraph memorandum. The entirety of the memorandum was worded in such a way as to give weight to Alvarado's story and the possibility of Cuban involvement, and unless Johnson himself carefully read the memorandum, he would miss that McCone stated in the fifth paragraph, "We doubt the story."

The sixth paragraph mentions Sylvia Duran's arrest, stating, "This arrest has caused several telephone conversations between the Cuban Ambassador in Mexico and President Dorticos in which Dorticos has expressed great concern over money matters."

McCone then blatantly lied about Dorticos's "great concern over money matters," stating, "It is somewhat obscure, however, whether his concern runs to a disclosure or an attempt by the Mexican authorities to bribe Sylvia Duran into making a damaging statement."

There was nothing "obscure" about what Dorticos said. Dorticos wanted to know if Sylvia Duran told Mexican authorities that the Cubans "had offered money to the American."[663] In another conversation that evening, Dorticos focused on whether "she had been threatened so that she would declare that the people at the Consulate had given money to this person, the American."[664]

McCone knew perfectly well that there was nothing in the conversation about "Mexican authorities" trying to "bribe Sylvia Duran," and the only other explanation that McCone proffered for Dorticos's "great concern over money matters" is that it is an amazing "disclosure" that Cuba paid Oswald to kill President Kennedy.

To further his objective of promoting how potentially ominous Alvarado's story was, CIA Director John McCone wrote in the seventh paragraph, "At the moment, it seems that Alvarado's

---

[663] National Archives Record Number 104-10404-10114, p. 16
[664] National Archives Record Number 104-10404-10114, p. 22

statement cannot be verified because of the dates or for other reasons. However, the investigation will continue."

"Seems" that it cannot be "verified" is a far cry from saying that Alvarado's story is patently false and ridiculous and that there is no need for further investigation.

McCone's memorandum "through Bundy" was clearly designed to keep President Johnson in the dark about Alvarado's deception so that Johnson would fear the possibility of Cuban involvement.

McCone did, however, call President Johnson on November 30, one day after Johnson established the Warren Commission, and said, "We had a phone call from Mexico City that this fellow Alvarado that I was telling you about this morning . . . signed a statement that all the statements that he made in connection with that matter had been false . . . . Apparently there is no such truth in it at all . . . . So this looks like it probably washes out entirely."[665]

The effort to implicate Castro began exactly one year before President Johnson established the Warren Commission.

The CIA intercepted a letter from Havana, Cuba postmarked November 29, 1962, stating, "If we are able to kill President Kennedy, it would be a great success, super extraordinary for Fidel and for the Communist Liberation Movement . . . . We have to rely on our own forces. Russia cannot do it all . . . . If we are able to do this, we will paralyze imperialism completely. They will respect Fidel and his government more . . . . We will also completely paralyze the future plans of the United States if we are successful in killing Kennedy . . . . Fidel is very anxious to know how the plans are progressing."[666]

But the FBI would not be investigating any possible Cuban involvement in the assassination, because the FBI's investigation was extremely short lived.

---

[665] Lyndon Baines Johnson Library, LBJ Phone Calls; Telephone Conversation between the President and Director McCone, 30 Nov 1963, 3:14PM, p. 1
[666] National Archives Record Number 104-10308-10250, pp. 3 & 4

At 9:20 p.m. on Friday, November 22, the FBI sent a message to all FBI field offices instructing them to "immediately contact all informants, security, racial and criminal, as well as other sources for information bearing on assassination of President Kennedy. All offices immediately establish whereabouts of bombing suspects, all known Klan and hate group members," and "known racial extremists."[667]

Then, less than two hours later, at 11 p.m. the FBI sent a second message to its field offices, stating, "The Bureau is conducting an investigation to determine who is responsible for the assassination. You are therefore instructed to follow and resolve all allegations pertaining to the assassination. This matter is of utmost urgency."[668]

At 11:20 a.m. on Saturday, November 23, barely twelve hours after the second message of November 22, the FBI told its personnel to completely disregard the previous day's messages and go back to what they were doing before the assassination.

The FBI sent a message to all FBI field offices stating, "Lee Harvey Oswald has been developed as the principal suspect in the assassination of President Kennedy.... All offices should resume normal contacts with informants and other sources."[669]

Less than twenty-four hours after the President of the United States was assassinated, the FBI was no longer interested in who else may have been involved in the assassination, and to add to the inanity of it, FBI Director J. Edgar Hoover called President Johnson on November 23 and stated, "The evidence that we have at the present time is not very strong.... The case as it stands now isn't strong enough to be able to get a conviction."[670]

---

[667] Church Committee: Book V, p. 39
[668] Ibid.
[669] Ibid.
[670] Lyndon Baines Johnson Library, LBJ Phone Calls; Telephone Conversation between the President and J. Edgar Hoover, 23 Nov 1963, p. 2

Oswald was killed the following day, Sunday, November 24, thus eliminating the need for a "conviction" when the "evidence" that Oswald is the assassin "is not very strong."

FBI Director J. Edgar Hoover spoke to White House aide Walter Jenkins "immediately following Oswald's murder" and told Jenkins, "The thing I am most concerned about, and so is Mr. Katzenbach, is having something issued so we can convince the public that Oswald is the real assassin."[671]

Hoover also wrote a memo on November 24 reiterating that he and CIA officer Nicholas Katzenbach wanted to "convince the public that Oswald is the real assassin . . . . Mr. Katzenbach thinks that the President might appoint a Presidential Commission of three outstanding citizens to make a determination."[672]

The next day, Monday, November 25, Katzenbach sent his memo to the White House stating, "The public must be satisfied that Oswald was the assassin; that he did not have confederates who are still at large; and that the evidence was such that he would have been convicted at trial."[673]

A memorandum to an Assistant FBI Director states, "The basic investigation showing how the assassination occurred was substantially completed by November 26, 1963," and all FBI actions after that date were to "further verify the information developed up to November 26, 1963."[674]

The FBI sent a "supervisor" to Mexico City on November 27 with orders to "coordinate the investigation and pursue it vigorously until the desired results are obtained," which "desired results" were, of course, to "convince the public that Oswald is the real assassin."[675]

The FBI, after quickly claiming that Oswald was the lone assassin, was clearly prevented from doing anything to either establish or refute a Cuban connection to the assassination. The CIA, which was

---

[671] Church Committee: Book V, p. 33
[672] House Select Committee on Assassinations, Volume XI, p. 250
[673] House Select Committee on Assassinations, Volume XI, pp. 411-412
[674] National Archives Record Number 124-10370-10003, p. 260
[675] Church Committee: Book V, p. 103

overrun with the very KGB officers who had assassinated President Kennedy, would be conducting the investigation. The CIA alone was tasked with determining whether anyone else was involved in the assassination. The FBI would be doing nothing but seeking to "further verify the information developed up to November 26, 1963."

The Warren Commission subsequently instructed the FBI and the Secret Service to send all their information to the CIA. An internal Warren Commission document states that on March 12, 1964, the CIA confirmed that "the FBI and the Secret Service were continuing to forward materials to the CIA as the Commission had previously requested."[676]

President Johnson was initially opposed to establishing a Presidential Commission and was highly in favor of a Texas State Inquiry into the assassination, which he made clear in a phone call to FBI Director J. Edgar Hoover on November 25, 1963, the same day that Katzenbach wrote his memo to the White House promoting a Commission.

Johnson told Hoover, "Some lawyer in Justice is lobbying with the *Post* because that's where the suggestion came from for this Presidential Commission, which we think would be very bad."[677]

Johnson promoted having the FBI work in conjunction with the Texas State Inquiry, telling Hoover, "The State Attorney General is young and able and prudent . . . . He's going to have associated with him the most outstanding jurists in the country . . . . They can expect Waggoner Carr, the Attorney General of Texas, to make an announcement this morning to have a state inquiry, and you can offer them your full cooperation and vice versa."

After telling FBI Director J. Edgar Hoover to have the FBI fully cooperate with the Texas State Inquiry, President Johnson further

---

[676] National Archives Record Number 104-10422-10284, p. 8
[677] Lyndon Baines Johnson Library, LBJ Phone Calls; Telephone Conversation between the President and J. Edgar Hoover, 25 Nov 1963, 10:30AM, pp. 1-2

disparaged "this Commission thing," stating, "Sometimes a Commission that's not trained hurts more than it helps."

In a phone conversation with newspaper columnist Joseph Alsop just ten minutes after speaking to Hoover, Johnson again promoted having the FBI work with the Texas State Inquiry, stating, "They're going to have FBI from outside Texas, but this is under Texas law . . . . We don't send in a bunch of carpet-baggers . . . . If we have another Commission, hell, you're gonna have people running over each other."[678] (Assassinating the President was not a "federal" crime in 1963, which is why Johnson stated that the investigation was "under Texas law.")

Later in the conversation, Alsop told President Johnson, "I now see exactly how right you are and how wrong I was about this idea of a blue ribbon commission," and Johnson replied, "Katzenbach suggested that and that provoked it."

CIA Director John McCone met with President Johnson the next day, Tuesday, November 26, and a CIA Memorandum for the Record disclosed, "The President noted with some considerable contempt the fact that certain people in the Department of Justice had suggested to him on Saturday that an independent investigation of the President's assassination should be conducted by a high level group of attorneys and jurists."[679]

The memorandum continued, "President Johnson rejected this idea, and then he heard that the identical plan was to be advanced in a lead editorial in the *Washington Post*. The President felt this was a deliberate plant and he was exceedingly critical. He personally intervened."

CIA officer Nicholas Katzenbach, using his "official cover" as Deputy Attorney General, obviously went into action on Saturday, November 23, suggesting the idea of a Presidential Commission to Johnson and then lobbying the *Post*. He then harped on the idea with

---

[678] Ibid., Telephone Conversation between the President and Mr. Joe Alsop, 25 Nov 1963, 10:40AM pp. 2 & 6
[679] National Archives Record Number 104-10408-10099, p. 5

J. Edgar Hoover on Sunday, November 24, and pressed the issue further by writing his memo to the White House on Monday, November 25.

Katzenbach's 3-day push for a Presidential Commission was clearly not yielding results, nor was the phony story about Oswald visiting the Soviet and Cuban Embassies in Mexico. President Johnson was apparently not moved when, on Sunday, November 24, McCone informed him of the CIA's "plans against Cuba," which included assassinating Fidel Castro, and then advised him to get "an early briefing on the Soviet long-range striking capability" and Soviet "air defense posture."

It all sounded so ominous, but President Johnson had absolutely no desire for a Presidential Commission and displayed his "considerable contempt" for the idea when he met with CIA Director and KGB officer John McCone on Tuesday, November 26.

The next day, Wednesday, November 27, McCone sent his cable to National Security Advisor McGeorge Bundy in which he pointed out every detail of Alvarado's story about Oswald receiving a payoff in the Cuban Embassy with absolutely no disparaging remarks about Alvarado. McCone clearly made it sound like Alvarado's story was an amazing development that changed everything.

On the following day, Thursday, November 28, President Johnson was apparently very much in favor of a Presidential Commission, which he made clear in a phone call to Senator James Eastland. Johnson told Eastland, "My thought is this . . . if we could have two Congressmen and two Senators . . . and maybe a Justice of the Supreme Court take the FBI report and review it and write a report . . . and do anything they felt needed to be done . . . . This is a very explosive thing, and it could be a very dangerous thing for the country . . . . What would you think about . . . getting somebody from the Court and somebody from the

House and somebody from the Senate and have a real high-level judiciary study of all the facts?"[680]

In a call to Senate Majority Leader Mike Mansfield on Friday, November 29, 1963, President Johnson stated, "Secretary of State is here with me now and he's quite concerned about it. We have given a good deal of thought, at least I have, to the suggestion of Katzenbach over at Justice to having a high-level Commission . . . to having someone from each side, House and Senate, and let them review the investigation that has been made by the Court of Inquiry and the thorough one by the FBI and let them staff it."[681]

Johnson then put Secretary of State Dean Rusk on the phone with Senator Mansfield, and Rusk told Mansfield of the "possible implications . . . that if the rumors were to leak out as fact, and if there were anything in this that had not been fully substantiated, it would cause a tremendous storm."

Rusk also said, "Trying to get . . . the absolute truth . . . is very much in my mind. This has already been commented on and picked up all around the world, and if we're not careful here, we could really blow up quite a storm."

But the CIA documented that the "alleged plots" to kill President Kennedy "are seen everywhere as racist and rightist,"[682] and the Soviet Union went as far as to repeatedly implicate Goldwater in a plot to kill President Kennedy.

The only thing that could possibly cause Johnson to worry that people are testifying "Khrushchev did this" and "Castro did that" is disinformation from CIA Director John McCone and the phony story about Oswald going to the Soviet and Cuban embassies in Mexico.

McCone's blatant disinformation is readily apparent in Johnson's phone call to Senator Richard Russell on November 29. Johnson told Senator Russell that Secretary of State Dean Rusk is "deeply

---

[680] Lyndon Baines Johnson Library, LBJ Phone Calls, Telephone Conversation between the President and Senator Eastland, 28 Nov 1963, 3:21PM, p. 1
[681] Lyndon Baines Johnson Library, LBJ Phone Calls; Telephone Conversation between the President and Senator Mike Mansfield, 29 Nov 1963, 11:10AM, p. 2
[682] Warren Commission Document 1135, p. 64

concerned" about the claim that "they're spreading throughout the communist world" that "Khrushchev has killed Kennedy."[683]

To repeat, the only claim "spreading throughout the communist world" was that there was a right wing conspiracy to kill President Kennedy. There was absolutely no one claiming that Khrushchev killed Kennedy.

McCone and his KGB minions easily hoodwinked the entire United States government hierarchy into thinking that if Lee Harvey Oswald is not pegged as President Kennedy's lone assassin, the United States would be risking nuclear war with the Soviet Union.

On November 29, White House aide Walter Jenkins sent a memo to President Johnson stating that CIA officer Nicholas Katzenbach, whose initial three-day push for a Presidential Commission failed, is now "preparing a description of how the Commission would function."[684]

On January 23, 1964, as the cover-up plan proceeded along, "The Warren Commission began requesting information from the CIA."[685]

The Church Committee reported that the Warren Commission staff "was given access to CIA files on the assassination, including material obtained from sensitive sources and methods." The CIA gave the Warren Commission "all significant information CIA investigators had."[686]

On April 6, 1964, a CIA cable made reference to "three members of Warren Commission legal staff" who would be going to Mexico as part of the investigation, and it states, "All have studied our reports in detail."[687]

---

[683] LBJ Library, LBJ Phone Calls; Telephone Conversation between the President and Senator Russell, 29 Nov 1963, 8:55PM, p. 5
[684] House Select Committee on Assassinations, Volume XI, p. 6
[685] Church Committee: Book V, p. 31
[686] Church Committee: Book V, pp. 58 & 59
[687] National Archives Record Number 104-10434-10390

CIA Director John McCone made it clear that the CIA handled the Warren Commission investigation. He sent a letter to his cover-up man, CIA officer Nicholas Katzenbach, in February 1965 stating that CIA operatives were in "close contact" with the Warren Commission staff "throughout the existence of the President's Commission."[688]

McCone's letter also states that CIA personnel "were instructed by me to cooperate fully with the President's Commission and to withhold nothing from its scrutiny." By that time, CIA officer Nicholas Katzenbach had an "official cover" as Attorney General of the United States, an "official" government position that provided "cover" for him while he carried out the CIA's agenda.

A 1971 CIA memorandum confirms that "CIA did not withhold any information from the Warren Commission."[689] CIA Director John McCone and Deputy Director for Plans Richard Helms "extended to the Commission full access to the Agency's most sensitive information and the sources and methods involved."[690]

On September 22, 1964, just a few days before the Warren Commission released its report, a CIA Bulletin titled "Propaganda Notes" stated that the U.S. State Department would be sending copies of the Warren Commission Report to "American Diplomatic Posts" for "selective presentation to editors, jurists, Government officials, and other opinion leaders."[691]

The Propaganda Notes Bulletin also states that CIA Headquarters would be sending "copies of this Government Printing Office edition" to CIA "field stations," where "covert assets should explain the tragedy . . . and counter all efforts to misconstrue it . . . . Divisions should make bulk purchases for field use through regular channels."

The American taxpayer would be paying various "divisions" of the Central Intelligence Agency to purchase "bulk" quantities of the Warren Commission Report. CIA "field officers" and their "covert

---

[688] National Archives Record Number 104-10412-10212
[689] National Archives Record Number 104-10320-10043
[690] National Archives Record Number 104-10009-10101, p. 3
[691] National Archives Record Number 104-10412-10121

assets" in the United States and abroad would then use the report to push the idea that Lee Harvey Oswald was the lone assassin and there was no conspiracy to assassinate President Kennedy.

By January 1967, less than two and a half years after the "Propaganda Notes" Bulletin, the CIA was so concerned about people thinking there was a conspiracy to kill President Kennedy that it issued a thirteen-page dispatch titled "Countering Criticism of the Warren Report."

The CIA dispatch stated that "speculation about the responsibility" for the assassination had been "stemmed by the Warren Commission report, which appeared at the end of September 1964. Various writers have now had time to scan the Commission's published report and documents . . . . There has been a new wave of books and articles criticizing the Commission's findings . . . . Conspiracy theories have frequently thrown suspicion on our organization."[692]

Under "Action," the dispatch instructs CIA officers to "discuss the publicity problem with liaison and friendly elite contacts, especially politicians and editors," and tell these "friendly elite contacts" that the "charges of the critics are without serious foundation."

It also instructs CIA officers to "urge" their contacts to "use their influence." CIA officers were told to "employ propaganda assets to answer and refute the attacks of the critics." They were also told that "book reviews and feature articles" would be "particularly appropriate" for "propaganda assets" to use.

In the end, the Warren Report was nothing but a work of propaganda designed to relieve the CIA of culpability in their one and only successful assassination of a United States President.

The Warren Commission was directed to make a case for no conspiracy while completely relying on and trusting the CIA to investigate the assassination. KGB officers inside the CIA easily used the CIA to supply the Warren Commission with information

---

[692] National Archives Record Number 104-10406-10110, p. 2 & 3

that would implicate their chosen patsies in the assassination, namely, anti-Castro Cubans. Those patsies are addressed in the next chapter.

Chapter 13: The KGB's Chosen Patsies in the Assassination

Warren Commission member Gerald Ford testified at the closed-door Congressional hearings in 1984 that the Warren Commission was absolutely certain that Cubans assassinated President Kennedy. Ford also testified that the CIA was the source of information that Cubans killed President Kennedy, and a CIA officer clarified that the alleged Cuban assassins to whom Ford was referring were anti-Castro Cuban exiles.

The CIA focused their attention on anti-Castro Cubans just four days after the assassination, which would be November 26, the day that the FBI "substantially completed" its investigation.

A CIA officer at the CIA's Miami field station wrote that he contacted a "political contact and Cuban exile leader" and several of his "assets," telling them, among other things: "Get me all possible data on any Cuban exile you know who disappeared just before or right after the Kennedy murder and has since been missing from Miami under suspicious circumstances.[693]

"Give me a list of all Cuban exiles or Cubano-Americans you consider to be capable of orchestrating the murder of President Kennedy in order to precipitate an armed conflict between Cuba and the USA.

"Give me a list of the richest Cubans in exile; Cubans possessing sufficient personal wealth and the possible inclination to bankroll the murder of President Kennedy."

---

[693] National Archives Record Number 104-10423-10226, pp. 5-6

The CIA officer wrote, "The above questions levied on my agents were not my own invention but were the results of talk sessions held in the FI [Foreign Intelligence] branch of my Station by our Branch Chief and my fellow case officers."

Anti-Castro Cubans were suspects in the assassination for good reason. The CIA, under the leadership of Soviet KGB officer John McCone, spent considerable time and effort making the anti-Castro Cubans look like they would have a reason to assassinate President Kennedy.

Secretary of State Dean Rusk wrote a letter to President Kennedy in March 1963, stating he was concerned about "hit and run raids by Cuban exiles," particularly an "exile attack that caused substantial damage to a Soviet vessel." CIA officers, of course, had to be intricately involved when their assets attacked and caused "substantial damage" to a "Soviet vessel."[694]

Secretary Rusk's letter resulted in President Kennedy having the National Security Council Executive Committee meet on March 29 to "discuss the problem posed by Cuban Refugee groups." Everyone was given a copy of the Rusk letter to use "as a basis for discussion."

Three weeks earlier, President Kennedy "approved" actions taken by "several departments and agencies" to "control the movement of subversives and subversive trainees." Action was also taken to put "controls on movement of propaganda material," along with "controls on movement of arms" and "controls on movement of funds."[695]

The CIA, under the leadership of KGB officer John McCone, specifically "increased its efforts designed to control the movement of persons, arms, and propaganda materials to and from Cuba."[696]

On March 30, one day after the NSC Executive Committee met to discuss the exile "problem," law enforcement agencies that dealt with

---

[694] National Archives Record Number 104-10306-10016, pp. 5 & 6
[695] National Archives Record Number 104-10310-10009, p. 2
[696] Ibid., p. 6

the Cuban exiles were directed to take "vigorous measures to assure that the pertinent laws of the United States are observed."[697]

Two days later, a CIA cable stated that Cuban exile leaders in Florida had been notified that they were prohibited from "travel outside Dade County," which resulted in the "exile colony" being in an "uproar" over the travel prohibition. The cable stated that exile reaction "appears universal over this issue" and is clearly "anti-U.S. and anti-Kennedy."[698]

Specific Cuban exile leaders who were being handled by the CIA were extremely vocal concerning the travel prohibition, stating that the United States "cannot be trusted as an ally" and "has abandoned Cuba." One exile leader told the FBI "to reserve space for him in local jail" as he has "no intention of accepting travel restriction."

Another exile leader stated, "Elimination of exile action," combined with Castro's "crackdown" on guerilla forces in Cuba, will bring "an end to internal resistance" and ultimately lead to the Cuban people's "acceptance of Castro."

Cuban exiles saw the travel restriction as an "alliance" between the United States and Russia, and a Cuban exile leader "expressed a general opinion" among Cuban exiles that the United States was "protecting" Castro. Another exile leader stated that "it looks like" the United States is now "against the anti-Castro cause."

A memorandum to KGB officer and CIA Director John McCone in early April 1963 states that the leader of the Cuban Revolutionary Council, Dr. Jose Miro Cardona, was resigning because of "no indication from Washington that there is a definite plan for the liberation of Cuba." The memo to McCone goes on to cite "great and wide-spread pessimism in exile groups" because of

---

[697] U.S. State Department Website https://1997-2001.state.gov/about_state/history/volume_vi/exchanges.html
[698] National Archives Record Number 104-10308-10330, pp. 2-3

"the restrictions imposed upon Cuban exile efforts to defeat Castro."[699]

McCone himself wrote a Memorandum for the Record on April 11, 1963, stating that the U.S. government and the CIA "more or less disenfranchised ourselves from the Cuban colony in Miami as a result of the Miro Cardona incident."[700]

On April 18, the CIA reported that Luis Conte Aguero, a radio commentator in charge of Cuban exile "propaganda" and a "semi-monthly bulletin" for that purpose, "seems to be taking stronger anti-U.S. stand in exile controversy and egging Miro on by criticizing him for resigning instead of denouncing Americans."[701]

The crackdown on Cuban exiles continued in the Summer of 1963. On July 31, 1963, the FBI raided "a Cuban exile training base and weapons cache near New Orleans."[702]

On August 10, just a few months after Soviet KGB officer John McCone's statement about the United States being "disenfranchised" from the Cuban colony in Miami, an anti-Castro Cuban had specific knowledge of plans to assassinate Fidel Castro, but according to a CIA cable, he would not reveal the identity of the individual in Cuba who was organizing Castro's assassination because, "These Cubans believe that U.S. policy toward Cuba had been so wrong that U. S. govt agencies must be penetrated by traitors."[703]

Back in November 1962, funds for Cuban exiles were "reduced or cut off," and "people were instructed to go out and seek employment."[704]

In January 1963, two months after the Cuban exiles were told to go out and get jobs and three months after the Cuban missile crisis, a group of exiles planned to use "dynamite" to blow up "cars and

---

[699] National Archives Record Number 104-10306-10015, pp. 2 & 4
[700] National Archives Record Number 104-10306-10003, p. 7
[701] National Archives Record Numbers 104-10235-10193 & 104-10166-10426
[702] National Archives Record Number 180-10142-10036, p. 52
[703] National Archives Record Number 104-10308-10126, p. 3
[704] National Archives Record Number 104-10308-10178, p. 2

buildings in NY and Miami" and blame it on Castro, believing it would "compel" the United States to take "action against Cuba."[705]

It would have been relatively easy to manipulate Cuban exiles into using dynamite to blow up "cars and buildings" in New York and Miami. One of the keys to manipulating assets is to let them think that the action they take is their idea. KGB officers inside the CIA could simply let Cuban exiles overhear them say that the real problem is Castro's inaction and that Castro has simply not given the United States a reason to invade Cuba.

First KGB officer: "It's been three months since Castro tried to put Soviet missiles in Cuba. I can't believe Kennedy let that slide without invading Cuba. It would be nice if someone could pull off something big and horrendous inside the United States and work it so that Castro would be blamed for it. The United States would then have to invade Cuba."

Second KGB officer: "Yes, but it would have to be really big, otherwise, no U.S. invasion."

Third KGB officer: "Seeing as how the exiles had to go out and get actual jobs, I'm sure they'd be interested in a 'job' that would result in Castro being blamed for some horrific action inside the United States. Maybe we should ask them if they'd like a job like that. They'd probably do it for free."

Fourth KGB officer: "We'd be in big trouble if we told the Cuban exiles to do something like that, but since some of our most loyal exiles are standing a few feet away, listening and smiling, maybe they'll think of it on their own. I'm sure they can't hear us, because like I said, whatever they do has to be their own idea. We can't tell them what to do."

A CIA Memorandum for the Record states that an anti-Castro Cuban named Dr. Jose La Saga met with a CIA officer from November 7 through November 10, 1963, just two weeks before President Kennedy's assassination, and according to the CIA, "It

---

[705] National Archives Record Number 104-10312-10324

was La Saga's firm position that while President Kennedy was in power, it would be impossible to defeat Castro."[706]

KGB officers inside the CIA had no problem manipulating anti-Castro Cubans into actively planning President Kennedy's murder with a hope that Castro would be implicated in the assassination.

The Cuban government took decisive action that would lead the CIA to look for President Kennedy's killers among the Cuban exiles.

As noted in the previous chapter, a letter from Havana, Cuba on November 29, 1962, almost a year before the assassination, told the recipient of the necessity to "kill President Kennedy" and that it would be a "great success" for Castro. The intended recipient was also told to "continue demonstrating yourself as anti-Communist, more specifically anti-Castro . . . . You have played your role very well, and you have been successful in completely deceiving the FBI.[707]

The letter telling the intended recipient to "kill President Kennedy" and "continue demonstrating yourself as anti-Communist, more specifically anti-Castro," means the CIA and the Warren Commission would have been grossly negligent in not looking for President Kennedy's assassins among the anti-Castro Cuban exiles.

Even more important, on November 26, 1963, a Cuban exile named Tony Cuesta told the FBI that someone had attempted to entice Cuban exiles into assassinating President Kennedy in order to put Vice President Lyndon Johnson into the Presidency. Cuesta was the military leader in the "exile attack" on a "Soviet vessel" back on March 27 in the "waters of the Atlantic."

Cuesta told the FBI that a few weeks after the March 27 attack, he received an anonymous letter from Texas dated April 18, 1963, stating: "To Tony Cuesta, active, ardent, and audacious Cuban patriot and his group . . . . Only through one development will you Cuban patriots ever live again in your homeland as freemen, responsible, as must be the most capable, for the guidance and welfare of the Cuban

---

[706] National Archives Record Number 104-10308-10080, p. 3
[707] National Archives Record Number 104-10308-10250, pp. 3 & 4

people: namely, if an inspired act of God should place in the White House within weeks a Texan known to be a friend of all Latin Americans."[708]

The letter then states that Vice President Johnson, "under present conditions," cannot help the exiles, but if "an Act of God" would "suddenly elevate him into the top position," the exiles would get their much-needed support in their efforts to defeat Castro.

It concludes by telling Cuesta, "There are sharks in the waters of the Atlantic. Perhaps one of them, or a group, may free you of the Kennedy-Khrushchev frustrations, which now deny you your right to restore your homeland to control of the Cuban people and their own loyal and rightful rulers."

The FBI report states that Cuesta told them he thought the letter was "the work of a 'crackpot'" and "attached no importance to it." But for some reason, Cuesta "kept it in his possession" for more than seven months and kept the envelope in which the letter had been sent, "postmarked April 18, 1963, Arlington, Texas." After the assassination, Cuesta "reflected back upon this letter and felt that it might have more significance than he had at first attached to it."

Tony Cuesta, an anti-Castro Cuban exile carrying out raids against Cuba, presented the FBI with documentation on November 26 that served to definitively implicate anti-Castro Cubans in the assassination. Recall that November 26 was the day that the FBI "substantially completed" its investigation, which means the CIA would be investigating Cuesta's information. To repeat, CIA investigators and the Warren Commission would have been grossly negligent if they had not taken a hard look at anti-Castro Cubans when they investigated the assassination.

---

[708] Warren Commission Document 1107, FBI Gemberling Report of May 15, 1964, pp. 1057-1059

Information alleging that anti-Castro Cubans assassinated President Kennedy became public in 1967 when New Orleans District Attorney Jim Garrison investigated the assassination.

Garrison's investigation was first publicized in February 1967, and five months later, on July 10, 1967, a CIA officer wrote that one of Jim Garrison's investigators had gone to the National Archives and obtained "the list of CIA classified documents made available to the Warren Commission."

The CIA officer met with Dr. Robert Bahmer, Archivist of the United States, and he informed Dr. Bahmer that a New Orleans newspaper had published "the list of CIA classified documents."[709]

The CIA officer also wrote, "Dr. Bahmer said that the list never should have been shown to Garrison's investigator or any other researcher in its present form," adding that the CIA "became aware of the problem late in May and took steps to correct it."

Another CIA memorandum stated there was an "original unexpurgated list of all Warren Commission material held by the National Archives," and "a new list without CIA titles was prepared by Archives at our request."[710]

The July 10 memorandum quotes Dr. Bahmer as saying that even though the original list of classified CIA documents would "no longer" be available, "It was like closing the barn door after the horse escaped."

Jim Garrison's investigation was first publicized in a New Orleans newspaper on February 17, 1967.[711] The focus of the investigation was a New Orleans pilot named David Ferrie, and on the following day, "District Attorney Jim Garrison issued a statement predicting 'arrests and convictions' in New Orleans."[712]

While Garrison was predicting arrests and convictions on February 18, David Ferrie, the target of the investigation,

---

[709] National Archives Record Number 104-10412-10286, p. 3
[710] National Archives Record Number 104-10400-10055, p. 2
[711] New York Times, 2-18-67, p. 19
[712] Ibid., 2-20-67, p. 28

"acknowledged that he was under investigation but called the inquiry 'a big joke.'"[713]

David Ferrie was found dead in his apartment at 11:40 a.m. on February 22, 1967. The coroner, Dr. Nicholas Chetta, said he had died on the evening of February 21, four days after Garrison's investigation became public.

The *New York Times* stated Ferrie was naked under a sheet in his bed, where he died of a "brain hemorrhage," initially stating: "What appeared to be a suicide note was on the dining room table in the apartment, according to Dr. Nicholas Chetta, the Orleans Parish coroner . . . . He quoted part of it as saying, 'To leave this life is, for me, a sweet prospect. I find nothing in it that is desirable, and on the other hand, everything that is loathsome' . . . . Mr. Chetta declined to reveal the full contents of the note."[714]

An FBI report on their investigation of Ferrie back in 1963 states that when they interviewed him on November 25, 1963, Ferrie stated that he had at one time been "associated with the Cuban Revolutionary Front," which, according to Ferrie, "was definitely an anti-Castro organization . . . . All persons connected with the organization were violently anti-Castro."[715]

Two days after Ferrie was killed in February 1967, the *New York Times* stated: "Housewives who lived near Mr. Ferrie at the time of the assassination told newsmen he had a strong interest in Cuba, and acquaintances reported him to be militantly anti-Castro . . . . According to a friend, Mr. Ferrie was 'a rabid anti-Castroite.'"[716]

In May 1967, Jim Garrison directly accused the CIA of complicity in President Kennedy's assassination, which is when the CIA "became aware" of their "problem."

---

[713] New York Times, 2-23-67, p. 22
[714] New York Times, 2-23-67, p. 22 & 2-25-67, p. 56
[715] National Archives Record Number 124-10371-10039, pp. 51-52
[716] New York Times, 2-23-67, p. 22

The *New York Times* reported on May 22, 1967: "District Attorney Jim Garrison says that Lee Harvey Oswald did not kill President Kennedy and the Central Intelligence Agency knows who did. 'Purely and simply, it's a case of former employees of the CIA, a large number of them Cubans, having a venomous reaction from the 1961 Bay of Pigs episode. Certain individuals with a fusion of interests in regaining Cuba assassinated the President,' Mr. Garrison says."[717]

Garrison said the CIA knew "the name of every man involved and the name of the individuals who pulled the triggers." He also said that it would take "'only 60 minutes for the CIA to give us the name of every last Cuban involved in this and that's how close we have been to the end for some time, but we are blocked by this glass wall of this totalitarian, powerful agency which is worried about its power.' He repeatedly accused the agency of blocking and attempting to block his investigation, begun last fall."

The CIA was obviously the source of information that anti-Castro Cubans killed President Kennedy. KGB officers inside the CIA clearly silenced Ferrie to cover their tracks, just like they silenced George H. W. Bush's old friend, George DeMohrenschildt, but Garrison was undeterred.

In an interview with Larry King on March 16, 1968, Jim Garrison stated, "John Kennedy was killed by employees of the Central Intelligence Agency . . . . This is the group that killed Kennedy . . . . Most individuals shooting were Cubans" under CIA "supervision."[718]

"We have found the involvement, systematically, of Central Intelligence Agency men servicing the assassination, convoying Oswald, setting it up," and "participating actively."

What Garrison did not know was that the CIA, more specifically KGB officers inside the CIA, "systematically" set it up so that anti-Castro Cubans would ultimately take the fall for assassinating President Kennedy.

---

[717] New York Times, 5-23-67, p. 20
[718] National Archives Record Number 104-10428-10179, p. 5-6

A January 1968 CIA memo states that eight people on whom Garrison focused his investigation had ties to the CIA's Directorate for Plans, and "eight more were DCS contacts," which means they worked in conjunction with the CIA's Domestic Contact Services, or more precisely, the CIA's Domestic Operations Division.[719]

The KGB's solution to the revelation of an anti-Castro Cuban connection was to kill Ferrie, but he was not the only one they killed in the effort to block the Garrison investigation.

An October 1967 letter from the CIA to the Justice Department's "Internal Security Division" states that a Cuban named Eladio Del Valle, who had been described as a "valuable witness" by Jim Garrison, had been "murdered in Miami on February 22, 1967," the same day that the body of Ferrie was discovered.[720]

Del Valle "had been involved in anti-Cuban operations."[721]

With David Ferrie and Eladio Del Valle both dead, which would be the original target of Garrison's investigation and a "valuable witness" in the investigation, Garrison focused his prosecutorial efforts on a man named Clay Shaw in order to make his case for a conspiracy.

Five months after Garrison pointed the finger of guilt at the CIA, accusing them of being directly involved in the assassination, the CIA told the Justice Department's Internal Security Division that Garrison's prosecution of Shaw was exposing "people who have been involved in Cuban operations."[722]

The Cuban exile connection that Garrison was exposing was instantaneously connected to President Kennedy's assassination. Anti-Castroite David Ferrie came under investigation "by local and Federal authorities only hours after the assassination."[723]

---

[719] National Archives Record Number 104-10404-10437, p. 2
[720] National Archives Record Number 104-10438-10217, p. 3
[721] National Archives Record Number 104-10435-10007
[722] National Archives Record Number 104-10438-10217, p. 4
[723] New York Times, 2-23-67, p. 22

The FBI report on their investigation of Ferrie in 1963 states that according to a witness, Ferrie had once said, "The President should be killed," and Ferrie had "outlined plans to this effect."[724]

"Secret Service records" show that Ferrie told the FBI shortly after the assassination that he was "'positive' he was in New Orleans" when President Kennedy was assassinated.[725]

"Three days after the assassination, when they received reports that Mr. Ferrie had made a quick trip to Texas immediately after the Presidential murder, Mr. Garrison's staff arrested him for questioning, but Federal interest in Mr. Ferrie waned, according to one investigative source, when the FBI determined that Mr. Ferrie had gone to Houston rather than Dallas."

On the day that anti-Castroite David Ferrie was found dead in February 1967, Jim Garrison stated: "Evidence developed by our office had long since confirmed that he was involved in events culminating in the assassination of President Kennedy. Although my office has been investigating Mr. Ferrie intensively for months, we have not mentioned his name publicly up to this point . . . . In a meeting in my house this morning, we had reached a decision to arrest him early next week. Apparently, we waited too long."

Ferrie, who was targeted by the FBI and the Secret Service after the assassination, was definitely "involved in events culminating in the assassination of President Kennedy," but those "events" were orchestrated by KGB officers inside the CIA in order to pin the assassination on anti-Castro Cubans.

It was "three days after the assassination" that David Ferrie's attention-grabbing antics resulted in Jim Garrison arresting him, and it was four days after the assassination that Cuban exile leader Tony Cuesta produced his letter about someone trying to entice Cuban exiles into assassinating President Kennedy, which is all evidence of the CIA's orchestration of setting up anti-Castro Cubans to be the patsies.

---

[724] National Archives Record Number 124-10371-10039, p. 77
[725] New York Times, 2-25-67, p. 56

The FBI sent a letter to Presidential aide Marvin Watson on February 20, 1967, informing him of Garrison's investigation. Six weeks later, Marvin Watson told the Assistant Director of the FBI that President Johnson "is convinced there was a plot in connection with Kennedy's assassination."[726]

The CIA gathered intelligence on Garrison and on all aspects of his investigation. An abundance of CIA memorandums and communications reveal top-level CIA officials focused on the Garrison investigation.

Two months after Del Valle and Ferrie were murdered, an April 26 CIA memo stated that there are "loads of possible concern to CIA because of what may be an intent to involve the Agency directly or indirectly."[727]

A June 1967 CIA memo, written shortly after the CIA realized they had a "problem," states, "The activity of District Attorney James C. Garrison of New Orleans shows no signs of abating . . . . We shall continue to study all available information about the New Orleans investigation."[728]

In September 1967, the CIA documented, "Since the Garrison investigation was first publicized in February 1967, we have kept book on all persons in the case: 139 to date."[729]

The CIA also established the "Garrison Group," consisting of some of the senior-most officials in the CIA; the Executive Director, the Deputy Director for Plans, the Deputy Director of Support, the CIA General Counsel, the CIA Inspector General, and Raymond G. Rocca, the Chief of Research and Analysis in the CIA's Counterintelligence Division.[730]

A CIA memo states that at the first meeting of the Garrison Group on September 20, 1967, "Rocca felt that Garrison would,

---

[726] Church Committee: Book V, p. 106
[727] National Archives Record Number 104-10404-10446
[728] National Archives Record Number 104-10404-10443, p. 3
[729] National Archives Record Number 104-10438-10004, p. 2
[730] National Archives Record Number 104-10428-10023

indeed, obtain a conviction of Shaw for conspiring to assassinate President Kennedy."

The memo also quotes the CIA Executive Director as having said, "The possibility of Agency action should be examined from the timing of what can be done before the trial, and what might be feasible during and after the trial."

The CIA also engaged in a world-wide propaganda campaign to discredit Garrison.

In July 1968, the CIA sent a dispatch to all CIA stations and bases around the world, and it contained a nineteen-page article critical of Garrison and his investigation. The dispatch states, "You may use the article to brief interested contacts, especially government and other political leaders." It also states that the article should be used to demonstrate "that there is no hard evidence of any such conspiracy."[731]

The CIA had previously issued a "Propaganda Notes" Bulletin when the Warren Report came out in September 1964, and copies of the Warren Report were sent to CIA "field stations" so that "covert assets" in the United States and around the world could "explain the tragedy" of President Kennedy's assassination.

The CIA also issued "Countering Criticism of the Warren Report" in January 1967, and now, in 1968, the CIA was engaged in a worldwide effort to disparage a New Orleans District Attorney and his investigation.

Jim Garrison did not know that anti-Castro Cubans were patsies, and the Warren Commission could not acknowledge the CIA's information alleging that anti-Castro Cubans were the assassins because of the cover-up mentality of the Warren Commission.

The CIA, of course, did not want it known that they pointed the finger of guilt at anti-Castro Cubans, but Garrison followed the Cuban connection right up to the CIA's doorstep and then publicized what he found out.

---

[731] National Archives Record Number 104-10412-10306, p. 2

Unlike Chief Justice Earl Warren, Garrison did not have a cover-up mentality drilled into him. He did not get instructions from the President of the United States stating that unless Lee Harvey Oswald is pegged as the lone assassin, it "might even get us into a war; a nuclear war."

The KGB officers foresaw that it would be said that there was a conspiracy to assassinate President Kennedy. Even the Warren Commission privately acknowledged a conspiracy. During an Executive Session on December 16, 1963, they questioned how Kennedy "could have been hit in the front" when Oswald was behind the President during the assassination.[732]

The KGB officers' foresight dictated that they would need someone on whom they could ultimately pin the assassination. Soviet KGB officers inside the CIA were more than happy to orchestrate a grand production blaming anti-Castro Cubans for assassinating President Kennedy.

But as noted earlier, if anti-Castro Cubans were the perpetrators, it would mean that the Soviets, their Eastern European satellites, and Cuban Premier Fidel Castro immediately knew that the assassination was a right-wing conspiracy orchestrated by "those demanding a stronger policy against Cuba." Chapter 9 clearly detailed the extensive propaganda campaign in which the Soviet Union and Cuba accused Barry Goldwater and "rightists" of killing President Kennedy.

On January 7, 1964, four days after Barry Goldwater announced his candidacy for President, Goldwater told reporters that if he were President, he "would be 'inclined' to provide air cover for Cuban exiles in any future invasion of their homeland," first telling the reporters, "I would help Cuban exiles. I would train them and

---

[732] Warren Commission Executive Session, Dec 16, 1963, pp. 34-35

supply them,"⁷³³ which means Cuban exiles would naturally want CIA officer Barry Goldwater elected to the Presidency.

Back on July 12, 1963, it was reported that Senator Barry Goldwater, in referring to the Castro regime in Cuba, told 500 of his supporters that President Kennedy wanted to "coexist with international communism wherever it thrives, even in the Western Hemisphere,"⁷³⁴ and when Goldwater received his grand reception in Texas six weeks before President Kennedy's assassination, he declared that Kennedy's policy was "blind in Cuba."⁷³⁵

Goldwater was most definitely the Cuban exiles' choice for President. Had the KGB officers succeeded in assassinating President Johnson immediately before the 1964 election to catapult Barry Goldwater into the Presidency, anti-Castro Cubans would have been the ideal patsies in that assassination, too.

CIA officer Barry Goldwater was noticeably silent on accusing Castro after President Kennedy's assassination, but a group of CIA-controlled Cuban exiles known as the "Cuban Student Directorate" published a four-page newspaper on November 23, 1963, stating that Oswald had killed President Kennedy on behalf of Fidel Castro.

Veteran *Washington Post* reporter Jefferson Morley wrote that the CIA funded all of the "Cuban Student Directorate's" activities and that declassified White House documents clearly state the CIA had total control over the Cuban Student Directorate at the time of the assassination.⁷³⁶

Morley wrote, "The agency's responsibility for the first JFK conspiracy theory is beyond dispute. By the admission of its own former leaders, the Cuban Student Directorate was totally dependent on CIA funding in 1963," all of which means the CIA used these

---

⁷³³ Prescott Evening Courier, 1-7-64. p. 1
http://news.google.com/newspapers?id=G7IKAAAAIBAJ&sjid=D04DAAAAIBAJ&pg=6441%2C178789
⁷³⁴ Washington Post, 7-13-63, p. 2
⁷³⁵ Dallas Morning News, 10-12-63, p. 6
⁷³⁶ Jefferson Morley essay, "What Jane Roman Said," at https://www.history-matters.com/essays/frameup/WhatJaneRomanSaid/WhatJaneRomanSaid_6.htm

particular anti-Castro Cubans to initiate pointing the finger of guilt at Castro.

CIA records show that less than two hours after the assassination, a Cuban intelligence officer in Mexico City knew that the plan to assassinate President Kennedy entailed having anti-Castro Cubans initiate the claim of Castro's involvement.

At 2 p.m. on November 22, 1963, an hour and a half after the assassination, a woman identified as "Yoya" called Cuban intelligence officer Luisa Calderon and said, "A good shot; direct. Listen. Now they are going to say that it was from here, that it was some Cuban."[737]

Calderon stated, "That is possible. Then if they don't say it; they will die."

Yoya replied, "That is certain."

Less than two hours after the assassination, Cuban intelligence officer Luisa Calderon and "Yoya" knew that it would be said that it was a Cuban conspiracy, and they both knew that if certain parties did not say that it was a Cuban conspiracy, those parties would die. Those parties were the anti-Castro Cubans who were controlled by the CIA and who were completely dependent upon CIA funding.

Calderon and Yoya were "certain" that "they will die" if they do not "say that it was from here, that it was some Cuban."

In another phone call to the Cuban Embassy four hours after the assassination, Luisa Calderon spoke to an "unidentified man" about accused assassin Lee Harvey Oswald and said, "They already know that he speaks Russian and belonged to the pro-Cuba committee."[738]

As noted in Chapter 9, Luisa Calderon and the unidentified man both had definitive foreknowledge of President Kennedy's assassination. Their conversation began when the unidentified man "calls Luisa" and "asks if she knows the latest news."

---

[737] National Archives Record Number 104-10404-10426, p. 23
[738] National Archives Record Number 104-10404-10426

Luisa Calderon responds by saying, "Yes, of course. I knew about it before Kennedy."

The unidentified man then "laughs and comments that that is very bad."[739]

Five days after the assassination, the CIA's Mexico City station sent a cable to CIA Director and KGB officer John McCone stating that the U.S. Ambassador to Mexico, Thomas Mann, wanted "Mexican authorities" to "arrest for interrogation Eusebio Azcue, Luisa Calderon, and Alfredo Mirabal." Ambassador Mann warned that "they may all quickly be returned to Havana in order to eliminate any possibility that the Mexican government could use them as witnesses."[740]

CIA Headquarters sent back a "Flash" cable (meaning it had the highest priority and was more than an emergency) making reference to "Ambassador Mann's message." Headquarters told the CIA's Mexico City station that they must "not take any action" to have anyone arrested "without approval from here."[741]

A CIA "Information Report" states that Luisa Calderon "made reservations to return to Havana on Cubana Airlines on December 11, 1963," exactly two weeks after Ambassador Mann warned that she could "quickly be returned to Havana" to prevent her from being arrested and interrogated. It also states, "Calderon said that she would not be returning to Mexico."[742]

An "Eyes Only" memo to the CIA's Counterintelligence Chief in May 1964 stated, "Luisa Calderon, since she returned to Cuba, has been paid a regular salary by the DGI [Cuban Intelligence] even though she has not performed any services."[743]

A CIA paper on Cuban operations states that two Cuban diplomats in Mexico were working for the CIA,[744] and Church Committee

---

[739] Ibid., p. 35
[740] National Archives Record Number 104-10404-10117, p. 5
[741] National Archives Record Number 104-10408-10303
[742] National Archives Record Number 104-10408-10144, p. 5
[743] National Archives Record Number 104-10408-10153
[744] National Archives Record Number 104-10310-10005, p. 6

staffers wrote that the CIA conducted "electronic surveillance of conversations" inside the Cuban Embassy.[745] As such, the CIA had detailed information on the "reactions" of "Cuban officials" to President Kennedy's assassination.

A CIA cable on November 25, 1963 states, "They appear happy about it, and sorry for Oswald." Cuban officials commented that "Oswald is 'dead duck' since to be judged in Texas," and it states "after Oswald was shot," a Cuban official said Oswald was a "poor boy" who "had nothing to do with Kennedy's murder."[746]

A CIA cable disclosed that on November 7, 1963, Ricardo Santos, a high-ranking official at the Cuban Embassy in The Hague, attended "a reception of the Soviet Ambassador." When Santos was "asked about the attacks of the Cuban refugees against the Cuban mainland," he replied, "'Just wait and you will see what we can do. It will happen soon' . . . . Asked to be more precise about what will happen, Santos merely answered, 'Just wait. Just wait.'"[747]

Santos' statements, fifteen days before President Kennedy's assassination, fit very well with Cuban intelligence knowing that President Kennedy would be assassinated and that it would ultimately be blamed on the "Cuban refugees."

As noted earlier, Cuba took action to make sure investigators would look for the assassins among the Cuban exiles long before the assassination. A letter from Havana, Cuba in November 1962 told the intended recipient of the necessity to "kill President Kennedy," as it would be a "great success" for Castro, and the intended recipient was instructed to "continue demonstrating yourself as anti-Communist, more specifically anti-Castro . . . . You have played your role very well, and you have been successful in completely deceiving the FBI."[748]

---

[745] National Archives Record Number 157-10014-10120, p. 78
[746] National Archives Record Number 104-10434-10223
[747] National Archives Record Number 104-10408-10199, p. 3
[748] National Archives Record Number 104-10308-10250, pp. 3 & 4

Recall that Warren Commission member Gerald Ford testified at the closed-door Congressional hearings in 1984 that the Warren Commission was absolutely certain that Cubans had assassinated President Kennedy. Ford also testified that the CIA was the source of information that Cubans had killed President Kennedy, and a CIA officer clarified that the alleged assassins to whom Ford was referring were "anti-Castro Cubans."

Ford's closed-door testimony and Jim Garrison's charges lead to the inescapable conclusion that the CIA worked with Cuban exiles to actively plan President Kennedy's assassination. But the KGB officers were not about to "outsource" the assassination, and once the deed was done, the Cuban exiles were left holding the bag. They and their CIA handlers then set about pointedly blaming Castro for the assassination.

The push to establish the Warren Commission and a "no conspiracy" mandate began with CIA officer Nicholas Katzenbach, but the ultimate catalyst was KGB officer John McCone's persistent behind-the-scenes pressure on President Johnson.

Recall that on November 23, McCone briefed President Johnson on "the information CIA Headquarters had received from its Mexico City station," and on November 24, McCone informed Johnson of the CIA's "plans against Cuba," after which McCone met with President Johnson "in his private residence" and suggested that he get "an early briefing on the Soviet long-range striking capability" and Soviet "air defense posture."

And on November 27, one day after observing Johnson's "considerable contempt" for a Presidential Commission, McCone vouched for the claim that Oswald was seen taking a payoff inside the Cuban Embassy. Only then did Johnson begin to fear that Soviet and Cuban involvement "might even get us into a war; a nuclear war."

Declassified CIA documents clearly show that the CIA controlled the Warren Commission investigation and supplied them with ample information.

In addition to what was noted in the previous chapter, Raymond G. Rocca, Chief of Research & Analysis in the CIA's Counterintelligence division, wrote a Memorandum in 1975 marked "Eyes Only" in which he stated that the CIA's "line of reporting" to the Warren Commission had "multiple" levels. Rocca also stated that "on sensitive matters of concern," Deputy Director for Plans Richard Helms and the CIA's Soviet Russia Chief, David Murphy, "dealt directly with the Commission."[749]

A CIA memorandum concerning a March 12 meeting that Helms and unnamed CIA "staff officers" had with the Warren Commission staff states, "The purpose of this meeting was to discuss the current status of the CIA contribution to the work of the Warren Commission."[750]

The Warren Commission lavished praise on the CIA just two months after it began "requesting information from the CIA." Raymond G. Rocca had a meeting with a Warren Commission staff member on March 27, 1963, after which Rocca wrote that the staff member said, "The Agency handling of the information in the Oswald case was unique among what the Commission had found had happened in every other agency."[751]

Rocca wrote that the Warren Commission staff member "stated flatly that no Federal component, except CIA, had been able to show the Commission hard documentation which indicated there had been immediate action on field reported information by headquarters, and full interaction by headquarters with the field on file trace data and instructions for follow-up," all of which means the CIA put on a grand show of "digging up" information to pin it on anti-Castro Cubans.

Another CIA memorandum shows that Chief Justice Earl Warren and another Warren Commission member, Senator John Sherman Cooper, met with CIA Director John McCone at CIA

---

[749] National Archives Record Number 104-10406-10113, p. 7
[750] National Archives Record Number 104-10312-10367
[751] National Archives Record Number 104-10441-10031, p. 4

Headquarters on April 16, 1964, three weeks after the Warren Commission staff member praised the CIA for being so helpful.[752]

Deputy Director for Plans Richard Helms wrote a chronology of meetings that he had with the Warren Commission. Helms stated he met with the Warren Commission twice in January, twice in March, and again on June 24, and the chronology of meetings "does not include the score of telephone calls I had with Mr. Rankin and the Commission staff."[753]

In addition to all the high-level meetings and the "multiple" levels of contact, the House Select Committee on Assassinations reported that the CIA provided the Warren Commission with "twelve full-time and part-time professionals. They also provided secretarial and clerical assistance."[754]

As noted in Chapter 1, the CIA is not some government "Temp" agency that sends employees on various assignments because there is a temporary need for them. The CIA is in the business of gathering intelligence and conducting secretive operations.

CIA officers employed as "full-time and part-time professionals" filled out intelligence reports on Warren Commission staff members and on everything that the Warren Commission was doing, and CIA officers detailed to "secretarial and clerical" positions filled out intelligence reports on the information they gathered each day.

By controlling the Warren Commission investigation, the CIA was able to supply details of a plot by CIA-controlled Cuban exiles to kill President Kennedy. But as noted earlier, KGB officers inside the CIA were not about to "outsource" the assassination, and once the deed was done, the Cuban exiles were left holding the bag.

The CIA had good reason to worry when Jim Garrison's investigation became public. As far as the CIA was concerned, detailed information implicating anti-Castro Cubans was meant only

---

[752] National Archives Record Number 104-10306-10011, p. 2
[753] National Archives Record Number 104-10412-10228
[754] National Archives Record Number 104-10427-10043

for the Warren Commission. The American people were not supposed to be privy to it.

Besides eliminating anti-Castroites David Ferrie and Eladio Del Valle when Garrison's investigation became public in 1967, and besides a world-wide propaganda campaign to discredit Garrison's high-profile claim that Cuban exiles killed President Kennedy, the CIA continued to eliminate Cuban exiles to keep them from talking.

Five Cuban exile leaders were killed after Congress set up the House Select Committee on Assassinations in 1976.

On January 14, 1977, the *Tampa Tribune* reported that they had been "assassinated" in Miami "in the last few months," including one who was "gunned down as he left his front door last week." It also reported that a total of seven Cuban exile leaders were "assassinated in Miami in the past three years."[755]

In Katzenbach's memo to the White House on November 25, as he pushed to establish a Presidential Commission, he wrote that the Commission not only needed to quash the idea that it was a "Communist conspiracy," but also quash any speculation that it was "a right-wing conspiracy to blame it on the Communists."[756]

When the Warren Commission was formed, covering up the CIA's information that anti-Castro Cubans killed President Kennedy was just as important as covering up the CIA's initial information implicating Castro in the assassination.

As it turns out, assassinating President Kennedy was not just a Communist conspiracy, it was a Communist conspiracy to blame it on the right-wing. Funny how Katzenbach did not say anything about that in his memo to the White House. He was just a CIA officer doing what he was told in the CIA takeover of the United States government.

By having the Chief Justice of the Supreme Court enlisted to head the cover-up, KGB officers inside the CIA achieved a

---

[755] National Archives Record Number 104-10160-10009
[756] House Select Committee on Assassinations, Volume XI, pp. 411-412

tripartite conquest of the three branches of the United States government. Chief Justice Earl Warren effectively gave Supreme Court approval to the workings of an Agency that was overrun with KGB officers, double agents, and renegade CIA officers, all of whom were bent on controlling the United States government.

Chapter 14: The CIA Continues Trying to Control the Presidency

As noted in chapter 4, none of this is about politics. This is about virulently corrupt elements of the CIA destroying our Constitution and corrupting our government far beyond what anyone could imagine. Renegade CIA officers have clearly perpetuated the KGB-initiated quest to control the government.

Those who might have a political motive for doubting the information in this chapter should consider the fact that they knew nothing about the CIA killing Members of Congress, nor did they know anything about Members of Congress being in the CIA. They did not know that President George W. Bush was a CIA asset who had at one time committed a felony on behalf of renegade CIA officers, and they did not know that KGB officers inside the CIA assassinated President Kennedy. No one, including those who might have a political motive for doubting the information in this chapter, knew that renegade CIA officers were behind the 9/11 terrorist attacks that killed 3000 Americans, and no one should have any doubts about the information in this chapter.

John Brennan, CIA Director during President Barack Obama's second term, is part of the "Democratic faction" of renegade CIA officers thriving off the corruption and vying for control of the United States government. Brennan joined the CIA in 1980 at a time when KGB officers inside the CIA were still in charge and two of their assets, CIA officers Jimmy Carter and Walter Mondale, held office as President and Vice President.

Brennan testified before Congress that while he was CIA Director, he initiated an FBI investigation into the Presidential campaign of Donald Trump. Brennan claimed that the Trump campaign was colluding with Russia to win the 2016 Presidential election. According to Brennan, he gave the FBI information that "served as the basis for the FBI investigation" into the alleged "collusion."[757]

CIA Directors are still in the CIA after ending their stints as CIA Director. As of January 2017, Brennan is a CIA officer using a "nonofficial cover" as a "former CIA Director."

Unlike any former CIA Director before him, renegade CIA officer John Brennan elevated the CIA's quest to control the United States government to an entirely new level. Using his "nonofficial cover" as a former CIA Director, Brennan became an attack dog for the Democratic Party.

Brennan laid the groundwork when he began feeding disinformation to the FBI in "July of 2016," the same month that Donald Trump won the Republican nomination for President.

On September 9, 2016, two months before the Presidential election, the *Guardian* reported that CIA Director John Brennan and other "key CIA leaders" are "seeking to run Langley [CIA Headquarters] under Hillary Clinton," the Democratic nominee for President in 2016.[758]

CIA officer John Brennan had direct input when Obama chose the infamous Leon Panetta for the position of CIA Director, as Brennan was a "leader" on President-elect Obama's "intelligence transition team."[759]

John Brennan came to see me prior to becoming CIA Director. I quickly surmised his alliance with Leon Panetta and directly asked him if he worked with Panetta to keep Osama bin Laden hidden, and he confirmed that he did.

In November 2005, after Osama bin Laden was moved to a newly built compound in Abbottabad, Pakistan, Brennan started using a "nonofficial cover" as CEO of a company called The Analysis

---

[757] Wall Street Journal, 7-19-2018, https://www.wsj.com/articles/brennan-and-the-2016-spy-scandal-1532039346

[758] https://www.theguardian.com/us-news/2016/sep/09/cia-insider-daniel-jones-senate-torture-investigation

[759] Wall Street Journal, November 11, 2008; https://www.wsj.com/articles/SB122636726473415991

Corporation,[760] located just seven minutes from CIA Headquarters in McLean, VA. Brennan was using that particular "cover" while he was a "consultant" to Barack Obama's Presidential campaign in March 2008, several months before becoming a "leader" on Obama's "intelligence transition team."[761]

On October 18, 2017, former CIA Director John Brennan, who had been "seeking to run Langley [CIA Headquarters] under Hillary Clinton," spoke at Fordham University, where NBC News correspondent Andrea Mitchell asked Brennan if it was his "theory" that "there was some connection" between the Trump campaign and a "Russian operation," to which Brennan laughed and replied, "It's a hypothetical . . . . Almost anything is in the realm of the possible" when it comes to "interference" in the 2016 elections.[762]

Brennan went on to say that he does not "know the extent of it," which means that in his "hypothetical," he had absolutely no knowledge of the Trump campaign working with the Russians. He also claimed the Russians were "maybe getting people to work with them," which he based on his knowledge that it "is part of their M.O."

In other words, because any intelligence agency, including the CIA, would want people in other countries to "work with them," the most Brennan could say about his "hypothetical" is that the Russians were "maybe getting people to work with them" because that is what intelligence agencies do and "almost anything is in the realm of the possible." Brennan clearly had no knowledge of a "Russian operation" involving the Trump campaign, and Brennan admitted it when he testified before Congress.

Six months after Trump won the 2016 election, Brennan's fellow CIA officer, former FBI Director Robert Mueller, was appointed Special Counsel to investigate Brennan's claim of the Trump campaign colluding with Russia.

As noted in Chapter 6, Robert Mueller told me in person that he is in the CIA. Mueller was, at the time, using his "official cover" as FBI Director. President and CIA asset George Bush appointed

---

[760] http://www.washingtonpost.com/wp-dyn/content/article/2006/06/21/AR2006062102044.html?noredirect=on
[761] http://www.cnn.com/2008/POLITICS/03/22/passport.files/index.html
[762] https://www.msnbc.com/brian-williams/watch/fmr-cia-boss-brennan-world-may-wonder-if-trump-s-just-reckless-1076612675538

Mueller to be Director of the FBI in the Summer of 2001 after FBI Director Louis Freeh "unexpectedly" resigned "two years ahead of schedule."[763]

CIA officer Robert Mueller was sworn in as FBI Director one week before the CIA-orchestrated 9/11 attacks, and he would be investigating the attacks working directly under his fellow CIA officer, Attorney General John Ashcroft, who reported directly to President and CIA asset George W. Bush.

Recall that the FBI, under FBI Director Louis Freeh, investigated the "accidents" and "suicides" that killed sixteen Members of Congress in a 34 year period from 1957 to 1991. FBI Director Louis Freeh acknowledged that the FBI now has all sixteen deaths categorized as homicides, but the Clinton Administration prevented the FBI from further pursuing the case or saying anything about it.

I found out directly from President Clinton that the infamous Leon Panetta used his influence with Clinton to put a stop to prosecuting anyone in the CIA.

Panetta would obviously not want Louis Freeh to be Director of the FBI when the FBI investigated Panetta's CIA-orchestrated terrorist attacks. Panetta would clearly want one of his CIA colleagues in charge of the FBI investigation, hence, the appointment of CIA officer Robert Mueller to be Director of the FBI.

In May 2017, CIA officer Robert Mueller adopted his "official cover" as Special Counsel investigating Brennan's claim that the Trump campaign colluded with Russia, and a few days later, former CIA Director John Brennan testified to the House Intelligence Committee and claimed to be "aware of information and intelligence that revealed contacts and interactions between Russian officials and U.S. persons involved in the Trump campaign."[764]

But when a member of the Committee asked Brennan if he had "evidence of a connection between the Trump campaign and Russian state actors," the former CIA Director replied, "I don't do evidence."

Brennan, of course, did not name any "Russian officials" that were allegedly contacting the Trump campaign, and he

---

[763] https://www.cbsnews.com/news/another-blow-to-the-bureau/
[764] https://www.realclearpolitics.com/video/2017/05/23/gowdy_grills_john_brennan_do_you_have_evidence_of_trump-russia_collusion_or_not_brennan_i_dont_do_evidence.html

acknowledged in his testimony that he "didn't know if 'collusion existed'" between Russians and anyone in the Trump campaign.[765]

Renegade CIA officer John Brennan accused Trump and the people involved in his campaign of being "unwittingly" led down a "treasonous path," regardless of the fact that Brennan had no "evidence" of a "connection between the Trump campaign and Russian state actors" and had absolutely no knowledge of any "collusion."[766]

With his admission that he worked with Leon Panetta to keep Osama bin Laden hidden, it is clearly Brennan who was "unwittingly" led down a "treasonous path."

Brennan testified that "U.S. persons are being contacted by Russian officials" and that there is "a particular intelligence operational campaign" in which "Russians are actively involved."[767] But Brennan clearly could not specify who the alleged "Russians" were, nor could he specify what the "particular intelligence operational campaign" was, and Brennan said nothing about the "U.S. persons" being connected to the Trump campaign.

Andrea Mitchell spoke with MSNBC news anchor Brian Williams after she interviewed Brennan at Fordham University in October 2017, and when the subject of Special Counsel Robert Mueller's investigation into a "Russia connection" to the Trump campaign came up, Andrea Mitchell stated, "It was Brennan's CIA that first referred this whole case in 'July of 2016' to the FBI,"[768] which Brennan confirmed when he testified before Congress.

Donald Trump officially became the GOP candidate for President in "July of 2016," the same month that Brennan initiated an investigation, and it was in "July of 2016" that former British spy Christopher Steele began feeding the FBI information from his

---

[765] https://www.npr.org/2017/05/23/529598301/former-cia-director-tells-lawmakers-about-very-aggressive-russian-election-meddl
[766] https://www.cnn.com/2017/05/23/politics/john-brennan-house-intelligence-committee/index.html
[767] https://www.forbes.com/sites/paulroderickgregory/2017/06/06/its-not-trump-but-public-intellectuals-lobbyists-who-are-advancing-putins-u-s-agenda/#251f61413d77
[768] https://www.msnbc.com/brian-williams/watch/fmr-cia-boss-brennan-world-may-wonder-if-trump-s-just-reckless-1076612675538

"Steele Dossier," a document clearly designed to hurt Donald Trump's chances of winning the 2016 Presidential election.[769]

As noted in Chapter 6, renegade CIA officers will use proxies to discredit a Presidential candidate or a sitting President, just as their KGB progenitors did when they orchestrated the Watergate scandal.

Renegade CIA officers will also use proxies to "conceal" any CIA funding, which explains why it was the Clinton campaign and the Democratic National Committee that hired Fusion GPS, which in turn hired ex-spy Christopher Steele to come up with his "dossier" of information from Russian sources.[770]

It is beyond dispute that the Clinton campaign and the Democratic National Committee paid Christopher Steele to enlist Russians for the purpose of interfering in the 2016 Presidential election, and any CIA involvement has obviously been "concealed."

The only thing verifiable in the whole "Russia collusion" claim is that there were a bunch of salacious claims about Donald Trump that were clearly designed to help Hillary Clinton win the Presidency.

One of the "key CIA leaders" that were "seeking to run Langley [CIA Headquarters] under Hillary Clinton,"[771] was renegade CIA officer Mike Morell, who served as "Acting Director" of the CIA immediately after the infamous Leon Panetta ended his reign in 2011 and immediately before Brennan began his reign in 2013. Panetta personally chose Morell to be Deputy Director of the CIA in April 2010.[772]

Morell wrote a *New York Times* op-ed on August 5, 2016, titled "I Ran the CIA. Now I'm Endorsing Hillary Clinton,"[773] and a senior

---

[769] https://www.washingtonpost.com/graphics/2018/politics/steele-timeline/?utm_term=.a012cd3cb5d5
[770] https://www.cnn.com/2017/10/24/politics/fusion-gps-clinton-campaign/index.html
[771] https://www.theguardian.com/us-news/2016/sep/09/cia-insider-daniel-jones-senate-torture-investigation
[772] https://web.archive.org/web/20190601201848/https://www.cia.gov/news-information/press-releases-statements/press-release-2010/senior-leadership-changes.html
[773] https://www.politico.com/story/2016/08/michael-morell-endorses-clinton-226707

CIA official wrote on the CIA's website that the op-ed was "an unprecedented step for a top CIA leader."[774]

The op-ed, written just seventeen days after Trump won the GOP nomination for President, alleges that Vladimir Putin "had recruited Mr. Trump as an unwitting agent."

Three days later, on August 8, as the flurry of activity to stop Trump from being elected President continued, Deputy Assistant FBI Director Peter Strzok and Lisa Page, Special Counsel to the Deputy Director of the FBI, sent text messages to each other stating that they intended to stop Donald Trump from being elected.

Page wrote, "[Trump's] not ever going to become president, right? Right?!" and Strzok replied, "No. No he won't. We'll stop it."[775]

One week after the two high-ranking FBI officials texted each other that they would "stop" Trump from becoming President, Strzok sent a text to Page stating, "There's no way he gets elected, but I'm afraid we can't take the risk," adding that they have an "insurance policy" in place in case he does get elected.[776]

Peter Strzok was in charge of the Brennan-initiated investigation at the FBI and later worked for Special Counsel and CIA officer Robert Mueller, as did Lisa Page.

Recall that CIA officers operate in the United States with "official covers" as employees of the FBI, the Justice Department, and "other United States government agencies,"[777] and they will enlist assets in the FBI and Justice Department to advance their agenda. They will also manipulate "proxies" to do their bidding when necessary.

I know first-hand that Lisa Page is a CIA officer who had an "official cover" in the FBI and that Peter Strzok was her "asset."

"In a late August briefing" in 2016, corrupt CIA Director John Brennan enlisted the Senate Democratic Leader, Harry Reid, in the CIA's quest to control the government. Brennan told Reid that

---

[774] https://web.archive.org/web/20200716103013/https://www.cia.gov/library/center-for-the-study-of-intelligence/csi-publications/csi-studies/studies/vol-62-no-3/pdfs/for-the-record.pdf
[775] https://www.foxnews.com/politics/ig-report-on-clinton-email-probe-reveals-fbi-agents-stop-trump-text-calls-comey-insubordinate
[776] https://www.foxnews.com/politics/trump-to-declassify-the-insurance-policy-in-the-strzok-page-text-nunes-says
[777] Rockefeller Report, p. 215

"Russia was trying to help Mr. Trump win the election and that Trump advisers might be colluding with Russia."[778]

Senator Reid then sent a letter to FBI Director and CIA asset James Comey stating, "The evidence of a direct connection between the Russian government and Donald Trump's presidential campaign continues to mount."[779]

CIA asset James Comey testified to the House Intelligence Committee that the FBI's position as of July 2016 was that it was a foregone conclusion that Russia interfered in the 2016 election, and the FBI was trying to "determine the extent" of it.[780]

In July 2017, one year into the CIA-orchestrated investigation, renegade CIA officer John Brennan proclaimed that "some" Trump Administration "officials" must "refuse to carry out" the President's orders if he fires Brennan's CIA colleague, Special Counsel Robert Mueller. Brennan alleged that Trump Administration officials have an "obligation" to disobey "some" of the President's "orders."[781]

In an interview in March 2018, Brennan was again asked if he had "any theories" on who in the Trump campaign had worked with the Russians in an alleged plot to control the election, and Brennan replied, "No," which means twenty months after initiating the investigation, he still had no knowledge of anyone in the Trump campaign working with the Russians.[782] Ten months earlier, Brennan was unable to name any "Russians" or "Russian officials" that were allegedly contacting "U.S. persons."

Brennan went on to say that "individuals either wittingly or unwittingly may have aided the Russians," but Brennan said nothing about the alleged "individuals" having any connection to the Trump campaign.

---

[778] Wall Street Journal, 7-19-2018, https://www.wsj.com/articles/brennan-and-the-2016-spy-scandal-1532039346
[779] Washington Times, 5-12-18, https://www.washingtontimes.com/news/2018/may/12/harry-reid-sent-sensitive-trump-collusion-letter-o/
[780] https://www.usatoday.com/story/news/politics/2017/03/29/two-russia-probes-churn-house-panels-investigation-stalls/99775528/
[781] https://www.thedailybeast.com/russian-election-hacking-pits-us-spy-against-spy
[782] https://archive.org/details/MSNBCW_20180302_210000_Deadline_White_House

Being completely devoid of any information that indicated the Trump campaign worked with "the Russians" on anything, Brennan, who initiated the investigation, added, "This is why it's so important" for "Robert Mueller and the investigators" to continue looking for something. Brennan also ranted during the interview that the President was "unstable, inept, inexperienced, and also unethical."

A "Russian operation" being run under CIA Director John Brennan in which CIA officers in Russia were in contact with Russian officials would account for Brennan's claim that "U.S. persons are being contacted by Russian officials." It would also account for "a particular intelligence operational campaign" in which "Russians are actively involved."

Since Brennan did not have any "evidence of a connection between the Trump campaign and Russian state actors," if Brennan's claims about "contacts" had any veracity, the only explanation would be that CIA Director John Brennan was running a "Russian operation" designed to make it look like the Trump campaign was colluding with the Russians. Brennan did say, "Almost anything is in the realm of the possible."

In "July of 2016," five days after Donald Trump was nominated to be the Republican candidate for President, the *Guardian* reported, "Hillary Clinton's campaign has accused Russia of meddling in the 2016 Presidential election."[783]

Five days later, in "July of 2016," CIA Director John Brennan sat for an hour-long interview at the Aspen Institute. Before the interview got under way, Brennan was told one of the topics to be discussed was "cyber in Russia." He was also told that they expect him to "make news."[784]

When the interview concluded with questions from the audience, an NBC reporter wanted information on "the hacks" because, by sheer coincidence, "As we have been sitting here, the news is broken that the Hillary Clinton campaign was hacked, and government

---

[783] https://www.theguardian.com/us-news/2016/jul/24/clinton-campaign-blames-russia-wikileaks-sanders-dnc-emails
[784] http://aspensecurityforum.org/wp-content/uploads/2016/07/a-candid-conversation-with-the-director-of-the-cia.pdf

officials are telling us and other news organizations that there is really not any doubt that Russian intelligence was behind this."

The Clinton campaign hack took place back on March 19, 2016,[785] but it was not discovered and publicized until by sheer coincidence, CIA Director John Brennan was doing his interview at the Aspen Institute in "July of 2016," the interview where they expected him to "make news" while discussing "cyber in Russia."

Brennan's use of the hallowed "intelligence sources and methods" in orchestrating all of it would obviously preclude public disclosure of the CIA's nefarious actions in fabricating the whole "Russian collusion" allegation. Renegade CIA officers will go to extraordinary lengths to hide or obfuscate their activities.

The Clinton campaign itself made the hack possible in March 2016 when campaign chairman John Podesta received a common phishing email in his personal gmail account stating that "another user" had "tried to access" his account. The phishing email instructed Podesta to click on a link and "change your password immediately."

But instead of deleting the email or marking it as spam, Podesta's chief of staff sent it to the "help desk," and an IT staffer replied, "This is a legitimate email. John needs to change his password immediately," which, coincidentally, is precisely what the hacker said in his phishing email.

The IT staffer also "provided a link to the real gmail security-management page,"[786] and stressed, "It is absolutely imperative that this is done ASAP."[787]

Instead of using the link provided by the IT staffer, someone in the Clinton campaign clicked on the link in the phishing email, which the IT staffer had said is "a legitimate email." Hackers then gained access to tens of thousands of Podesta's emails, and the entire Clinton campaign hacking episode was explained away as a "typo" by

---

[785] https://www.cnn.com/2016/12/26/us/2016-presidential-campaign-hacking-fast-facts/index.html
[786] http://fortune.com/2016/10/29/clinton-email-phishing-attack/
[787] https://slate.com/technology/2016/12/an-interview-with-charles-delavan-the-it-guy-whose-typo-led-to-the-podesta-email-hack.html

the IT staffer,[788] who supposedly meant to say that the phishing email was "illegitimate" or "not a legitimate email."[789]

But it would make absolutely no sense for the IT staffer to emphatically reply, "This is not a legitimate email. John needs to change his password immediately," and then stress, "It is absolutely imperative that this is done ASAP."

The IT staffer later claimed he pushed Podesta to change his password "out of an abundance of caution," but everyone receives spam and phishing emails, and in no way does it necessitate changing your password.

As for the idea that Clinton campaign staffers purposely facilitated hacking the Clinton campaign, recall that "campaign workers" acting on behalf of KGB officers inside the CIA were intrinsic to killing Congressmen Boggs and Begich in 1972. Renegade CIA officers would have no trouble becoming Clinton campaign staffers or enlisting Clinton campaign staffers to act on their behalf.

David Axelrod, a senior advisor to President Obama and a top strategist in his 2012 re-election campaign, stated that there is "an old tradition of throwing a brick through your own campaign office window and then calling a press conference to say that you've been attacked."[790]

And what a coincidence it was that the Clinton campaign accused Russia of meddling in the election just five days before it was "discovered" that "Russian intelligence" allegedly hacked the Clinton campaign.

In July 2018, Russian President Vladimir Putin stated he wanted Trump to win the 2016 election because Trump "talked about bringing the U.S.-Russia relationship back to normal."[791]

The CIA would have known in 2016 that Putin wanted Trump to win, which would have spawned Brennan's plan to make it look like Trump was colluding with Russia while he, CIA Director John

---

[788] https://www.cnn.com/2016/12/26/us/2016-presidential-campaign-hacking-fast-facts/index.html
[789] https://slate.com/technology/2016/12/an-interview-with-charles-delavan-the-it-guy-whose-typo-led-to-the-podesta-email-hack.html
[790] https://www.npr.org/templates/story/story.php?storyId=126114960
[791] https://www.politico.com/story/2018/07/16/putin-trump-win-election-2016-722486

Brennan, worked in conjunction with other renegade CIA officers to get Hillary Clinton elected.

CIA officers in Russia could easily enlist their assets in Russia to promote a "Trump for President" agenda, and they could easily have "Kremlin linked" CIA assets trying to contact the Trump campaign to give the appearance of "collusion."

CIA officers acting under orders to give information to their assets, including "Russian intelligence officers," would account for Brennan's statement, "Individuals either wittingly or unwittingly may have aided the Russians."

If there actually were any sort of "contacts" between any Russians and anyone at all associated with the Trump campaign, it was surreptitiously orchestrated by President Obama's CIA Director, John Brennan, and his corrupt CIA colleagues.

On October 7, 2016, one month before the Presidential election, the Obama Administration "formally blamed Russia for recent political hacking attacks, saying they were 'intended to interfere with the U.S. election process,'"[792] but the "October Surprise" failed to prevent Trump from being elected President on November 8.

CIA Director John Brennan, however, was undeterred and pressed forward with his plans to go after Trump.

On December 10, 2016, it was reported that Brennan's CIA "has concluded that the Russian government aimed to help Donald Trump win the Presidency by hacking his opponents during the U.S. election."[793]

Putin's desire to see Trump win the election would have also spawned the idea of having CIA officers in Russia facilitate hacking both the Clinton campaign and the Democratic National Committee. If all went according to plan, "President-elect Hillary Clinton" would hit the ground running after the election and push a "Russia tried to help Trump get elected" issue, thanks to CIA Director John Brennan, whose value to "President Hillary Clinton" could not be overstated.

---

[792] https://www.cnbc.com/2016/10/07/us-officially-blames-russia-for-political-hacking-attempts.html
[793] http://fortune.com/2016/12/10/cia-concludes-russia-interfered-with-u-s-election-to-help-trump/

When President Trump fired CIA asset and FBI Director James Comey in May 2017, someone inside the FBI was pushing the idea that "Trump fired Comey at the behest of Russia."[794]

Peter Strzok, the FBI Deputy Assistant Director, and CIA officer Lisa Page, using her "official cover" as Special Counsel to the FBI Deputy Director, got involved "in the hours after Comey's firing."

Strzok anxiously texted Page that they "need to open the case we've been waiting on," adding that they need to do it "now" while Andrew McCabe "is acting" FBI Director, which means they could count on McCabe, who served as Deputy Director under Comey until Comey was fired, to be party to their efforts to bring down the Trump Presidency.[795]

Recall that Strzok sent a text to CIA officer Lisa Page in August 2016 emphatically stating that they intended to "stop" Trump from winning the election, and, because they "can't take the risk" of Trump winning, they have an "insurance policy" in place in case he wins.

They were obviously "waiting" to implement the "insurance policy" in an attempt to bring down the Trump Presidency.

CIA officer Robert Mueller was appointed to be Special Counsel eight days after CIA asset Peter Strzok told CIA officer Lisa Page that they "need to open the case we've been waiting on."

Eight months later, in January 2018, two months before Brennan admitted that he knows nothing of the Trump campaign working with the Russians, Brennan sent out a tweet calling on Congress to "enact legislation" to prevent his CIA colleague, Robert Mueller, from being fired so that Mueller could do anything he wants in an effort to bring down the Trump Presidency.

Brennan stated that he wanted the "investigative chips" to "fall where they may"[796] in his CIA-orchestrated investigation, which ultimately led to a slew of allegations against various individuals that had nothing to do with Brennan's fabricated claim that "the Trump campaign colluded with Russia."

Renegade CIA officer Chuck Schumer, a United States Senator in violation of the Constitution, supported Brennan's position.

---

[794] https://www.cnn.com/2019/01/14/politics/trump-fbi-debate-investigation/index.html
[795] Ibid.
[796] John Brennan twitter feed, https://twitter.com/johnbrennan

On November 7, 2018, Schumer stated, "Protecting Mueller and his investigation is paramount,"[797] but it was "paramount" only to the CIA's quest to control the United States government, a quest in which renegade CIA officer Chuck Schumer has been intricately involved since his election to Congress in 1980 under the auspices of his KGB handlers, the original architects of the CIA's quest to control the government.

Recall that back in January 2017, Schumer used his "nonofficial cover" as the newly elected Senate Democratic Leader to warn President-elect Trump not to "take on the intelligence community" because, according to Schumer, "They have six ways from Sunday at getting back at you."[798]

On March 21, 2018, nineteen days after CIA officer John Brennan's interview in which he admitted that he did not have "any theories" on who might have been involved in any alleged "collusion," Brennan changed his attack strategy and claimed that President Trump is "afraid" of Russian President Vladimir Putin because, according to Brennan, the Russians "may have things" on him, which would "make his life more difficult."[799]

Brennan admitted that this particular rant was a result of President Trump congratulating Vladimir Putin on winning a fourth term as President of Russia. Ironically, it was Brennan who did his best to make Trump's life "more difficult" after Trump won the GOP nomination for President in "July of 2016."

On April 5, 2018, Brennan continued his new attack strategy during an interview in which he stated, "Donald Trump will do what he can to protect Mr. Putin" from U.S. efforts to make sure the Russian government does not interfere with U.S. elections.[800]

Again, the irony is made manifest. Brennan and his ilk have been killing Members of Congress and interfering in U.S. elections with

---

[797] https://fox13now.com/2018/11/07/schumer-on-sessions-firing-protecting-mueller-and-his-investigation-is-paramount/
[798] TheHill.com, 1-3-17 http://thehill.com/homenews/administration/312605-schumer-trump-being-really-dumb-by-going-after-intelligence-community
[799] http://www.dailymail.co.uk/news/article-5527813/Former-CIA-chief-Brennan-says-Russians-Trump.html
[800] https://www.msnbc.com/brian-williams/watch/john-brennan-reacts-to-syria-strikes-comey-book-1210773059872

impunity for more than sixty years, and they "will do what they can" to "protect" the CIA's long-running operation to control the United States government.

In 1980, the year that Brennan joined the CIA, four of his corrupt CIA colleagues, Jimmy Carter, Walter Mondale, Edward Kennedy, and George Bush, all of whom were KGB assets, were contending for the White House, not to mention that quite a few of his CIA colleagues were Members of Congress in violation of the Constitution.

Brennan's fabricated "Russia collusion" claim was clearly designed to "interfere with U.S. elections" in 2016 so that renegade CIA officers would once again control the Presidency.

Eight days after claiming President Trump was protecting Vladimir Putin, Brennan blew a gasket and raged with a frothing-at-the mouth tweet directed at President Trump. The President had sent out a tweet critical of disgraced former FBI Director James Comey, who "leaked classified information" and "lied to Congress under oath."

Brennan's frothing-at-the mouth response claimed that Trump was running a "kakistocracy" [government by the worst people] and that it is "collapsing after its lamentable journey."[801]

Brennan also claimed that Trump had "tragically deceived" those who support him, and he called the Trump Presidency a "nightmare" for the nation.

This book clearly documents the "nightmare" that renegade CIA officers like John Brennan have been foisting upon the American people since the early 1950s in an effort to establish a corrupt CIA "kakistocracy."

Two weeks later, when President Trump quoted a just released House Intelligence Committee Report showing "no evidence" that the Trump campaign "colluded, coordinated or conspired with Russia," Brennan called the House Intelligence Committee "broken" and attacked their report as "highly partisan, incomplete, and deeply flawed."[802]

---

[801] John Brennan's twitter feed, https://twitter.com/johnbrennan
[802] John Brennan's twitter feed, https://twitter.com/johnbrennan

Back on August 4, 2016, the month after CIA Director John Brennan implemented his plan to attack GOP nominee Donald Trump with his CIA-engineered allegation of "colluding," Brennan met with the Director of the Russian FSB, Russia's main intelligence agency and successor organization to the Russian KGB.

Brennan told the FSB Director that "all Americans," regardless of party, "cherish their ability to elect their own leaders without outside interference."[803] In light of the information documented throughout this book, Brennan's hypocrisy in that statement is unfathomable, not unlike Barry Goldwater's statement in 1974 that the CIA should be allowed to keep "domestic subversives" under surveillance.

And Brennan attempted to provide cover for renegade CIA officers operating inside the United States while maintaining his own cover. In an interview on July 9, 2017, six months after he was replaced as CIA Director, Brennan stated that there are "no domestic intelligence authorities,"[804] which is directly contradicted by a mountain of evidence and documentation throughout the chapters of this book.

Brennan, while still functioning as CIA Director in November 2016, mounted his first "public" attack on President-elect Trump twenty-two days after the election.

Brennan, by sheer coincidence, became the first sitting CIA Director to be interviewed by "the British media," which afforded him the opportunity to attack Trump's campaign promise to get rid of the nuclear deal with Iran. Brennan proclaimed that it "would be disastrous" and "the height of folly."[805]

Five days before President-elect Trump took the oath of office, John Brennan, again, while functioning as CIA Director, mounted an attack alleging that Trump does not have "a full appreciation and understanding" of protecting "U.S. and national security interests,"[806] as if renegade CIA officers like Brennan, who are engaged in killing elected officials and getting CIA officers elected to

---

[803] http://freebeacon.com/politics/cia-sought-fbi-probe-russian-targeting-trump-campaign/
[804] https://www.nbcnews.com/feature/meet-the-press-24-7/meet-press-july-9-2017-n781106
[805] http://www.bbc.com/news/world-us-canada-38149088
[806] New York Daily News, 1-15-2017 http://www.nydailynews.com/news/world/cia-head-brennan-blasts-trump-plans-ease-russian-relations-article-1.2946973

Congress, are the ones protecting "U.S. and national security interests," not to mention the lunacy of a sitting CIA Director trying to undermine the American people's confidence in an incoming President.

It is no surprise that former CIA Director John Brennan proclaimed that the CIA would reign supreme over the United States government. Not since the assassination of President Kennedy has the CIA's quest to control the United States government reached such an extraordinary level.

Brennan's Goldwater-style attacks on the President (see Chapter 8) were facilitated by the twitter account he set up in September 2017 devoted mostly to attacking President Trump.

On December 21, 2017, the first day Brennan began tweeting, he accused President Trump of being a "narcissistic, vengeful autocrat" specifically because the President threatened to cut aid to countries that condemned the United States for moving its embassy in Israel from Tel Aviv to Jerusalem. Brennan claimed that Trump was expecting "blind loyalty and subservience" from nations that openly condemn the United States.[807]

Two days later, Brennan claimed that Trump's actions against two disgraced FBI officials meant that he was afraid of the FBI officials and afraid of the entire FBI. Brennan's tweet states that President Trump "fears them, along with the rest of FBI."[808]

It was three months later that Brennan claimed President Trump is "afraid" of Russian President Vladimir Putin. Former CIA Director John Brennan and his corrupt CIA colleague, Senator Chuck Schumer, clearly wanted President Trump to fear the CIA, because, as Schumer warned, "They have six ways from Sunday at getting back at you."[809]

Brennan started off his 2018 tweets with a January 2 claim that there are "reformists" in Iran who could destroy Iran's nuclear program and stop Iran from developing nuclear weapons. Brennan claimed that President Trump's "condemnation" of Iran and the

---

[807] John Brennan's twitter feed, https://twitter.com/johnbrennan
[808] http://www.dailymail.co.uk/news/article-5527813/Former-CIA-chief-Brennan-says-Russians-Trump.html
[809] TheHill.com, 1-3-17 http://thehill.com/homenews/administration/312605-schumer-trump-being-really-dumb-by-going-after-intelligence-community

"nuclear deal" ended all "prospects" that the hallowed "reformists" would be able to halt Iran's pursuit of nuclear weapons.[810]

On January 18, 2017, as the anniversary of being replaced as CIA Director approached, Brennan continued to swing wildly when he accused President Trump of "destructive behavior." He also revamped his call for Trump Administration officials to be blatantly defiant and insubordinate to the President, stating that "members" of the President's "Cabinet" need to work with "Congress" against President Trump.[811]

Brennan's vitriol makes it abundantly clear why he fabricated the entire "Russian collusion" allegation in "July of 2016." Renegade CIA officer John Brennan did what he could to assassinate the character of President Trump. Fortunately, Brennan, unlike renegade CIA officer Barry Goldwater, did not have three assassins with telescopic rifles finishing the job for him.

CIA officer John Brennan broadened his efforts to bring down the Trump Presidency on February 4, 2018, when he adopted a "nonofficial cover" as "senior national security and intelligence analyst" for NBC News,[812] which is not unlike CIA officer Mike Morell having a nonofficial cover as "senior national security analyst" for CBS News.[813] And it is not unlike CIA officer Tulsi Gabbard using a "nonofficial cover" with Fox News.[814] Media control is essential to CIA efforts to control the government.

Recall that CIA Director William Colby testified that there are "full-time employees" of the CIA who are also "full-time employees of major domestic media outlets."[815]

The CIA will use its media control to push any narrative it wants. It will use the media to push any propaganda or disinformation that facilitates the CIA takeover of the government.

---

[810] John Brennan's twitter feed, https://twitter.com/johnbrennan
[811] Ibid.
[812] https://www.nbcnews.com/meet-the-press/meet-press-february-4-2018-n844541
[813] https://www.cbsnews.com/video/does-the-travel-ban-make-america-any-safer/
[814] https://www.latimes.com/entertainment-arts/business/story/2022-11-14/tulsi-gabbard-signs-as-a-contributor-for-fox-news
[815] Hearings Before The Select Committee On Intelligence, Part 5, p. 1589 https://www.maryferrell.org/showDoc.html?docId=146901#relPageId=27&tab=page

When President Trump bemoaned that over the past thirty years, the United States has lost six million manufacturing jobs and has "accumulated trade deficits of more than 12 trillion dollars," including a 2017 "trade deficit of almost 800 billion dollars," former CIA Director John Brennan responded that the world has been "transformed" by "technology, automation, and the attendant evolution of economics and societies." Brennan also asserted that President Trump has "an amazing albeit unsurprising ignorance" of it all.[816]

According to Forbes, "manufacturers added 467,000 jobs" in the "first two years" of the Trump Administration compared to "the 73,000 manufacturing jobs added" during the "last two years" of the Obama Administration.[817] Perhaps Brennan did indeed study the methods of Barry Goldwater, who, like Brennan, was a renegade CIA officer wildly attacking the President of the United States with insults and nonsensical statements.

Brennan followed up his nonsensical tweet ten days later and essentially proclaimed that a CIA disinformation campaign would bring down the Trump Presidency, tweeting, "When the full extent of your venality, moral turpitude, and political corruption becomes known, you will take your rightful place as a disgraced demagogue in the dustbin of history."[818]

One would not think that a former CIA Director would go off the deep end and constantly rage uncontrollably at the President of the United States, but as noted earlier, John Brennan had elevated the CIA's quest to control the United States government to an entirely new level.

On April 4, 2018, Brennan boasted that he had been a CIA employee during the preceding six Presidential Administrations, or as Brennan put it, he "served 6 Presidents." He then stated that he "admired and respected all of them," but because President Trump tweeted out a news article concerning his approval numbers, which

---

[816] John Brennan's twitter feed, https://twitter.com/johnbrennan
[817] https://www.forbes.com/sites/chuckdevore/2019/02/01/manufacturers-added-6-times-more-jobs-under-trump-than-under-obamas-last-2-years/#26263f6f5635
[818] John Brennan's twitter feed, https://twitter.com/johnbrennan

was obviously meant for his followers on twitter, Brennan accused Trump of "self adoration."[819]

As for allegedly "serving" six Presidents, Brennan literally worked for Soviet KGB officers when he joined the CIA in 1980, and he has since joined renegade CIA officers in carrying on with the KGB-initiated quest to control the United States government.

And two of the six Presidents that Brennan "served," Presidents Jimmy Carter and George H. W. Bush, were themselves renegade CIA officers who were addicted to cocaine. Another President that Brennan "served," George W. Bush, was a witting CIA asset, and the other three Presidents, Ronald Reagan, Bill Clinton, and Barack Obama, literally became unwitting CIA assets in the CIA's quest to control the government.

Twenty-three days after Brennan's boast that he "served 6 Presidents," the House Intelligence Committee, as noted earlier, reported that there was "no evidence" that the Trump campaign "colluded, coordinated or conspired with Russia," which resulted in renegade CIA officer John Brennan's bitterness and anger again being made manifest in a tweet directed at President Trump.

Brennan tweeted, "You diminish the Office of the Presidency," and he accused Trump of "hypocrisy" and of not being "a man of integrity, honesty, ethics, and morality."

Brennan's hypocrisy is, again, unfathomable. His actions and those of his corrupt CIA colleagues, documented throughout this book, clearly show who it is that lacks "integrity, honesty, ethics, and morality."

Regarding renegade CIA officer Robert Mueller, his "official cover" as FBI Director was supposed to end on September 4, 2011, pursuant to the legally mandated 10-year term for FBI Directors. But in May 2011, President Obama announced that Mueller would serve as FBI Director for an additional two years.

One month earlier, Attorney General and CIA officer Eric Holder proclaimed that "Mueller was 'a hard person to replace,'" and when Obama announced his intention to keep CIA officer Robert Mueller in the position of FBI Director for another two years, CIA officer Eric

---

[819] John Brennan's twitter feed, https://twitter.com/johnbrennan

Holder proclaimed that "there is no better person" for the position of FBI Director than "Bob Mueller."[820]

Reuters reported that when Obama announced he was keeping CIA officer Robert Mueller as FBI Director beyond the legally mandated ten-year limit, it "caught officials in Washington off guard. Many were expecting Obama to choose a replacement for Mueller in the coming weeks."[821] (Congress had to pass special legislation to make it legal to keep Mueller for an additional two years.)

Renegade CIA officer John Brennan was Deputy Executive Director of the CIA and then had an "official cover" as Director of the National Counterterrorism Center prior to having a "nonofficial cover" at The Analysis Corporation in 2005.[822]

Recall that "a distinct feature of the CIA" is that there are no "'outsiders' in top-level management." In any other United States "executive agency," the "chief officer" and "top-level assistants" are "appointed from the outside," but "no such infusion occurs in the CIA." Future CIA Director John Brennan was obviously a top-ranking CIA official while advising Presidential candidate Barack Obama in 2008.

After the 2008 election, Brennan was given an "official cover" as President Obama's "Deputy National Security Advisor and Assistant to the President for Counterterrorism and Homeland Security."[823]

Brennan, like CIA officer Eric Holder, regularly used his "official cover" to fill out intelligence reports on President Obama and the Obama Administration, and in 2013, President Obama appointed John Brennan to be Director of the CIA.

When Mueller's report came out in March 2019 stating that no one in the Trump campaign "conspired or coordinated" with Russia, Brennan claimed that he may have "received bad information,"

---

[820] https://www.reuters.com/article/us-obama-fbi/obama-makes-surprise-request-that-fbi-chief-stay-idUSTRE74B50P20110512
[821] Ibid.
[822] http://www.washingtonpost.com/wp-dyn/content/article/2006/06/21/AR2006062102044.html?noredirect=on and http://www.cnn.com/2008/POLITICS/03/22/passport.files/index.html
[823] https://globenewswire.com/news-release/2018/04/12/1469347/0/en/Former-CIA-Director-John-O-Brennan-Joins-SecureAuth-Core-Security-Advisory-Board-to-Fortify-Gaps-in-Cybersecurity-Battle-Lines.html

adding, "I think I suspected there was more than there actually was."[824]

In the end, the most Brennan could do is orchestrate circumstances to make it look like Trump conspired with Russia and then obstructed justice by refusing to give any credence to the phony charges. Brennan and his corrupt CIA colleagues are clearly unhappy and frustrated that the investigation that Brennan initiated did not stop Trump from becoming President and that, with Hillary Clinton's election loss, Brennan's reign as CIA Director came to an end in January 2017.

With the "Russia Hoax" failing to get Hillary Clinton elected, the world's most powerful spy agency would have four years to make sure they could install CIA "asset" Joe Biden as President and make sure they could conceal the "evidence" of a stolen election.

---

[824] The Washington Times, 3/25/2019
https://www.washingtontimes.com/news/2019/mar/25/john-brennan-ex-cia-chief-offers-mea-culpa-on-trum/

Chapter 15: An Even Bigger Picture

Since the exposure of the KGB officers and double agents in 1984, renegade CIA officers have gone full bore in an unbridled quest to control the United States government, a quest that includes the September 11 terrorist attacks that killed 3000 people. Like their KGB progenitors, renegade CIA officers have regularly killed Members of Congress.

Renegade CIA officers are acutely aware of how successful the KGB officers were over the course of several decades in controlling the United States government. Renegade CIA officers have, themselves, controlled or occupied the highest offices in the land.

They know that, like their KGB progenitors, they are viewed as loyal Americans and completely trusted within the CIA. And renegade CIA officers in Congress, who consistently fill out intelligence reports on other Members of Congress, know that they are completely trusted within their own political party.

Like their KGB progenitors, renegade CIA officers have held substantial sway, if not definitive control, in Congress and the Executive Branch for more than thirty years.

The KGB-dominated CIA most certainly held sway during the Eisenhower and Kennedy Administrations. They also held sway during the Johnson Administration even though the KGB admitted it was their intention to kill President Johnson so that their asset, CIA officer Barry Goldwater, would be elected to the Presidency in 1964. Not only did the Johnson Administration cover-up the obvious conspiracy in President Kennedy's assassination, but it was also during the Johnson Administration that KGB officers inside the CIA killed civil rights leaders Martin Luther King and Senator Robert F. Kennedy in an ongoing effort to start a race war.

Killing Martin Luther King on April 4, 1968 was, according to the KGB officers, supposed to be the precursor to a "race war" in 1968. Senator Robert F. Kennedy's assassination on June 5, 1968, immediately before he was to head to Chicago to win the Democratic nomination for President, was meant to be the catalyst for their "race war." The KGB officers had a double agent in the room help Sirhan Sirhan assassinate Senator Kennedy.

As cited in Chapter 7, manipulating Sirhan, an Arab nationalist, into carrying out the assassination was an easy task. Senator Kennedy had spoken out in favor of Israel, and Sirhan Sirhan was vehemently anti-Israeli. The Jordanian-born Sirhan had at one time lived in Jerusalem while it was partially under Jordanian control, and Sirhan assassinated Senator Kennedy on June 5, 1968, the anniversary of the 1967 six-day war in which Israel defeated Jordan and took over the rest of Jerusalem and the West Bank.

A book about the assassination, *RFK Must Die!* has as its cover a photocopy of Sirhan's diary writings in which Sirhan repeatedly writes over and over, "RFK must die. RFK must be killed. Robert F. Kennedy must be assassinated before 5 June 68."[825]

Prior to assassinating Martin Luther King and Senator Kennedy, the KGB officers used the long tentacles of the CIA to foment racial strife as they strove toward their vision of a race war in the 1960s. They promoted vehement opposition to civil rights and integration in Southern Democratic states, and they easily stirred up violence within African American communities.

Summers of violence followed the advent of growth in the civil rights movement in the early 1960s, largely because KGB officers saw racial strife and polarization of society as a means of inciting the masses in the United States. They were behind much of the violence

---

[825] "RFK Must Die!" (E. P. Dutton & Co., Inc., New York, 1970)

targeting African Americans, including a Ku Klux Klan church bombing that killed four African American schoolgirls in Birmingham, Alabama in September 1963.

The Rockefeller Commission documented the CIA's inroads with African American militants who stirred up violence and anger in the African American community.

As noted in Chapter 1, "certain corrupt elements" of the CIA were focused on inciting "racial" unrest in the United States, and as such, the CIA's Operation CHAOS joined with the Domestic Operations Division when it gathered intelligence on "United States Black Militants," intelligence that would facilitate KGB efforts to promote racial violence.

The Rockefeller Commission, which focused only on *CIA Activities Within the United States*, stated, "In 1963 and 1964, civil rights disturbances occurred in Birmingham, Savannah, Cambridge (Maryland), Chicago, and Philadelphia. Early in 1965, serious disorder took place in Selma, Alabama, and in August of 1965 the Watts section of Los Angeles became the scene of massive rioting and destruction. By 1966, news coverage of domestic turmoil had almost become a part of everyday life in the United States . . . . Although severe racial rioting had occurred in United States cities in previous summers, it had never been as widespread or as intense as it became in 1967."[826]

The information on "massive rioting and destruction" and "severe racial rioting" was in the report of the Commission on *CIA Activities Within the United States* because the CIA was behind the "domestic turmoil." Otherwise, there would be no reason for the information to be in the Commission's report.

In the "hardest hit" cities of Newark and Detroit, "conditions of near-insurrection developed in ghetto areas."[827]

---

[826] Rockefeller Report, p. 285
[827] Ibid., p. 287

The Commission on "*CIA Activities Within the United States*" also reported that the 1967 riots were "the worst racial disturbances in the history of the United States."

Two African American militants, Stokely Carmichael and H. Rap Brown, "called for 'guerilla warfare' in urban ghettos."

The fact that Stokely Carmichael and H. Rap Brown are mentioned in the report of the Commission on "*CIA Activities Within the United States*" means they were both CIA assets, or more specifically, KGB assets.

On August 6, 1967, KGB asset H. Rap Brown "told a rally in New York that the summer's racial riots were 'only dress rehearsals for revolution,'"[828] which clearly means the KGB's "race war" was supposed to take place in 1968.

The Commission, which desperately tried to downplay the CIA's domestic operations, admitted that it was "activities of the Central Intelligence Agency" that caused the Commission to address "political unrest, disturbances, disorder, and violence in the United States."

It claimed that the CIA "activities" took place only during "the late 1960s and early 1970s,"[829] even though the Commission on "*CIA Activities Within the United States*" was specifically addressing profound racial disturbances from 1963 through 1968.

KGB officers inside the CIA looked forward to the years of "rioting" and "destruction" culminating in a race war in 1968. Toward that end, as noted earlier, they assassinated Martin Luther King on April 4, 1968, and they assassinated Senator Robert F. Kennedy on June 5, 1968.

One day after they assassinated Martin Luther King, African American militant and KGB asset Stokely Carmichael proclaimed, "We Negroes must arm ourselves with rifles and pistols and launch

---

[828] Ibid., p. 287
[829] Rockefeller Report, p. 285

an assault on the streets of the cities of the United States in reprisal for King's assassination."[830]

The Rockefeller Commission, which, again, focused only on *CIA Activities Within the United States*, stated that by the "middle of July, serious racial disorders had occurred in 211 cities."[831]

In their quest to control the government, the CIA clearly instigated and coordinated rioting across the United States from 1963 to 1968.

The KGB officers failed to realize their "race war" in 1968, and they exhausted all efforts along those lines by killing the two most prominent civil rights leaders of the day.

CIA officers bent on carrying out the KGB-initiated quest to control the government undoubtedly instigated and coordinated the nationwide riots that took place in 2020. They were trying to inflame racial tensions. The CIA obviously specializes in orchestrating riots.

As for CIA officers in Congress who knew that the CIA had killed Members of Congress, Senator Thomas Eagleton of Missouri, the KGB's intended Vice Presidential candidate for the Democratic ticket in 1972, informed me in 1984 that he knew that his CIA colleagues had killed his fellow Missourian, Congressman Jerry Litton, in 1976. Senator Eagleton did not disclose whether or not he had foreknowledge of plans to kill Congressman Litton. As noted in chapter 5, the plane crash that killed Congressman Litton also killed his entire family.

It bears repeating that when CIA officer George H. W. Bush became President in 1989, renegade CIA officers picked up where the KGB left off in killing Members of Congress. They killed Congressman Mickey Leland, Congressman Larkin Smith, Senator John Heinz, and former Senator John Tower in four separate plane crashes in less than two years, and as noted in Chapter 7, FBI Director Louis Freeh stated that these four deaths are now

---

[830] National Archives Record Number 104-10137-10316, p. 4
[831] Rockefeller Report, p. 289

categorized as homicides, as are the thirteen deaths of Members of Congress that the KGB killed.

There is no reason to believe that each and every Member of Congress is not vulnerable to being killed by renegade CIA officers at any time, regardless of who is in the Oval Office.

Candidates for office are also vulnerable to being killed. Recall that renegade CIA officers killed Missouri Governor Mel Carnahan on October 16, 2000, twenty-two days before the election, in a failed effort to get CIA officer John Ashcroft re-elected to the United States Senate.

Two years later, in a failed attempt to get CIA officer Walter Mondale elected back into the Senate, they killed Senator Paul Wellstone eleven days before his 2002 re-election bid. Mondale replaced Wellstone on the Democratic ticket but lost the election after four days of campaigning.

Beyond killing Members of Congress and perpetrating terrorist acts, KGB officers and renegade CIA officers have had someone targeted for the Oval Office in every Presidential race from 1964 through 2020, with the exception of 1996 when renegade CIA officers were still grooming George W. Bush for the Oval Office. There were at least twelve CIA officers and CIA "assets" targeted for the Oval Office: Barry Goldwater, George H. W. Bush, Thomas Eagleton, Jimmy Carter, Walter Mondale, Edward Kennedy, George W. Bush, John Kerry, Chris Dodd, Michele Bachmann, Hillary Clinton, and Joe Biden.

As has been clearly explained in much of this book, assassinating President Kennedy was the first step in the KGB's effort to have their asset, Senator and CIA officer Barry Goldwater, elected to the Presidency in 1964. The second step, assassinating President Johnson immediately before the election, was averted when Suffolk County police arrested Robert Babcock, the man who was supposed to be the accused assassin, parked along the motorcade route with a telescopic rifle and shotgun.

In 1968, renegade CIA officer George H. W. Bush was being heavily promoted as the man Richard Nixon should choose as his Vice Presidential running mate, even though Bush, the "Houston oil man" who lost his 1964 Senate bid, had been a member of the House of Representatives for less than a year and a half.

The KGB officers were not able to get a candidate into the 1968 race, mainly because they were more focused on realizing their fantasy of a race war erupting after they assassinated Senator Kennedy. Promoting Bush was a "We have to at least try" effort, and it's hardly a coincidence that the lengthy article detailing the extensive Bush-for-Vice-President campaign was on June 5, 1968, the day they shot Senator Kennedy.

In 1972, CIA officer and Senator Thomas Eagleton was chosen to be Democratic Presidential nominee George McGovern's running mate, but less than three weeks after choosing Senator Eagleton, McGovern had to make a second choice when CIA officer Thomas Eagleton's psychiatric history came to light.

The objective of the June 1972 Watergate break-in was to discredit President Nixon. The hope was that they could have a McGovern-Eagleton ticket elected, which would be followed by the assassination of President McGovern to catapult Vice President Eagleton into the Presidency. Not only did they fail to get Eagleton onto the ticket after the Watergate break-in, Nixon was re-elected in a landslide regardless of the Watergate scandal.

Tony Chavez, a KGB officer who had been the CIA's head of domestic operations for several years until he went to prison in 1984, admitted that the Watergate scandal was orchestrated to discredit President Nixon with the intention of having a McGovern-Eagleton ticket elected in 1972.

Chavez also admitted that the KGB officers were responsible for would-be assassin Arthur Bremer shooting Presidential candidate George Wallace in May 1972. Wallace was running for the Democratic nomination for President.

I wondered if it might somehow be connected to their racial agenda, as Wallace was a prominent segregationist when he was elected Governor of Alabama in 1962. I asked them why they wanted to kill George Wallace, and the reply was that Arthur Bremer "shot the wrong guy! He was supposed to shoot Nixon!"

If everything had gone as planned in killing President Nixon, the unpopular Vice President Spiro Agnew would become President, after which he and his running mate would lose the 1972 Presidential election to the Democratic McGovern-Eagleton ticket, and the KGB would then assassinate "President McGovern."

Research into the *New York Times* bears out what the KGB officers said and that Bremer intended to kill Nixon in April 1972, the month before he shot Wallace.

The *Times* reported that "Bremer wrote in his diary that he entered Canada with two guns hidden in his car and that he intended to shoot Mr. Nixon during the President's state visit to Ottawa April 13-15.

"Bremer never got close enough to pull the gun from his coat pocket. Either the security was too tight or the President sped past before Bremer was ready, the diary disclosed."[832]

Eagleton was not the only CIA officer being targeted for the White House in 1972. As noted in chapter 4, CIA officer George H. W. Bush, a Member of Congress for less than four years, was being promoted in October 1970 as Nixon's choice for Vice President in 1972.

Plans to get Bush into the Vice Presidency in 1968 and 1972 included assassinating President Nixon to catapult Bush into the Presidency, just as they tried to kill President Reagan sixty-nine days after he and Bush took the oath of office in 1981. But plans to get Bush onto the 1972 ticket evaporated when Bush lost his second Senate bid in the 1970 election.

It turns out that for the year 1972, having Bush elected as Nixon's Vice President was Plan A; having Nixon killed to get the McGovern-Eagleton ticket elected was Plan B; and orchestrating the Watergate

---

[832] New York Times, 8-3-72, p. 13 and New York Times, 8-4-72, p. 1

scandal to get a McGovern-Eagleton ticket elected was Plan C. Plans A, B, and C all failed, but the KGB officers were still in charge and they pressed on.

KGB assets Jimmy Carter and Walter Mondale were elected President and Vice President on the Democratic ticket in 1976. It was the first and only time that the KGB had one of their assets in the Oval Office, and it was the first time that they had an asset in the Vice Presidency.

In the 1980 election, the KGB not only had CIA officers Carter and Mondale running for re-election, they also had Senator and CIA officer Edward Kennedy challenge the unpopular President Carter for the Democratic nomination, and they had CIA officer George Bush running for the Republican Presidential nomination, which he lost only to be chosen as Reagan's running mate. Four of the five top contenders for the White House were CIA officers, and three of the four candidates in the general election were CIA officers.

The 1980 election marked the second time that the KGB officers managed to get one of their assets elected to the Vice Presidency.

In the 1984 election, President Reagan, with CIA officer George Bush as his running mate, defeated Walter Mondale, who was trying to become the second CIA officer elected to the Presidency. Mondale chose another CIA officer, Congresswoman Geraldine Ferraro, to be his running mate. Once again, three of the four candidates in the general election were CIA officers.

After the 1984 election, President Reagan, working in conjunction with renegade CIA officers, began paving the way for CIA officer George Bush to run in the 1988 Presidential election. Reagan told me early in 1984 that there was absolutely no way he would replace Bush as his running mate. As noted in Chapter 7, the Reagan Administration and the United States Congress had no intention of exposing massive bipartisan corruption in 1984.

In 1988, renegade CIA officer George H. W. Bush, whose meteoric rise was unaffected by losing his two Senate bids in 1964 and 1970, became the second CIA officer to attain the nation's highest office.

He was defeated in his bid to be re-elected President of the United States in 1992, it being the seventh consecutive Presidential election since 1968 in which Bush was targeted for either the Presidency or the Vice Presidency.

Renegade CIA officers knew that they could do exactly what the KGB officers had done in targeting the Presidency, and in 1984, Leon Panetta led a faction of renegade CIA officers that entered into a secret agreement with George H. W. Bush's son, George W. Bush. They would facilitate Bush Jr.'s political career if he would show his loyalty to them by acting on their behalf and supplying cocaine to his father, Vice President George H. W. Bush.

Initially, the Panetta faction of renegade CIA officers followed the same pattern of their KGB progenitors, who never tried to get one of their own Soviet-born KGB officers into the Oval Office. The KGB officers had simply handled American CIA officers and targeted them for political office.

Likewise, Panetta's faction, instead of trying to get one of their own renegade CIA officers into the Oval Office, simply handled George W. Bush's political career. Panetta could count on Bush not to do anything about the corruption because Bush, himself, had committed a felony as part of their secret agreement.

Panetta succeeded in having Bush elected to the Presidency in 2000 to be in place for Panetta's CIA-orchestrated 9/11 terrorist attacks, but when Bush declined Panetta's offer to get Osama bin Laden if Bush would appoint him to be CIA Director, Panetta set his sights on 2004.

In the 2004 election, CIA officer John Kerry, a United States Senator in violation of the Constitution, was the Democratic nominee for President. Kerry was a KGB asset targeted for political office before he and his corrupt colleagues took charge of the CIA's quest to control the government in 1984.

The KGB officers were never able to have two CIA officers under their control running against each other as Presidential nominees, but the infamous Leon Panetta accomplished the next best thing in 2004 when Kerry, his CIA colleague, ran against his asset, President George W. Bush. When Kerry lost the election, Panetta knew that he would have to wait another four years before becoming CIA Director.

On January 11, 2007, with two years remaining in the second term of President George W. Bush, renegade CIA officer Chris Dodd of Connecticut, who had been a Member of Congress in violation of the Constitution for thirty-two years, announced that he would seek the Democratic nomination for President in 2008. He dropped out of the Primaries after finishing last in the Iowa caucuses on January 3, 2008.

Three weeks later, CIA-controlled "asset" Joe Biden announced his candidacy for the Democratic nomination for President. Biden was subsequently chosen for the Vice Presidential position.

On June 13, 2011, renegade CIA officer Michele Bachmann, who had served only two terms in Congress, announced that she would seek the Republican nomination for President in 2012. Like all CIA officers with "nonofficial covers" as Members of Congress, she began violating the Constitution as soon as she took the oath of office to become a Member of Congress. Ironically, Bachmann touted herself as a "Constitutional Conservative."

In the 2016 election, it was abundantly clear that renegade CIA officers were surreptitiously working to get Hillary Clinton elected while making a concerted effort to use Russia in a failed effort to interfere with Donald Trump's chances of winning the Presidency.

As for the 2020 Presidential election, if the CIA can get away with everything documented throughout the pages of this book, can it get away with stealing a Presidential election and covering it up?

The two people responsible for finding any "evidence" that the CIA stole the election were CIA officers Chris Wray and Bill Barr, who were operating with "official covers" as FBI Director and Attorney General under Trump. As noted earlier in this book, the CIA's "Republican faction" got Trump to appoint Wray and Barr.

Officially, the FBI is responsible for investigating all of the CIA's crimes, and the Justice Department is responsible for prosecuting the crimes, but the CIA has wielded substantial control within the FBI and the Justice Department since 2001. There have been CIA officers with "official covers" as FBI Director and Attorney General in every Presidential administration since 2001.

CIA officer Chris Wray is now Biden's FBI Director, and he works directly under CIA officer Merrick Garland. I know first-hand that Garland is a CIA officer using an "official cover" as Attorney General.

Garland had "official covers" with the Justice Department when his fellow CIA officers Jimmy Carter and George H. W. Bush were President.[833]

He also held high-ranking positions in the Justice Department under President Clinton until Clinton gave him a "nonofficial cover" as a federal judge on the D.C. Court of Appeals, the nation's second highest court,[834] which has influence over federal policy and national security matters.[835]

Recall that CIA officers with "official covers" have "official" positions with "other United States government agencies," and CIA officers with "nonofficial covers" are those who do not have "official" positions with "other United States government agencies."

Garland used his "nonofficial cover" as a federal judge for twenty-four years from 1997 until he resigned in 2021 when President and CIA "asset" Joe Biden gave him his "official cover" as Attorney General of the United States.

The National Security Act of 1947, the legislation that created the CIA, prohibits CIA officers from having "law-enforcement powers."[836] Attorney General Merrick and FBI Director Chrostopher Wray are literally breaking the law.

---

[833] https://www.govinfo.gov/content/pkg/CDIR-2020-07-22/pdf/CDIR-2020-07-22-JUDICIARY.pdf

[834] https://www.npr.org/2016/03/16/126614141/merrick-garland-has-a-reputation-of-collegiality-record-of-republican-support

[835] https://www.columbian.com/news/2016/mar/16/congressional-sources-obama-to-nominate-merrick-garland/

[836] National Security Act, section 102D
https://web.archive.org/web/20180606172154/https://www.cia.gov/library/readingroom/docs/1947-07-26.pdf

As for the CIA's desire to have government officials live in fear of the CIA, CIA officer Chuck Schumer used his position as Senate Democratic Leader to threaten Supreme Court Justices Neil Gorsuch and Brett Kavanaugh in March 2020, stating, "I want to tell you, Gorsuch, I want to tell you, Kavanaugh, you have released the whirlwind and you will pay the price," and then adding, "You won't know what hit you."[837]

I wrote this book because I love my country. Every American needs to understand what the CIA is doing to our country. Please leave a review on Amazon.

THE END

---

[837] https://www.usatoday.com/story/news/politics/2020/03/04/chief-justice-john-roberts-scolded-chuck-schumer-comments-kavanaugh-gorsuch/4956861002/

Made in United States
Troutdale, OR
03/29/2024